DICTIONARY
OF
CLICHES

14 | 44

£4-

g

DICTIONARY OF CLICHES

BETTY KIRKPATRICK

BLOOMSBURY

For Stewart and Trina, the apples of my eye,
the jewels in my crown, my pride and joy,
the salt of the earth and my towers of
strength, otherwise known as my son
and daughter.

First published1996 by
Bloomsbury Publishing Plc,
2 Soho Square, London, W1V 6HB

Copyright © Betty Kirkpatrick 1996

The moral right of the author has been asserted

A copy of the CIP entry for this book is available from the British Library

ISBN 0 7475 2030 5

10 9 8 7 6 5 4 3 2 1

Designed by Hugh Adams, AB3
Typeset by Hewer Text Composition Services, Edinburgh
Printed in Britain by Clays Ltd, St Ives plc

✳ Introduction ✳

It has become something of a linguistic cliché to say that it is difficult to define a cliché. Several writers have pointed to the elusive nature of this well-known fracture of our language.

In his Introduction to *A Dictionary of Clichés*, first published in 1940, Eric Partridge observed that it is impossible to get the average person, even 'the averagely well-educated person' to provide an articulate definition of a cliché. According to Partridge, the aforementioned average person when asked to explain the nature of the cliché would say 'Oh, well, you know what a cliché is,' and hesitate and stumble, and become incoherent.

If we took a random sample of 'averagely well-educated persons' today, we would find that, as far as defining a cliché is concerned, things have not changed radically in the half century since Partridge was writing. Most people in this category would know instinctively what a cliché is, but few would commit themselves to an exact definition.

Frank Muir in his Introduction to *The Methuen Dictionary of Clichés*, compiled by Christine Ammer, and published in 1992, comments on the general inadequacies of dictionaries in providing assistance with the task of getting to grips with the cliché. Muir is of the opinion that all they usually do is refer us to 'stereotype' which in turn leads to a description of making cast metal printing plates 'from a mould of wet newspaper into which a frame of moveable type has been pressed and sat upon.'

John Ayto in *The Bloomsbury Dictionary of Word Origins*, published in 1990, explains this allusion further. 'Originally, French *clicher* meant literally "stereotype" – that is "print from a plate made by making a type-metal cast from a mould of a printing surface".' He goes on, 'Hence a word or phrase that was a cliché had literally been repeated time and time again in identical form from a single printing plate.' In non-literal terms a cliché came to describe an expression that was repeated so often that it lost its freshness and became hackneyed.

Frank Muir is perhaps a little unfair to dictionaries as most of them do make the point that clichés are items of language that are overused. *Collins English Dictionary*, for example, defines cliché as 'a word or expression that has lost much of its force through over-exposure'. *The Oxford Advanced Learner's Dictionary* takes up the same theme with 'phrase or idea which is used so often that it has become stale or meaningless'.

H W Fowler in his *Dictionary of Modern Usage*, first published in 1926, makes much the same point in a more literary way. 'Cliché means a stereotype;' he writes, 'in its literary sense it is a word or phrase whose felicity in a particular context when it was first employed has won it such popularity that it is apt to be used indiscriminately.'

In his description of the cliché in *The Oxford Companion to the English Language*, published in 1992, the editor Tom McArthur also emphasizes overuse and consequent loss of freshness and makes the point that cliché is usually a pejorative term. The editors of *The Bloomsbury Guide to Better English*, first published in 1988 as *The Bloomsbury Good Word*

Guide, also dwell on the undesirable aspect of the cliché, indicating that the term 'is almost always used pejoratively'.

Partridge's definition agrees with this judgement. 'A cliché is an outworn commonplace; a phrase, or short sentence, that has become so hackneyed that careful speakers and scrupulous writers shrink from it because they feel that its use is an insult to the intelligence of their audience or public.'

B A Pythian in *A Concise Dictionary of Correct English*, published by Hodder and Stoughton in 1979, testifies to the pejorative nature of the word cliché. His definition, 'an overused expression, so hackneyed as to be both a tired substitute for original thought and an offence to the intelligence of the reader or listener', could hardly be construed as being complimentary.

Perhaps popular feeling against the cliché is best summed up by David Crystal in *English Language*, published by Penguin in 1988. He writes, 'The worst judgement people can pass on an expression is to call it a cliché.'

Thus we have the cliché convincingly established as the bad guy of the English language. Furthermore it is the worst kind of bad guy – the bad guy that used to be a good guy before it suffered a fall from grace or, in the case of the cliché, a fall from freshness. Such a cliché is described in *The Bloomsbury Guide to Better English*, 'Some clichés were quite apt when first used but have become hackneyed over the years.'

Even bad guys have their defendants and McArthur in *The Oxford Companion to the English Language* reminds us that the general dislike of the cliché is founded on a desire for originality of expression and that a desire to strive for linguistic novelty is a fairly modern one. He reminds us that in earlier times some usages and formulas such as stock expressions in literature, proverbs, and quotations from famous writers 'were admired precisely because they were unoriginal, and writers or speakers used them because they were familiar to their audiences'.

With this in mind it is perhaps relevant that the word cliché came into the language as recently as 1890. Before that people seem not to have required an expression with which to express their condemnation of non-originality. They were quite happy to follow their leaders

McArthur is not the only writer to offer a few words in defence of the cliché. Rather surprisingly Fowler does also at a considerably earlier date in *Modern English Usage*. 'What is new is not necessarily better than what is old,' he writes, and goes on to quote J A Spender as saying, 'The hardest worked cliché is better than the phrase that fails.' He even chastises those who are too censorious of clichés, pointing out that 'The enthusiasm of the cliché-hunters is apt to run away with them.'

Frank Muir, writing in *The Methuen Dictionary of Clichés*, also has some words of praise for the cliché, regarding it as vital to those members of the community who are not very literate or to people, namely politicians, who require a means of hiding their real opinions. More importantly he views clichés as being 'an important part of our spoken language, warm and colloquial, a kind of shared, shorthand way of conducting a conversation'.

Thus we have the cliché – a pejorative term for an expression that has lost its first bloom and thus its potency but is nevertheless widespread and sometimes even loved. Partridge refers to the fact that '[their] ubiquity is remarkable and rather frightening,' and muses 'Why are clichés so extensively used?'

He goes on to answer his own question by giving a variety of possible reasons. Haste, mental laziness, convenience, 'a half-education – that snare of the half-baked and the ready-made', and 'a love of display' are all put forward as possible causes.

However much we may learn about clichés, they have a habit of remaining rather shadowy figures in our language. Unlike with, say, the simile, we cannot simply supply a succinct and readily comprehensible definition that will enable everyone instantly to recognise them when they are encountered. They are impossible to pigeonhole. Classifying something as being overused and stale does not immediately call to mind a distinctive linguistic category.

With most linguistic categories there is not much room for individual opinion. A simile is either a simile or not; its classification is not dependent on the personal persuasion of the reader or the user. In less clear-cut cases, such as metaphor, there may be scope for occasional arguments as to category but nothing like the scope for disagreement that exists with regard to the categorization of a cliché.

Partridge refers to the potential for dispute with regard to clichés by citing a conference 'of learned and able men' in November 1939. 'Someone brought up the subject of clichés; everyone's opinion was different: what one included, another excluded; what one excluded, another included. In short, it is **a vexed question** (cliché).' Some might call it **a hornet's nest** (cliché or is it?).

Webster's Dictionary of English Usage, edited by W Ward Gilman and published in 1989, agrees that individual interpretation is central to the categorization of the cliché. It suggests that one realistic way of approaching the subject is 'simply to call a cliché whatever word or expression you have heard or seen often enough to find annoying.'

Given the level of personal interpretation necessary to categorize the cliché, this suggestion has great merit. There is, however, a problem. If the category is as amorphous and unwieldy as this suggestion indicates, how did it ever get to be a category in the first place? We could all have commonplace books of tired linguistic phrases which we find annoying and which we feel warrant the category of cliché but would they ever coincide, even in part, with everyone else's? A slightly more rigid classification seems necessary, although the personal angle has to remain at the forefront of this.

The major problem with the cliché category is that, rather like the English language itself, it is an inveterate borrower. Shamelessly it takes items from other well-documented categories and converts them into clichés. It might be seen as the magpie of the language, taking for its own glittering phrases that properly belong elsewhere but, unlike the magpie, destroying the glitter as it does so.

In order to achieve a sufficient degree of staleness to qualify for the rather dubious title of cliché, it is usual for an expression to have had a first life in some other linguistic category. There are several of these categories and several authorities have written about them. Since it seems to be in the nature of clichés to sow dissension among their observers, it is perhaps inevitable that the categories of the various authorities often do not coincide to any great extent.

Partridge distinguishes four categories of cliché. These are 1. Idioms that have become clichés. 2. Other hackneyed phrases. 3. Stock phrases and familiar quotations from foreign languages. 4. Quotations from literature. Of these he claims that groups 1 and 2 form at least four-fifths of all clichés.

Group 1, which he also calls idiom-clichés, he defines as 'those idioms which have become so indiscriminately used that the original point has been blunted or even removed entirely'. He cites **to leave the sinking ship** and **to take pot luck** as examples of the category. Of course this categorization raises the question of the definition of an idiom which could give further grounds for dispute.

In Partridge's Group 2 he includes what he calls 'non-idiomatic clichés, phrases so hackneyed as to be knock-kneed and spavined', a terrible condemnation indeed. These he subdivides into General, examples cited being **down to the last detail** and **to nip in the bud**; Sociological, Economic, Political, examples cited being **beyond the pale** and **leave the door open**; Journalism, examples cited being such familiar friends as **a reliable source of information** but also including such unusual phrases as **laying heretical hands on our imperishable constitution**; Literary, examples cited being **a sop to Cerberus** and **Pandora's box**, as well as the now rare **the eternal verities**.

I must say I get quite confused in the course of this category and I suspect that Partridge does also. But then I think that some degree of confusion is an inevitable accompaniment of any attempt at categorizing clichés. They are a maze just waiting to trap us.

Partridge seems on slightly firmer ground with his Group 3 and Group 4. Group 3 consists of phrases and quotations from dead and foreign languages, whether these be of the 'tag' variety, that is 'phrases apprehended without reference to an author', including **in flagrante delicto** (in the very act of committing a crime), **terra firma** (dry land), and **je ne sais quoi** (I don't know what) or what he calls 'the full-blooded quotations' variety.

Into this latter category he puts **sic transit gloria mundi** (thus passes the glory of the world), **timeo Danaos et dona ferentes** (I fear the Greeks even when they bring gifts) and **plus ça change plus ça reste la même chose** (the more it changes the more it is the same thing). Several of his examples in this category, and indeed in the 'tag' category, have passed from common use with the general decrease in familiarity with the classical languages and so have forfeited their cliché status.

Partridge's fourth and final category comprises quotations from literature, also dubbed quotation-clichés. From the Bible he cites among others **their name is legion**, many of the others having slipped from cliché status as knowledge of the Bible declined.

His quotations from literature include **there are more things in heaven and earth** . . . (from Shakespeare), **a dim religious light** (from Milton), **a thing of beauty is a joy for ever** (from Keats) and **Barkis is willin'** (from Dickens). He also includes misquotations, and lists as examples **fresh fields and pastures new** based on Milton's 'fresh woods and pastures new' (from *Lycidas*) and **a little knowledge is a dangerous thing** based on 'a little learning is a dangerous thing' from Alexander Pope's *An Essay on Criticism*.

I have dwelt at such length on Partridge's categorization for several reasons. First, it is inherently interesting – or at least I think so; second, it seems only fair that all this early spadework should receive due recognition in any work on clichés, and, third, it serves as a valuable jumping off point for any more modern attempt at definition and categorization.

Fowler's *Modern English Usage* also recognized that there were several divisions within the cliché category. It contends that there is a kind of hard core of clichés 'that always deserve the stigma – those threadbare and facetious ways of saying simple things and those far-fetched and pointless literary echoes'. To illustrate this category, it cites **filthy lucre**, **tender mercies**, and **suffer a sea change**, as well as the now rare **own the soft impeachment**, an accusation of a not very serious fault.

In other cases, however, Fowler declares that whether or not they deserve the stigma of cliché depends on the manner of their use. 'That depends on whether they are used mechanically, taken off the peg as convenient reach-me-downs, or are chosen deliberately as the finest way of saying what needs to be said.' He argues that writers 'would be needlessly handicapped' if they felt unable to use such potential clichés as **Hobson's choice**, **a white elephant** or **feather one's nest**.

The distinction which Fowler draws between these two suggested categories is not all that easy to comprehend and could easily give rise to dispute. If a writer can use **Hobson's choice** 'as the finest way of saying what needs to be said' rather than as a cliché, why should he/she not be able to use **suffer a sea change** in the same way? Or has time destroyed some subtle distinction between them?

In the course of his article on the actual word cliché, Fowler refers us to several other articles for examples of different kinds of cliché. These include Hackneyed Phrases, Battered Ornaments, Irrelevant Allusions, Siamese Twins and Vogue Words. All of these categories can be clichés.

His article on Hackneyed Phrases in fact seems to be more or less an article on clichés themselves, since he cites a host of them, including **blessing in disguise**, **conspicuous by his absence**, and **damn with faint praise**. Fowler instructs the writer to beware if hackneyed phrases should spring to mind. 'He should take warning that when they suggest themselves it is because what he is writing is bad or it would not need such help. Let him see to the substance of his cake instead of decorating with sugarplums.' For those feminists who are concerned with the implication here that all writers are men, it should be pointed out that Fowler's *Modern Usage* was first published when the fair sex were still slaving over a hot stove and rocking cradles.

The Battered Ornament category suggests a knick-knack that has not stood up very well to moving homes or changes of ownership. But Fowler uses it to describe what he calls a rubbish heap. In it he includes **alma mater** (a phrase used to describe one's old school or college), **hoi polloi** and **suffer a sea change**.

His Irrelevant Allusion category deals with the fact that certain words always spark off in some people particular allusions, usually of a literary nature, which are not necessarily apposite to the situation. For example, when something relating to method arises, **method in [the] madness** will be mentioned, however inappropriate. Likewise, the concept of rottenness will give rise to a reference to **something rotten in the state of Denmark**, an allusion to Shakespeare's *Hamlet*.

The article on Siamese Twins indicates that this category 'is a fruitful source of clichés'. Fowler writes that the term Siamese Twins is 'a suitable term for the many words, which, linked in pairs by "and" or "or", are used to convey a single meaning'. He makes the point that many general Siamese Twins are purely tautological, a synonym or near-synonym being added simply for emphasis. His list of examples includes **betwixt and between**, **bits and pieces**, and **leaps and bounds**.

As Fowler points out, some Siamese Twins are indivisible because one of the pair is used in an archaic sense and would not be understood if used alone. These include **kith and kin**, **hue and cry**, **might and main**, **odds and ends**. He further comments that in the case of some Siamese Twins the two words involved may not be actual synonyms but associated ideas. These include **flotsam and jetsam**, **frills and furbelows**, and **thick and fast**.

He cautions writers against them as he cautioned them against Hackneyed Phrases. He warns that 'such clichés are always lying in wait to fill a vacuum in the brain'.

Fowler also cites Vogue Words as a source of clichés, saying that a Vogue Word 'emerges from obscurity, or even from nothingness or a merely potential and not actual existence, into sudden popularity', and gives as examples **blueprint** and **breakthrough**. He comments that the meaning of such words is by no means immediately comprehensible to the average person 'who has to find out its meaning as best he can'. As a result of this struggle, the Vogue Word frequently undergoes a change of meaning. 'It does not mean quite what it ought to, but to make up for that it means some things that it ought not to, by the time he has done with it.'

Modern commentators on the language will recognize this phenomenon immediately. In the modern world, Vogue Words and expressions are constantly being spawned, and frequently changing their meaning, or even becoming virtually meaningless, as they get handed on from user to user. One has only to think of **the bottom line** with its various meanings to appreciate this point.

A special warning to young people is given in Fowler's article on Vogue Words. They are exhorted 'that their loose use is corrupting the vocabulary, and that, when they are not chosen as significant words but gatecrash as clichés they are repulsive to the old and the well-read'. Nowadays, at least, it would be unfair to single out the young, as the Vogue Word cliché is extensively used by a wide range of people, irrespective of age. The young might bring us some slang terms that we would rather not know about but they really cannot be saddled with the blame for clichés.

Both Partridge's *Dictionary of Clichés* and Fowler's *Modern Usage* dwell quite extensively on the nature, sources and categorization of clichés. Modern usage guides tend to have less space to devote to the task but *The Bloomsbury Guide to Better English* gives some guidance on categorization.

The editors list various categories with examples. One of these consists of 'overworked metaphors and similes' and is illustrated by **leave no stone unturned** and **as good as gold**. Another suggested category is 'overused idioms', examples being **add insult to injury** and **a blessing in disguise**. A category is devoted to the clichés of public speakers, examples of which include **someone who needs no introduction** and **in no uncertain terms**. Quotations, or misquotations, from the Bible and Shakespeare form another category and are illustrated by **pride goes before a fall** and **a poor thing but mine own**. Journalists are singled out as being among the worst offenders in cliché use, being much given to such expressions as **strife-torn countries**, and **categorical denials**. Lastly comes the newly coined phrase that can easily become a cliché overnight, examples being **keep a low profile** and **at this moment in time**.

At the end of this round-up of the views of commentators on clichés, it is quite clear that the cliché, although a major part of our language, is difficult to sum up. The main problem seems to lie in its categorization and in getting people to agree on this. I am prepared to attempt to establish some kind of proposed solution to the first of these problems, although not to the second. The propensity of the cliché to cause dissension seems too deep-rooted. We seemed doomed to disagree about what is a cliché and what is not.

When faced with a problem of supreme difficulty, I am essentially one of those who search diligently for the easy option. Therefore, as my first category, I have selected the Simile Cliché. Most people either know or once knew what a simile is, the signpost 'as' or 'like' being a dead giveaway.

In the Simile Cliché category I have included **cool as a cucumber**, **deaf as a post**, **good as gold**, and **as old as the hills**. Also included are **like a breath of fresh air**, **like a house on fire** and **like two peas in a pod**.

There is not much room for disagreement over my second category. This I have dubbed Foreign Clichés, and the category encompasses those clichés which retain their foreign form although they have been welcomed with open arms into the English language. Most come from French and include **cause célèbre, coup de grâce, de rigueur, je ne sais quoi** and **pièce de résistance**. Latin phrases are also represented but there are fewer of these than would have been common before the decline in popularity of classical languages in our schools. They include **terra firma** and **deus ex machina**.

Many clichés start life as proverbs or sayings, thereby giving rise to the category which I have called Proverb Clichés, although it also includes sayings. Examples are **the early bird catches the worm, forewarned is forearmed, little pitchers have big ears, make hay while the sun shines, many hands make light work** and **one good turn deserves another**.

Several proverbs and sayings appear only in part as clichés. The whole saying might occasionally appear but a truncated form is more common. To this I have assigned the category Allusion Cliché and in it I have included **a bird in the hand**, an allusion to the proverb a bird in the hand is worth two in the bush, **birds of a feather**, an allusion to the proverb birds of a feather flock together, **new broom**, an allusion to the saying a new broom sweeps clean, **the grass is always greener**, an allusion to the saying the grass is always greener on the other side of the fence and **there's many a slip**, an allusion to the saying there's many a slip between cup and lip.

The Allusion Cliché category is not restricted to proverbs and sayings. I have also used it to cover those clichés which are references to quotations, but do not comprise the whole quotation, as **the best-laid schemes** which is a reference to a quotation from a poem by Robert Burns, *To a Mouse*, the whole quotation being 'The best-laid schemes of mice and men gang aft agley'. It also includes references to legends and anecdotes, Bible stories, etc, as **the Midas touch**, a reference to the king in Greek legend who was given the gift of having everything that he touched turn to gold, **kill the fatted calf**, a Biblical reference to the story of the prodigal son in *Luke* 15, **forbidden fruit**, a reference to the Biblical story of Adam and Eve, and **manna from heaven**, also a Biblical reference.

My Quotation Clichés category includes full quotations and misquotation. These include quotations from literature, such as **damn with faint praise** from Alexander Pope's *Epistle to Dr Arbuthnot*, **for this relief much thanks** from Shakespeare's *Hamlet* and **the unkindest cut of all** from Shakespeare's *Julius Caesar*. It also includes ecclesiastical quotations such as **cover a multitude of sins** from *1 Peter 3:8* and **for better or worse** from *The Book of Common Prayer*.

It is common in English for quotations to be misquoted. If such misquotations become common enough, they become clichés and have been included under the Quotation Cliché classification. These include **a little knowledge is a dangerous thing**, a misquotation of 'a little learning is a dangerous thing' from Alexander Pope's *An Essay on Criticism* (1709), **fresh fields and pastures new**, a misquotation of 'fresh woods and pastures new' from Milton's *Lycidas*, and **money is the root of all evil**, a misquotation of the 'love of money is the root of all evil', a Biblical quotation from *1 Timothy* (6:10).

Another category corresponds to Fowler's Siamese twins classification, which I have chosen to call Doublet Clichés. As is the case with Siamese twins, this covers doublets containing synonyms, those containing near-synonyms and those containing associated ideas. Examples include **bag and baggage, bits and pieces, leaps and bounds, odds and ends, over and done with, safe and sound** and **the dim and distant past**.

Another category is Euphemism Clichés. Since many euphemisms are used so frequently, they qualify as clichés on the grounds of over-use. Many people use them automatically without giving thought to using a more down to earth, or even more honest, expression. Examples are **economical with the truth, kick the bucket, powder one's nose,** and **spend more time with one's family**.

For my next category, and one which is extremely extensive, I have decided to adopt Partridge's Idiom Cliché classification. As with his classification, this will include metaphor clichés. The category includes **the light at the end of the tunnel, make waves, on the warpath, paper over the cracks, par for the course, ring the changes** and **take the bull by the horns**.

In common with Euphemisms, many Catchphrases are so commonly used that they become clichés and thus they also represent a category. By their very nature catchphrases, phrases that in some way catch our attention and are repeated frequently, often as a kind of slogan, are usually topical and short-lived. The Catchphrase Cliché is one of the categories most likely to change with fashion, but it often stays on in the language as part of the folk history of a particular time.

Catchphrase Clichés are commonly found in areas such as advertising campaigns, memorable remarks made in films, or quotations from television programmes that gain popular appeal. They include such phrases as **does your mother know you're out?, don't call us, we'll call you, a man's gotta do what a man's gotta do, no names, no pack drill, no show without Punch, tell that to the marines** and **you can't take it with you**.

Vogue expressions, also known as buzz words, can also very quickly become clichés. As with catchphrases, they, as their name suggests, are very much part of the fashion of the day and tend to be ephemeral. Sometimes Vogue Clichés start life in a technical or specialist area of language, where they are perfectly acceptable, only acquiring cliché status when they are transferred to the general language and are subject to overuse. **The bottom line, gameplan, the generation gap** and **the name of the game** are cases in point.

Very many clichés are simply put in to fill up sentences (since the sentences are complete without them). I have designated these Filler Clichés, in view of the fact that they are just filling space. Sometimes the space involved is paper space but more frequently it is air space, Filler Clichés being frequently used in speech.

Clichés in this category are almost the equivalent of a signature tune as far as some people are concerned. We all have friends who insert **the thing is, just between you and me, you know what I mean, believe it or not, needless to say** and so on into practically everything they say.

The use of Filler Clichés is far from restricted to informal speech. You will find it not only in gossip between neighbours but in public speaking, as in the speeches of politicians and in the remarks of after-dinner speakers. Indeed, I would include **unaccustomed as I am to public speaking** in this category and such time-wasters as **at this moment in time**, since many speakers turn to it while they are thinking of something else to say.

As I have pointed out, the cliché does not relish being pigeonholed and there are a great many clichés which do not readily come within the confines of the above categories. To them I have assigned another category and have decided to adopt Fowler's Hackneyed Phrase as its designation. Arguably this could encompass the whole of the cliché linguistic category but I intend to restrict it to those overused phrases which have lost their freshness and which cannot be neatly or justifiably slotted in elsewhere, phrases that have gained widespread popularity over a period of time and sometimes seem to have come out of nowhere.

It is a difficult category to pinpoint exactly and will inevitably involve some degree of cross-over with other categories. It will be helpful to cite a few examples. These include **better late than never**, **a blazing inferno**, **by the same token**, **the blushing bride**, **a can of worms**, **common or garden**, **the end of an era**, **the envy of the world**, **a general exodus**, **the happy couple**, **in the cold light of day**, **make an offer that one cannot refuse**, **the one that got away**, and **pale into insignificance**.

I was tempted to subdivide some of these categories, particularly the last of these, the Hackneyed Phrase, but I resisted the temptation, partly because I felt that once I had started subdividing it would have been difficult to draw the line and avoid over-fragmentation. For example, I was tempted to have separate categories for sport and medicine, but then what about other specialist areas? Since clichés only really become clichés when they are part of the general language and send their tentacles out to affect all of us I decided to stick with the general category. If potential clichés stay within their specialist areas then it would be more accurate to describe them as jargon.

Journalese would seem an obvious separate category. Admittedly sports commentators are guilty of doing to death such eminently forgettable phrases as **game of two halves** and **get a result**, but for the most part the sin of journalists with regard to clichés is simply one of degree. This is perhaps not surprising when they are faced every day of their lives with a blank page to fill for the general public. Given the scope of journalists, most members of the general public would be just as cliché-ridden. You only have to listen to someone being interviewed on radio or television to get evidence of this. Alternatively, listen to the average public speaker, not to mention the average politician who frequently uses clichés to sidestep issues.

Tabloid journalists, however, are another matter, especially when dealing with headlines. Anyone under about three years old is 'a tot', any scientist is 'a top boffin', any fire, however small is 'an inferno', anyone who is trying to prevent a crime is described as 'having a go', and anyone in hospital is 'battling for life'. Sometimes this headlinese affects the rest of us and expressions such as **tug-of-love** come into being as clichés.

Instead of subdividing the broad categories, I compromised by pointing out which clichés are likely to have a particular relevance to a particular field. For example, **as well as can be expected** has distinct medical leanings since it is a favourite piece of information given to a patient's relatives by medical personnel. Likewise **till the fat lady sings** often has sporting associations, and **unavoidable delays** appeared in business and transport contexts.

Since it is difficult to pigeonhole clichés, it is inevitable that there will be some degree of cross-over between the categories. Some, for example can be both Hackneyed Phrases and Filler Cliches.

There are just two other categories that I would like to mention, both more nebulous than the rest and difficult to encapsulate in a dictionary. One is what I shall call the Situational Cliché. This is a kind of verbal Pavlovian response invariably given by someone when encountering a certain situation. It is perhaps best instanced by the neighbour who is progressing down the street, just as you are washing your car, and who almost inevitably comes out with, 'When you've finished that you can come and do mine' or 'It's bound to rain now'. Some situations are just bound to inspire unnecessary comment. Another one is occasioned by one happening to mention that one is going to church. Here the Pavlovian reponse, usually among non-church-goers is 'say one for me'.

The last category is not really one that is likely to make an appearance in a reference book for the general public, since it is the In-group Cliché. All families have them, phrases which have all the people familiar with the background to them having either a quiet smile or a loud guffaw – or occasionally a long sigh – and everyone else looking blank. Examples here are somewhat superfluous since they vary so much from family to family and group to group.

According to my children, I indulged in so many of these when they were growing up that they contemplated collecting and publishing them. Their least favourite and most annoying they claim was 'It comes from within'. This was said in relation to studying and was usually prefaced by 'I'm not going to nag you about studying'. My defence is that it was a successful cliché. They are now both graduates with jobs.

To return to the theme of more general clichés, in this collection I have included some information on the use of clichés and their likely users. This indicates whether they are more likely to be found in informal contexts, whether they are likely to be restricted to any one section of the population, such as older people or younger people, and so on.

As far as clichés are concerned usage is everything. With this in mind I have included examples of usage showing the clichés in action in an attempt to capture the flavour of the individual clichés.

Also included, where appropriate, is information on the derivation of the cliché. This is particularly so in the case of Idiom Clichés.

Information is also given as to the time-scale of clichés. This is not easy to do, given that clichés, by their very nature, exist in a pre-life before they become clichés.

I started this Introduction with a linguistic cliché and so I shall end with another one. No dictionary would be complete without it being pointed out that it is not claiming to be comprehensive, this being impossible in view of the constraints imposed by space. This is an almost de rigueur comment by reference book editors. It is, however, not only a cliché, it is also true, but then there is no suggestion that clichés, although they lack freshness, lack verity.

All that I have attempted to do is to bring you a selection of clichés which indicate the sheer width and diversity of the range. It is this aspect of the cliché that gives it the edge over other linguistic categories. Being an inveterate borrower, the cliché category has succeeded in making itself into either a treasure trove or a rag bag, depending on your point of view.

This book is neither a defence of clichés nor a condemnation of them. It simply contains some reflections on this most controversial of linguistic categories and an attempt to impose some degree of order on what is essentially a lawless part of the English language. At the very least I hope it contains food for thought. Enjoy!

BETTY KIRKPATRICK 1996

A

absence makes the heart grow fonder is a proverb cliché indicating that, if two people who love each other are separated, the separation is likely to intensify their love for each other, as *They work in different cities and are together only at weekends. Still absence seems to make the the heart grow fonder.* The sentiment can also be extended to absence from a place or situation, as *I am actually glad to be back at work again. Absence makes the heart grow fonder.* The expression was originally the first line of an anonymous poem published at the beginning of the seventeenth century. It became a cliché towards the end of the nineteenth century and is still used today, although often in an ironic or humorous context, as *I see you have come back to work. Absence must have made the heart grow fonder.*

accident waiting to happen, an is a hackneyed phrase used to describe a potentially dangerous situation that could very easily turn into a disaster, as *The council should board up that old house to stop the children playing there. It's an accident waiting to happen,* and *That rickety bridge is in dire need of repair. It is an accident waiting to happen.* As a cliché it became very popular in the 1980s and 1990s, especially among journalists and other commentators on society.

accidents will happen is a proverb cliché indicating in a philosophical way the inevitability of mishaps, no matter how much care is taken to avert them. It is often used with the intention of soothing the person involved in the mishap, but it frequently serves to annoy said person who is busy coping with the aftermath of the mishap. The expression has been a cliché since the late nineteenth century and is still common today, being used especially by those with a taste for platitudes and by those who feel that every situation requires a comment.

accidents, a chapter of see *chapter of accidents, a.*

Achilles heel is an allusion cliché meaning a weak spot, a flaw that makes one vulnerable, as *He was a brilliant and brave statesman but his Achilles heel, his love of beautiful women, led to his downfall.* The expression has been used figuratively, often in literary contexts, from the eighteenth century, gradually becoming a cliché. It is still used as a cliché today, especially by people of a literary bent. The allusion is to a Greek legend in which the mother of the Greek hero Achilles held him by the heel and dipped him in the River Styx so that he would be invulnerable. Only his heel remained unprotected and he was eventually killed by an arrow which pierced his heel.

acid test is an idiom cliché referring to a test which will either prove or disprove the truth or worth of something, as *The footballer appears to have recovered from his injury but the training session will be the acid test of his fitness.* The expression was first used literally to denote a test for distinguishing gold from other metals.

across the board is a hackneyed phrase meaning applying in all cases or categories, as *The unions insist that the percentage increase apply across the board, to management as well as shopfloor workers.* It became a popular cliché around the 1960s and is still common today, especially in situations involving money or economics, such as wage bargaining. In origin it referred to horse-racing in America where it described a bet placed on a horse to cover all possible winning places, second and third place as well as first place.

act together, get one's see *get one's act together*

actions speak louder than words is a proverb cliché indicating that what people do is more important than what they say, the implication being that it is easy to talk but actions require effort, as *She is always going on about the plight of the homeless but she never gets involved in any of our fundraising for them. She should realize that actions speak louder than words.* The sentiment appeared in an ancient Greek proverb but the actual wording of the present saying dates from the nineteenth century. As a cliché it is still quite common today, often being used critically against those who prefer talk to action.

add fuel to the fire is an idiom cliché meaning to inflame or exacerbate a situation, often one involving hostility or dispute, as *Our disagreement was not serious until the other side added fuel to the fire by accusing us of hiding the truth.* An alternative form of the expression is **add fuel to the flames**, both phrases referring to the fact that added fuel increases the strength of flames. The concept has been around since Roman times and as clichés both expressions are still common today.

add insult to injury is a hackneyed phrase meaning to insult or cause harm to someone whom one has already harmed, as *His car bumped into her when she was on a pedestrian crossing and then he added insult to injury by calling her careless.* The concept is an old one but the cliché dates only from the twentieth century.

after due consideration is a hackneyed phrase often used as a business cliché. It is most commonly found in rather formal written contexts and supposedly indicates that the user has given the matter a great deal of thought before coming to a decision. In fact it is usually virtually meaningless, being simply a polite convention, as *After due consideration we regret to have to tell you that your application for employment has on this occasion been unsuccessful.* It has long been a business cliché but is becoming rather dated as business letters, in common with most aspects of modern life, become less formal.

after one's own heart is an allusion cliché applied to someone or something that holds particular appeal, as *He is a man after her own heart. He loves good food and wine.* The expression has been a cliché since the late nineteenth century and is still common. In origin it is a Biblical allusion to *1 Samuel* (13:14) 'The Lord hath sought Him a man after His own heart, and the Lord hath commanded him to be captain over His people'.

against the grain, go see *go against the grain*

age before beauty is a catchphrase cliché supposedly used when allowing someone older to go before one into a room, etc, although this seems rather arrogant if used seriously. It is often nowadays used humorously or ironically, as *The old man held* the door open for the young women saying with a smile, 'Age before beauty!' As a cliché it dates from the late nineteenth century, its use today being rather dated.

alarums and excursions is an allusion cliché meaning confused activity, commotion or hullabaloo, as *It was a case of alarums and excursions in the Smith household when Mary announced that she was moving in with a married man.* As a cliché it dates from the twentieth century, being used by people of a literary bent, and nowadays used by them in a humorous context. In origin the expression refers to a stage direction in Elizabethan plays, such as Shakespeare's history plays, to indicate a vague representation of the edge of a battle.

alive and kicking is a doublet cliché, both words in the context meaning much the same thing, as *I thought he had died but I met him at a school reunion and he was alive and kicking.* As a cliché it has been popular since the middle of the nineteenth century and is still common today, its use being restricted to informal or slang contexts. In origin it was a term used by fishmongers to emphasize the freshness of their wares. A less colourful form of the expression is **alive and well**.

all and sundry is a hackneyed phrase meaning everyone, both collectively and individually. It is almost a doublet cliché, since sundry, while not quite meaning all, means several. It has been a cliché since the early nineteenth century but as a concept it is much older. Nowadays it is often used in a derogatory way, as *We don't want all and sundry joining this club.*

all chiefs and no Indians is a hackneyed phrase which refers to a situation or organization in which there are too many people issuing instructions and too few people carrying them out, as *With so many*

additional managers this place is all chiefs and no Indians. As a cliché in Britain the expression dates from the middle of the nineteenth century. It originated in America and has the variant form **too many chiefs and not enough Indians**.

all ears, be is an idiom cliché meaning to pay close attention, as *If you want to talk about what's bothering you, I'm all ears.* The idea has been common for a long time and is still popular today in an informal, and often in a humorous, context. The expression may derive from *Comus* (1634) by John Milton: 'I am all ear and took in strains that might create a soul under the ribs of death.'

all Greek to me is an allusion cliché used to refer to something that is completely unintelligible. The allusion is to Shakeapeare's *Julius Caesar* (1:2) where Casca says of Seneca's speech 'For mine own part it was Greek to me'. Seneca actually did speak in Greek so that some people would not understand what he was saying, but the expression began to be used figuratively. It is still used as a modern cliché, mostly by people of a literary bent, and often to describe something technical or specialist in nature, as *They tried to explain the new computing system but it was all Greek to me.*

all in a day's work is a catchphrase cliché indicating, somewhat philosophically or resignedly, that whatever happens has to be taken in one's stride, since it is part of one's job or duty, as *Firefighters' lives are often at risk but they know it is all in a day's work.* As a cliché it dates from the twentieth century. It is still quite common today and is sometimes used in humorous or ironic contexts, as *You always have to clear up after him, but it's all in a day's work.*

all intents and purposes, to is a doublet cliché meaning in practical terms, in all important ways, virtually, as *He occasionally spends a night at home but to all intents and purposes he and his wife are separated*. It has been a cliché since the middle of the nineteenth century and is still common in fairly formal contexts.

all mod cons is a hackneyed phrase which is a shortened form of 'all modern conveniences'. The expression was originally applied to property and meant up-do-date plumbing, such as bathrooms, and was part of estate agents' jargon, as *a desirable rural cottage with all mod cons*. It is still used with this meaning but as up-to-date plumbing has become more or less the norm in modern housing the phrase has come to be used in a wider, although mostly in a humorous or ironic, context as *Her home office has all mod cons – word processor, fax, answering machine*, and *Talk about all mod cons. The office the agency sent me to didn't even have an electric typewriter*.

all over bar the shouting is a catchphrase cliché which refers to a situation where the outcome is certain although it is not yet generally known, and so all that is to come is the official announcement or reaction, such as the applause or retribution. It was originally applied to sports events, as *The team is so far ahead that no other team can win the league now. It's all over bar the shouting*. But then its meaning was extended to cover wider contexts, as *The jury are considering their verdict. It's all over bar the shouting*. The expression has been common since the late nineteenth century and is still widely used today in all but the most formal contexts. An earlier form of the expression was **all over but the shouting**.

all part of life's rich pattern is a catchphrase cliché used in a satirically resigned or philosophical way as a comment on the trials of life, as *After work I have go to the supermarket, collect the drycleaning and pick up my daughter from her friend's house. Ah well, it's all part of life's rich pattern!* As a cliché it became popular in the second half of the twentieth century. An alternative, and now rarer, form is **all part of life's rich tapestry**.

all part of the service is a catchphrase cliché originally used commercially to customers, as *Certainly we deliver free of charge. All part of the service, sir.* This meaning still exists but the cliché is also used in a non-commercial, humorous or light-hearted way, as *Of course it's no trouble to run you home after dinner. All part of the service!* As a cliché it became popular about the middle of the twentieth century and had its origins in an advertising slogan used by the clothing company, Austin Reed, in the 1930s.

all present and correct is a catchphrase cliché meaning that everything is in order, as *I have checked that everyone is back in the bus. All present and correct!* and *All present and correct. I've checked today's takings.* The expression has a military origin, having been used by sergeant majors on parade when reporting to the officers in charge. As a cliché it was popular around the 1930s. It is still used today but its use tends to be restricted to older men with a military background or by people being deliberately satirical.

all right for some, it's is a hackneyed phrase used to express disgruntlement or mock jealousy of someone else's good fortune, as *Look at all those people sitting in the park sunning themselves while we're working. It's all right for some!* The cliché dates from the twentieth century and is still common in informal contexts.

all right on the night, it'll be is a catchphrase cliché originally used in consolation after a bad dress rehearsal of a play or show and dating from the later part of the nineteenth century. From about the 1920s it began to be used in wider contexts referring to things that had gone wrong initially but were optimistically thought to be going to turn out all right when the occasion demanded, as *The football team were absolutely hopeless at their last training session before the big match. Still, it'll probably be all right on the night*. As a modern cliché it is used in informal contexts.

all's well that ends well is a proverb cliché putting forward the point of view that as long as something turns out all right one can forget about any troubles that are involved in getting to that point, as *We had a lot of trouble setting this house to rights but it's perfect now. All's well that ends well*. The proverb is one of long standing and the same sentiment is found in proverbs in other languages. As a cliché it is still widely used today.

all singing, all dancing is a hackneyed phrase which was originally applied to a stage show to emphasize the splendid scale of the performance in order to tempt audiences to go and see it, as *You just have to come and see the all-singing, all-dancing show at the Playhouse!* As a cliché it was extended to a wider context in the late twentieth century, particularly to machines or systems of some kind, as *I just want a car that gets me to work. I don't want one of these all-singing, all-dancing expensive models*, and *They bought an all-singing, all-dancing camera for their holiday and then they couldn't work out how to use it*.

all systems go! is a catchphrase cliché used to refer to a state of readiness for imminent action. It had its origins in the launching of American rockets for space exploration, and especially for the moon landings in the 1960s and 1970s which received world-wide television coverage and helped to bring the expression to a wide audience. It then came to be used to refer to any state of readiness, as *Are the children ready to take part in the swimming contest. It's all systems go here!* It was frequently used in a humorous context, as *It's all systems go here! The bride is having hysterics about her taxi being late and her father has lost his speech*. As a cliché the term is not as popular as it was, perhaps because the space programme is not as active or as publicized as it once was.

all things considered is a hackneyed phrase which refers to the ultimate summing up of something when all aspects of it have been taken into account, as *All things considered, I think our play was quite successful*. As a cliché it became popular in the late nineteenth century and it is still widely used today. It is less formal than → **after due consideration**.

all things to all men, to be is an allusion cliché indicating that someone is willing to adapt so as to be liked by, or to please everyone or as many people as possible, as *You cannot count on his support. He keeps changing his mind. He tries to be all things to all men*. This rather dubious way of gaining popularity is usually referred to in negative terms nowadays, as *You will have to decide which side you are going to support. You cannot be all things to all men*. The allusion is to a Biblical passage, to 1 *Corinthians* (9:22) 'I am made all things to all men, that I might by all means save some.'

all-time low is a hackneyed phrase referring to a record low level. It can be used either literally, as *Temperatures have reached an all-time low for the time of year*, or figuratively, as *Morale reached an all-time low in the team as we lost match after match.* The opposite is **an all-time high,** as *House prices have reached an all-time high in the area,* and *Enthusiasm for the sport has reached an all-time high.* As clichés the expressions date from the twentieth century.

all to the good is a hackneyed phrase indicating something ultimately advantageous, although this fact might not at first be obvious, as *It's all to the good that you couldn't get a booking in Greece in August. It would have been far too hot for you.* It has been a cliché since the late nineteenth century. In origin, 'good' as an accounting term referred to profit or worth.

and that's that! is a hackneyed phrase used to emphasize that what one has said is to be regarded as final, and is not to be argued with, as *You are not going out before your homework is finished and that's that!* As a cliché the expression dates from the nineteenth century and is still common, often being used by irate parents when delivering ultimatums. An alternative form of the expression, possibly even more emphatic in its use, is **and that's flat!**

any port in a storm is an idiom cliché indicating that if one is in trouble one is not too particular about the form potential relief takes, as *He didn't want to take the job as nightwatchman but he was unemployed and it was a case of any port in a storm.* The expression dates from the eighteenth century and is still common today. The origin is the obvious one that in extremely stormy weather a ship would go into any port that would provide shelter.

anything that can go wrong will go wrong is a catchphrase cliché which is self-explanatory. It originated in America around 1950, probably in the form of **if anything**

can go wrong it will. It is still used as a cliché today but in Britain nowadays it is more usually known as Sod's Law and less commonly as Murphy's Law, as *Sod's Law dictates that if a piece of buttered bread falls it falls buttered side down.*

apple of one's eye, the is an allusion cliché used to refer to someone who is very much loved and cherished, one's favourite, as *She loves all her children but her youngest is the apple of her eye.* The expression has been popular since the eighteenth century and is still common today. The allusion is to a Biblical passage, to *Deuteronomy* 'He kept him as the apple of his eye.' The term refers to the fact that the pupil of the eye was once thought to be a solid apple-shaped body.

apron strings, tied to is an idiom cliché used to refer to someone who is too much under the influence of a woman, especially a mother or wife, as *He never goes out with the people from work. His mother doesn't like them and he's tied to her apron strings.*

cost an arm and a leg, is an idiom cliché used to refer to the high price of something, as *Houses in that area cost an arm and a leg.* The cliché originated in America and has probably been popular in Britain since the 1970s, being used in informal or slang contexts. The same sentiment is contained in the expression **cost the earth**.

armed to the teeth is an idiom cliché meaning fully equipped to the extent of being overequipped. It originally referred to weapons used in battle and the concept of being armed to the teeth dates back to the fourteenth century. It was popularized by Richard Cobden, the English economist and politician, in a speech against what he saw as Britain's excessive expenditure on armaments (1849) and became a cliché around that time. It then became used in more general contexts. Nowadays it is used mostly informally and often in a humorous or satirical way, as *The tourists were armed to the teeth with photographic equipment*, and *Whenever he gets home late he is armed to the teeth with excuses*.

as a matter of fact is a hackneyed phrase sometimes used to preface a piece of additional or explanatory information, as *He certainly has not left town. As a matter of fact, I saw him last night*. It is also frequently meaningless through habitual use.

asking for it is a hackneyed phrase used to suggest that a woman who has been raped, or has otherwise received unwelcome sexual attention, has been acting or has been dressed in a provocative way so as to give the man involved the impression that she wanted to have sexual intercourse with him. It is only fairly recently when more women are bringing accusations of rape to the notice of the courts that this supposed justification for rape has been challenged. The cliché, however, remains very common, and because of the increased number of rape trials currently enjoys a high profile.

ask me another is a catchphrase cliché used in an informal context when one does not know the answer to a question, *Why is he so nasty? Ask me another!* It dates from the late nineteenth century but is now rather dated.

as well as can be expected is a hackneyed phrase most commonly found as a medical cliché. It is used by people involved in the care of the sick when they do not wish to commit themselves to being too optimistic about a patient's condition but equally do not wish to sound too pessimistic. It tends to irritate the relatives of the patient who feel that they are being deprived of information, as *She phoned to ask how her father was after his operation but all she was told was that he was as well as could be expected*. The cliché dates from the late nineteenth century.

at a loose end, see *loose end, at a*

at daggers drawn see *daggers drawn, at*

at long last is a hackneyed phrase meaning finally, after a lengthy wait or delay, as *We waited for ages at the bus stop and at long last the right bus appeared*. In the sixteenth century the expression was **at the long last**. The modern form has been a cliché since the beginning of the twentieth century.

at one fell swoop is an allusion cliché to Shakespeare's *Macbeth* (4:3) 'Oh Hell-kite! All? What, all my pretty chickens and their dam at one fell swoop?' The word 'fell' in this context means 'savage', the kite being a bird of prey. As a cliché the expression dates from the nineteenth century and means at one stroke or operation, as *He lost all his money on the stock market at one fell swoop*.

at this juncture is a hackneyed phrase simply meaning now. It frequently appears in formal reports, such as are issued by the police, politicians, etc and are quoted in the press, as *At this juncture we cannot say whether foul play is involved*. As a cliché it dates from the twentieth century. It predates **at this moment in time** and is not subjected to the satire with which the latter is treated.

at this moment in time is a hackneyed phrase and filler cliché which simply means now. It was a vogue cliché of the 1970s, being much used in the course of the Watergate investigation in the United States. It is still used today, sometimes seriously by people who misguidedly think it sounds impressive or by people who are playing for time while, for example, thinking of a convincing reply in the course of an interview, as *At this moment in time we have not yet finalized our education policy.* Sometimes people use it satirically. An expression which shares its meaning but enjoys slightly more credibility is **at this juncture**.

at your earliest convenience is a hackneyed phrase mostly used in business contexts such as in formal letters, as *We should be grateful if you would reply to our letter at your earliest convenience.* It is frequently a request for payment of a bill and as such is a kind of euphemism cliché since the phrase really indicates that the bill should be paid at once.

avoid like the plague is a simile cliché meaning to avoid contact as much as possible, as *Avoid him like the plague. He is such a bore*, and *I avoid the town centre like the plague on Saturday afternoons.* The cliché is common today in rather informal contexts. The expression is a very old one,

having been used by St Jerome (AD 345– 420), and originally referred to the need to avoid contact with anyone suffering from an infections or contagious disease.

away from one's desk is a hackneyed phrase which is often also a euphemism cliché in business contexts. It is mostly used by secretaries, assistants, colleagues, etc as a reason or excuse for someone not taking a telephone call. It is frequently used as a euphemism for 'does not wish to speak to you'. It became popular as a cliché in the 1980s. See also **in a meeting**.

axe to grind, an is an idiom cliché meaning a personal or selfish motive, as *He is very much in favour of the proposed carpark but he has an axe to grind. He owns a shop right beside the site.* It has been common as a cliché since the middle of the nineteenth century. Its origin is thought to lie in a story about a boy who was fooled into turning a grindstone while the owner sharpened his axe on it. The story has been attributed to Benjamin Franklin, the American politician (1706–90).

❧ B ❧

baby, left holding the is an idiom cliché meaning left with all the responsibility for something that is really either a shared responsibility or the responsibility of someone else, as *We were supposed to rent the house together but the others backed out leaving me holding the baby*, and *My brother volunteered to do our grandmother's garden and then went to the cinema leaving me holding the baby*. Originally the expression was applied literally to an abandoned mother. It is still a common cliché today, being used in informal contexts.

baby with the bathwater, to throw out see *throw the baby out with the bathwater*

back number is an idiom cliché used to refer to someone who is no longer popular, effective, etc, as *He was quite a well-known singer in the seventies but is a bit of a back number now*. In origin the expression refers to back issues of newspapers which of course do not carry items of current news. As a cliché the figurative use of the term has been used since the beginning of the twentieth century. As the meaning suggests it is used in a derogatory way.

backroom boys is a hackneyed phrase used to describe the people who work away in the background and hardly ever get the acknowledgement their work deserves, this being reserved for those associated with the same project who are more in the public eye. The term dates from World War 2 and was used originally to refer to the scientists and technicians who contributed so much to warfare but went largely unnoticed as they were not in the front line. The expression is still used today to refer to essential but unobtrusive workers of either sex, as *When the actor won an Oscar for his film appearance he acknowledged the invaluable role played by the backroom boys*. It is more likely to be used by older people who may remember the origin of the phrase and it has rather a dated ring.

backseat driver is an idiom cliché used to describe someone who interferes in some project without having any involvement in it and usually without any knowledge of the subject, as *We would get this meal cooked a whole lot faster if you backseat drivers would stop telling us what to do*. The expression is also used literally to refer to someone in a vehicle, often someone who cannot drive, who offers unwanted advice to the driver. The term dates from the early twentieth century and in origin refers to the passenger in a chauffeur-driven car who gave the driver directions.

back to basics is a hackneyed phrase used to refer to a return to a simple, rudimentary method of doing something. It has been used to refer to educational methods, as *There are some people who believe that more children would learn to read and write if we got back to basics in the classroom*. In the 1990s it became used politically by the British government in their advocacy of a reinstatement of moral values supposedly common in the past.

back to square one is an idiom cliché used to indicate that it is necessary to go back to the beginning again or think something through again from the beginning, since the original attempt has not been successful, as *This timetable isn't going to work. It's back to square one!* and *He's hit a snag in his research project and so it's back to square one*. The expression may have been popularized in the 1930s by reference to the numbered grid, representing a football pitch and printed in the programme guide, which was used by radio sports commentators when giving a commentary on a match. In origin it probably refers to board games, such as snakes and ladders, where a player has to go back to the first square after incurring a certain penalty. Alternatively it may originally have been a reference to hopscotch. It is still a common cliché today, usually being used in rather resigned tones. Some of the same sentiment is conveyed by the expression → **back to the drawing board**.

back to the drawing board is an idiom cliché used to indicate that something has gone wrong with a scheme and one will have to start again and reappraise the situation, as *The rota system for overtime is not working. I suppose it's back to the drawing board*. In origin it refers to an architect or designer redrawing plans. It was popularized during World War 2 by the caption to a cartoon by Peter Arno in *The New Yorker* which depicted an aircraft exploding into the ground while a designer with a roll of blueprints stood by. As a cliché it is still popular today, usually said in rather resigned tones. Some of the same sentiment is conveyed by the expression → **back to square one**.

back to the wall, have one's is an idiom cliché meaning to be in an extremely difficult or dangerous situation, so that one has to make a final defensive stand in order to survive, as *During the recession a lot of small firms had their backs to the wall*. If one has one's back to the wall, no retreat or escape is possible and one has no alternative, if one wishes to remain alive or undefeated, but to stand and fight, with the wall acting as a defence from the rear. The expression dates from the sixteenth century but it was popularized by an order given to British troops by General Haig near the end of World War 1: 'With our backs to the wall and, believing in the justice of our cause, each one of us must fight on to the end.' As a cliché it is still common today and is often used to refer to a difficult financial situation.

bag, in the is an idiom cliché meaning certain, as *The export order's in the bag*, and *The league cup's in the bag. No other team can catch them now*. As a cliché the expression dates from the twentieth century and probably has its origin in a game bag used for holding the hunter's catch. The cliché is still common today, being used in informal or slang contexts.

bag of tricks is an idiom cliché referring to the equipment that someone uses to do a job. In origin the expression refers to the bag of tricks that a travelling magician would carry around to be used in his show. As a figurative expression it usually carries the suggestion that there is some mystique about the equipment as it is used by someone with a specialist skill that others do not share, as *There is something wrong with our central heating. We'd better send for Mr Jack and his bag of tricks*, and *The child had a very sore throat but the doctor arrived with his bag of tricks and gave him an antibiotic*. The expression dates back to the late seventeenth century and became common in the nineteenth century. It is still quite common today. An alternative form is **box of tricks**.

balance, hang in the is an idiom cliché which is used to describe a situation where there is doubt or suspense about the outcome of something, and often where the uncertainty is between two opposite possibilities, as *The condition of the accident victim is hanging in the balance. He is in intensive care*, and *His career is hanging in the balance. If he is found guilty of drink driving he will lose his job.* Frequently the expression is associated with fate, as *The fate of the workers is hanging in the balance while they are waiting for the outcome of the proposed merger.* The balance referred to is the old weighing device consisting of two pans, in one of which was placed the thing to be weighed and in the other of which was placed weights of known measure, some being added or taken away until the two pans balanced and the weight of the contents of the first pan was established. The expression dates from the fifteenth century and has been used ever since. It is still popular as a modern cliché.

bald as a coot is a simile cliché meaning completely bald, as *He has been bald as a coot since he was quite a young man.* It is the standard description of total baldness. In origin it refers to a water bird with black plumage but which has a white beak extending to its forehead, giving it the appearance of baldness.

ballgame, a different is an idiom cliché which was a vogue cliché of the 1970s and 1980s and is used to indicate a completely different situation, with a different set of considerations to be thought of, as *You can't compare the political situation then and now. It's a totally different ballgame.* The cliché is American in origin, ballgame being much more common in American English than it is in British English, and has never really become naturalized. As a cliché in Britain it is now fading slightly in popularity as is the way of vogue clichés, having always been regarded as rather jargonistic.

ballpark figure is an idiom cliché which became a vogue cliché in Britain in the 1980s, meaning an approximate estimate, a rough guess. The expression is American in origin, being derived from baseball, **in the ballpark** meaning within certain limits. It has come to be a cliché chiefly in the sphere of finance and business which is, of course, international, and one that frequently uses American English. The cliché has never become widespread in general British English.

ball's in your court, the is an idiom cliché indicating that it is up to the other party in a situation to act. In origin the expression refers to tennis. As a cliché it dates from the middle part of the twentieth century and it is still common today, being used in informal or slang contexts.

banana skin, a is an idiom cliché which refers to something which, figuratively, might make you fall flat on your face and therefore look foolish. The image of someone slipping on a banana skin, usually while everyone else present laughs heartily, is an old one, being a favourite of compilers of comics and cartoonists. It was popular in a political context in 1980s Britain during the Thatcher administration. As a cliché it is one of those that seems to come and go, as though people forget about it for a while and then suddenly remember how appropriate it is. It is a term which appeals to journalists and is often used by them in connection with the world of politics where there is usually no shortage of people indulging in the kind of behaviour that warrants the use of the cliché, as *This latest scandal involving a Cabinet Minister is yet another banana skin for the Government.*

11

bandwagon, jump on the see *jump on the bandwagon*

bang one's head against a brick wall is an idiom cliché meaning to try assiduously but in vain, or with little hope of success, to achieve an objective. It is often used of someone who is trying to get someone else to understand something or to follow a piece of advice, as *You'll just be banging your head against a brick wall if you try to persuade him to stay on at school*, and *We tried to get her to see a doctor but we were just banging our heads against a brick wall*. The expression is long established and its origin suggests going to a lot of trouble (and pain) and achieving nothing. As a cliché it is still widespread today in all but the most formal contexts.

baptism of fire is an idiom cliché which refers to someone's introduction to, or first encounter with, something that is likely to be an ordeal, as *She has finished her teacher training course and is about to face her baptism of fire in the classroom*. The expression was first used figuratively of soldiers being exposed to gunfire for the first time, and as a cliché with this meaning dates from the nineteenth century, the wider meaning being a later development. It is still common today in a wide range of contexts, sometimes being used humorously.

barking up the wrong tree is an idiom cliché meaning directing one's efforts or energies in the wrong direction, as *The police have taken in him for questioning but they are barking up the wrong tree. I know who the real culprit is*. As a cliché the expression dates from the nineteenth century and is still popular today in rather informal contexts. In origin it refers to the former American practice of raccoon hunting when trained dogs would bark up trees at night to indicate where the raccoons were. Sometimes they made a mistake and quite literally barked up the wrong tree.

bark is worse than his bite, his is an idiom cliché indicating that someone appears and sounds much fiercer and sterner than he or she actually is, as *All the children are scared of the new teacher, but people say that her bark is worse than her bite and that she can be very kind to her pupils*. The expression dates from the middle of the seventeenth century and is a common cliché today. In origin it refers to a dog that might growl and snarl but will not actually bite people. The cliché is sometimes reversed for humorous or satirical purposes, as *Watch out for the new boss. She looks very gentle but her bite is worse than her bark*.

barrel, have someone over is an idiom cliché indicating that one has someone totally in one's power, as *He has the workers over a barrel. He pays them rock-bottom wages because he knows they wouldn't get other jobs*. As a cliché it dates from the twentieth century and is still common today, being used in informal or slang contexts.

batten down the hatches is an idiom cliché meaning to make oneself as secure as possible in expectation of trouble. In modern times it is frequently associated with an economic or financial situation, as *Small firms that cut their expenditure and batten down the hatches will stand the best chance of surviving the recession*. The expression has been used figuratively since the late nineteenth century and is still quite common today. It is nautical in origin, referring to the preparation of a ship for stormy weather by fastening down the battens (strips of wood that were nailed to the masts) and spars, and covering the hatchways of the ship with tarpaulin.

battle royal, a is an idiom cliché which refers to a fierce quarrel or row, often involving several people, as *There was a real battle royal when the landlord of the pub refused to serve one of the customers.* In origin the phrase refers to cockfighting in the seventeenth century, a battle royal being a fight in which more than two birds were involved. The expression was used figuratively from the eighteenth century. As a cliché it is less commonly used today than it once was.

be-all and end-all is a hackneyed phrase meaning the thing that is of most importance, as *Money isn't the be-all and end-all of life, you know*, and *She thinks that getting married is the be-all and end-all of a woman's existence.* As a cliché it has been in common use since the nineteenth century. It is still used today but in rather a restricted range of contexts. Its most famous literary use is in a passage from Shakespeare's *Macbeth* (1:6) when Macbeth in a soliloquy is thinking about murdering Duncan 'that but this blow might be the be-all and end-all here'.

beat about the bush is an idiom cliché meaning to approach something in a roundabout or ultra-cautious manner, to shilly-shally, as *I wish the boss would tell people directly if they're being made redundant. He keeps beating about the bush.* The expression dates from the sixteenth century and became a cliché in the late eighteenth century. Both it and the practice it refers to are very popular today. In origin it refers to beating bushes in order to flush out game birds from their hiding place so that they may be shot.

beat a hasty retreat is a hackneyed phrase meaning to depart or get out of the way as quickly as possible, as *The children beat a hasty retreat when they realized that they had* broken a window. The expression is military in origin, where it originally referred to the practice of beating a drum as a signal to the troops to retreat. Later in military terms it came to mean simply to retreat and later still came to be used figuratively. It was a cliché from around the middle of the nineteenth century but nowadays usually has 'hasty' in the expression.

beaten track, off the see *off the beaten track*

beats cock-fighting, it is a catchphrase cliché indicating that something is either superior or desirable in some way or that it is remarkable, as *A fortnight in the Bahamas may not be everyone's ideal holiday but it sure beats cock-fighting*, and *He's broken the record for the course again. Doesn't that beat cock-fighting?* As a catchphrase the expression dates from the early nineteenth century. As a cliché it is still found today but it is becoming rather dated.

beats me, it is a hackneyed phrase indicating that one is absolutely baffled by something, as *It beats me why she stays with him. He's always after other women.* The expression has been common in Britain since the 1920s and is still a common cliché today, being used in an informal context.

because it's there is a catchphrase cliché used in defence of taking part in something the motivation for which other people cannot understand, regarding the venture as too dangerous, uncomfortable, boring, etc. The phrase was used by George Leigh Mallory (1886–1924), a famous mountaineer, with reference to his attempt on Mount Everest, an attempt which was unsuccessful and from which he disappeared. It was later popularized by Edmund Hillary, whose attempt to climb the same mountain was successful (1953). As a modern cliché it is still frequently used with reference to mountaineering, as *So many people risk their lives on Scottish peaks in the winter but when you ask them why they do it they say, 'Because it's there'.* It is also used of other sporting activities, as *When we asked him why he wanted to swim the channel all he could come up with was 'Because it's there'.* More recently it has extended its use to cover less obvious areas of interest, mostly in a humorous or ironic way, as *They say they drink such a lot of whisky because it's there.*

bed of roses, a is an idiom cliché used to refer to a very pleasant, comfortable or trouble-free situation, a bed of roses being a very beautiful place to be, if you do not take into consideration the thorns. The expression is mostly found in the negative, as *Life on the dole isn't exactly a bed of roses,* and *Being a single mother is hardly a bed of roses.* As a metaphor it has been in use since the sixteenth century and has been a cliché since the middle of the nineteenth century. The cliché is widespread today, especially in view of the fact that the absence of trouble-free situations grows ever more common.

bee in one's bonnet, a is an idiom cliché meaning to have a fixation or obsession about something, as *I should warn you before you start the job that the boss has a bee in his bonnet about punctuality.* As a cliché the expression dates from the eighteenth century, although the idea is older. It is still very common today. In origin a comparison is being made between a bee buzzing around in a panic-stricken way when caught inside a hat and an idea that goes round and round irrationally in one's head.

beer and skittles is an idiom cliché meaning a life of ease and enjoyment. The expression is often negative in its implications, as *He thinks that the life of a student is all beer and skittles,* and *Being a courier for a holiday company is not all beer and skittles.* The game of skittles is associated with beer, since it is often played in pubs. As a cliché the expression dates from the middle of the nineteenth century and is still in common use today.

bee's knees, the is an idiom cliché meaning the very best, as *She is a very poor singer but she thinks she's the bee's knees.* The expression is American in origin and probably dates from the 1920s. As to derivation it seems likely that the knees of the bees are popular only because the two words happen to rhyme. The cliché is still popular in an informal or slang context.

before you can say Jack Robinson is a catchphrase cliché used to indicate great speed, usually with more optimism than actuality, as *I'll have this room decorated before you can say Jack Robinson.* The identity of Jack Robinson remains obscure, despite much speculation. His earliest recorded written appearance is in Fanny Burney's *Evelina* (1778) 'I'd do it as soon as say Jack Robinson'. A likely explanation seems to be that both elements add up to a very common name, in much the same way that John Smith does. As a cliché the expression probably dates from the nineteenth century and is still in common use today.

beg, borrow or steal is a hackneyed phrase meaning to obtain by any means possible, as *Our car's broken down. We'll have to beg, borrow or steal transport to get to the wedding on time.* The expression dates from the time of Chaucer in the fourteenth century and as a cliché is still popular today, often being used in humorous contexts.

beggars can't be choosers is a proverb cliché referring to the fact that people who are greatly in need of something are not in a position to pick and choose or to be critical of what is offered, as *We are not particularly fond of the house but it was the only one in our price range and beggars can't be choosers*, and *She did not want to work in a factory but she has no qualifications and beggars can't be choosers*. The proverb appeared in John Heywood's collection of proverbs in 1546 and has remained popular as a saying ever since. As a modern cliché it is extremely common, often being used in rather sanctimonious tones of another person's misfortune.

beginning of a new era, the is a hackneyed phrase meaning the start of some completely new stage or development, as *In technological terms the invention of the computer was the beginning of a new era*. The phrase suggests some major new development but in fact the cliché is frequently used to refer to minor changes, or even trivial changes, as *The discarding of the uniform heralded the beginning of a new era for the school*, and *We believe that our current publicity campaign marks the beginning of a new era in marketing*. The cliché dates from the end of the nineteenth century and is widely used today, especially by journalists, politicians and those making public speeches. An alternative form is **the beginning of an era**.

beginning of the end, the is a quotation cliché, being a translation of a remark made by Talleyrand to Napoleon after the battle of Leipzig was lost (1813) '*C'est la commencement de la fin*', although he may not have originated the phrase. The expression refers to a situation or event that marks the start of ruin, disaster, or some other misfortune, as *They only divorced this year but it was the beginning of the end when he had an affair with his secretary a few years ago*, and

The building of the new supermarket was the beginning of the end for many of our local shops. It has been a cliché since the middle of the nineteenth century and is still common today, often said in rather lugubrious tones.

be good is a catchphrase cliché used as a parting greeting in informal, humorous expressions, as *I must be off now. Have a good holiday and be good!* The expression often carries sexual connotations and is still sometimes found as **be good and if you can't be good be careful**, although this longer form is now rather dated. The expression dates from the beginning of the twentieth century in America when it was the title of a song 'If you can't be good be careful' written by Harrington and Tate. The same sentiment is found in → **don't do anything I wouldn't do**.

behind the scenes is a hackneyed phrase used to refer to activities that take place away from the public eye. The expression sometimes carries the suggestion that the activity is secret or even underhand, as *The official talks received a lot of media attention but we think most of the negotiations went on behind the scenes*, and *A great deal of lobbying went on behind the scenes before the new leader was elected*. This is not necessarily the case and it can be used with the same sentiment as → **backroom boys**, as *She always take the credit for the organization but most of the work is done by people slaving away behind the scenes*. The expression can also be used adjectivally, as *We think that there was a great deal of behind-the-scenes wheeling and dealing before the merger of the companies took place*. In origin the expression refers to the fact that in the seventeenth and eighteenth century theatre, especially in France, a great deal of the violent action, such as murders, took place literally behind the scenes. The expression has been used figuratively since the late eighteenth century, becoming a cliché around the middle of the nineteenth century. As a cliché it is still in common use today.

believe it or not is a filler cliché used to alert one's listener to the fact that one is about to say something surprising, as *Believe it or not, he was considered the best applicant for the job.* It is sometimes used virtually meaninglessly by people to whom it has become a habit. It has been a cliché since the middle of the nineteenth century, perhaps having been popularized by a London show entitled *Believe It or Not* (1939–40). In America it was popularized by the cartoonist Robert Leroy Ripley who used the expression as the title of a cartoon series first published in 1918. As a cliché it is still widespread today, being used in informal contexts.

believe one's eyes, cannot is a hackneyed phrase used to emphasize the surprising or unusual nature of what is revealed, as *I could not believe my eyes when I saw a well-dressed woman calmly take a dress off the rack and put it in her briefcase*, and *The children couldn't believe their eyes when they saw the huge Christmas tree*. The expression probably dates from the seventeenth century and became a cliché around the late nineteenth century. It is still common today in informal contexts.

be like that is a hackneyed phrase used to someone who will not agree to do as one wishes, as *Be like that! I'll borrow someone else's book*, and *Be like that! We'll go to the cinema without you*. It is found in informal contexts and is frequently used by children who are peeved by the lack of cooperation on the part of their friends.

be mother is a hackneyed phrase used to mean to pour out tea or coffee or generally act as hostess, as *I'll be mother. Do you take milk and sugar?* It is still used nowadays but it is often regarded as being rather 'twee'. People who use it often do so in a deliberately humorous way.

be my guest is a catchphrase cliché used to indicate that one does not mind someone borrowing or taking something, as *Of course you can borrow my magazine. Be my guest!* and *Yes, you can have the last cake. Be my guest!* The expression has been popular since the 1950s and is still a common cliché used in informal contexts. It is often now used ironically to indicate that someone has borrowed or taken something that one thinks properly belongs to one, or has done something rather high-handedly, as *Actually that was my trolley but be my guest!*

belle of the ball is a hackneyed phrase used to refer to the most beautiful or best-dressed woman at a social gathering, not now necessarily a ball or dance, as *You'll be the belle of the ball in that dress*. It is often now used ironically to describe someone who thinks she is the most beautiful or elegant woman present and who puts on airs. *Belle* as a noun in French means beautiful woman, and the word was adopted into English early in the seventeenth century.

bells and whistles is a hackneyed phrase used to refer, usually in a derogatory way, to features that are purely decorative, being neither functional nor necessary. The term is often applied to machines or gadgets, such as computers, as *I just want an efficient basic model. I don't want any bells and whistles*, and *He just wants a car that will get him from A to B. He doesn't want to pay extra for a lot of bells and whistles.*

bend over backwards is an idiom cliché meaning to go to a great deal of trouble, often excessively so, as *We bent over backwards to make her feel at home but she never really settled in.* The expression often carries the implication that the undue exertion is in vain. It originated in America around the 1920s and is much used as a cliché today. In origin it refers to the physical exertion required to bend backwards. An alternative form is **lean over backwards**.

benefit of the doubt, give the is a hackneyed phrase meaning to treat someone as innocent, even though there may be some doubt or some evidence to the contrary, as *We can't prove that he stole the money and so we must give him the benefit of the doubt, but he was the only person with access to it.* It is sometimes used in a humorous or ironic context, as *If you say you were ill yesterday we'll give you the benefit of the doubt but it was a scorching day and you've got a suntan.* In origin the expression refers to the fact that in law a person is presumed innocent until proved guilty beyond doubt. It has been used figuratively since the nineteenth century and has been a cliché since around the turn of the century, being still commonly used today.

be seeing you! is a catchphrase cliché used as a standard informal greeting on parting from someone, as *There's my bus! I must go! Be seeing you!* It has been common since the middle of the 1940s and is still used today, often being shortened to **see you!** Unlike the more modern **see you later!** it does usually mean that the user will see the person so addressed again.

best bib and tucker is a hackneyed phrase used to refer to one's best clothes, as in *If you're going to dinner with her parents you'd better look out your best bib and tucker.* The expression is used in informal or slang contexts and is now rather dated. It dates from the eighteenth century. In origin it refers to parts of clothing worn only to rather formal events. A bib was a man's formal shirt front or a frill worn on a shirt front, and a tucker was a piece of lace worn on the neck and shoulders by women.

best-laid schemes, the is an allusion cliché used to reflect the fact that the most carefully made plans can go wrong, as *She had the holiday planned down to the very last detail and then there was a ferry strike. Ah, well, the best-laid schemes . . .* The allusion is to a passage from a poem by Robert Burns. In *To a Mouse* (1786) he wrote 'The best laid schemes o' mice and men gang aft agley'. Sometimes the cliché is extended to include the whole quotation as *We had booked a weekend break and then our daughter got chicken pox and we had to stay at home. It's true that the best laid schemes o' (of) mice and men gang aft agley.* The longer version is less common than the shorter one. As a cliché it dates from the late eighteenth century and may have been common before its use by Burns, although he certainly popularized it. The expression, like the concept, is still common today.

best of British, the is a catchphrase cliché, short for **the best of British luck**. It is now used ironically, to indicate that the situation referred to is very difficult or impossible, as *Well, if you think you can get that stain off the carpet, the best of British to you.* The expression is probably military in origin, dating from World War 2, and may have been used ironically from its inception. As a cliché today it is found in informal or slang contexts and is somewhat dated.

best thing since sliced bread, the see *greatest/best thing since slice bread, the*

best things in life are free, the is a catchphrase cliché whose meaning is self-evident. The phrase is the title of a song from the Broadway musical *Good News* (1927) and the title of a film which was released in 1956. Both of these helped to establish the phrase as a common twentieth-century cliché and catchphrase. It is frequently now used ironically, since only people who are comfortably off are in a position to make this claim.

be that as it may is a hackneyed phrase which is also used as a filler cliché. It is equivalent to 'that may be true', as *You say that he is basically honest. Be that as it may, we are almost certain that he took the money.* Sometimes it is used virtually meaninglessly by people to whom it has become a habit. The expression dates from the nineteenth century. It is still common today and although it has rather a formal ring, it is found in informal as well as formal contexts.

better half, one's is a hackneyed phrase used by some men to refer to their wives, as *Thanks for the invitation. I'll have to ask my better half.* The idea of two people being two halves of a whole goes back to Roman days, when Horace used it to refer to friends. The term dates from the sixteenth century. Originally it, too, referred to close friends or lovers, eventually coming to mean a wife. As a jocular cliché it has been common since the middle of the nineteenth century. It is rather dated today when many women would regard it as patronizing although it is ostensibly a compliment.

better late than never is a hackneyed phrase used in an attempt to minimize the inconvenience caused by lack of punctuality. As a sentiment it dates from Roman times. The expression appears in several early collections of English proverbs, sometimes given in the extended form **better late than never, but better never late**. As a modern cliché it is extremely

common, a reflection of the fact, no doubt, that lateness is extremely common. The expression is used by people who are late themselves in cheerful disregard of the effects their poor time-keeping may have on others. It is also used by those at the receiving end of the unpunctuality seemingly in cheerful or polite acceptance of the unpunctuality but sometimes said through gritted teeth.

better safe than sorry is a hackneyed phrase advocating the virtues of safety and caution and pointing to the dangers of ignoring these, as *You'd better go back and check that you locked the back door. Better safe than sorry*, and *Have you checked the tyres and oil? Better safe than sorry.* As a cliché it dates from the twentieth century but the idea is considerably older. The cliché has a marked tendency to sound smug as though the person giving the advice knows best, and is frequently a source of annoyance to recipients of the advice.

between a rock and a hard place is an idiom cliché meaning a situation in which one is faced with a choice of two equally unpleasant or unacceptable choices, a rock and a hard place meaning the same in this context, as *I'm between a rock and a hard place. If I stay with my present company I have to move to another branch at the other end of the country. If I leave I'll have to take a job with a firm that doesn't pay so well.* It dates from the early twentieth century in its native America but its appearance in British English is fairly recent and even now it is sometimes used by people who are consciously using it as an Americanism. The phrase conveys the same sentiment as the older idioms **between Scylla and Charybdis** and **between the devil and the deep blue sea**.

between jobs is a euphemism cliché meaning unemployed. It sometimes genuinely means that someone has left one job and is waiting to take up another which has already been negotiated. Frequently, however, it is used to avoid having to admit to being unemployed or redundant, as *My husband is between jobs at the moment and so he is concentrating on the garden.* The cliché dates from around the late 1970s when general unemployment became a serious issue in Britain. It is a more general form of the theatrical euphemism **resting**, used of an actor who is without work for a while.

between you and me is a hackneyed phrase used to impress on someone the need for secrecy. In fact, it is more usually taken as a signal for the revelation of a really juicy piece of gossip which the hearer will then rush to pass on to someone else, as *They're supposed to be married, but between you and me I know for a fact that he is married already.* A later alternative form is **between you, me and the gatepost** which means much the same as the original form and dates from the late nineteenth century. Dating from around the same time is **between you, me and the bedpost** but this is no longer common. It is very common for people to use the phrase ungrammatically, as **between you and I**.

beyond our ken is a hackneyed phrase meaning beyond our understanding or experience. It is often used to refer to the understanding of mortals generally, as *I would never dare dabble in spiritualism. Some things are beyond our ken.* Indeed the expression **beyond the ken of mortal men** also exists, although it is not now commonly used. The expression is also used to refer to the particular rather than the general, as *It is beyond our ken what she sees in him but she is going to marry him*, and is sometimes used in humorous contexts.

As a cliché it dates from the late nineteenth century.

beyond the pale is a hackneyed phrase meaning morally or socially unacceptable, as *Her parents are very broad-minded but the conduct of her fiancé's drunken friends at the party was beyond the pale.* As a cliché the expression dates from the late nineteenth century. It is still common today and is often used in humorous or ironic contexts, as *I'm sure that we won't be invited to the wedding. It's to be a big society event and we are beyond the pale.* In origin the expression refers historically to the Pale in fourteenth-century Ireland which was the part within the bounds of English rule and therefore thought by them to be an area of civilization or superiority, anyone living outside this being deemed vastly inferior. A pale was first a stake of the kind used to build a fence, then its meaning extended to describe an area separated by a fence.

bide one's time, to is a hackneyed phrase meaning to wait for the right opportunity before taking any form of action, as *Now is not a good time to ask your father for a loan. You should bide your time and wait until he's in a better mood.* It often carries some rather sinister connotations, as *The landlord is being too nice. I think he's just biding his time to find a reason to throw us out.* The expression has been a cliché since the later part of the nineteenth century and is still common today. The verb 'to bide' is obsolete in English except in this expression, although it is still common in Scots.

Big Brother is watching you is a quotation cliché warning of the power that the authorities have over us, including that of surveillance, as *I know that surveillance cameras in the city centre might make the place safer but it does savour a bit of Big Brother is watching you.* The quotation is from

George Orwell's *Nineteen Eighty-Four* (1949). As a cliché it has been generally used since about 1960, although it was used by people of a literary bent before then. Before Orwell, 'big brother' was a synonym for kindly protection.

bigger they are, the harder they fall, the is a catchphrase cliché referring to the fact that the downfall of someone important is much more dramatic than the downfall of someone of lesser status. It is usually said with approbation, the user of the phrase being glad of the downfall, as *He is in a position of power just now but after the merger there will be a management shake-up and he will be out. The bigger they are, the harder they fall.* As a catchphrase it dates from the late nineteenth century and is still common as a cliché today. In origin it probably refers to boxers, since someone who is large and heavy falls down harder than a lighter person.

bird in the hand, a is an allusion cliché which refers to some kind of advantage that one already has or that one is sure of being preferable to something that one might acquire, as *You should stay in this job until you get another one. You know what they say about a bird in the hand.* The allusion is to the proverb **a bird in the hand is worth two in the bush**. The full version is also used as a cliché, as *We must find a flat before we give the landlord notice. A bird in the hand is worth two in the bush.* The proverb first appeared in English in the fifteenth century and appeared in Greek and Latin before then. Both the full proverb and the truncated version are commonly used today, particularly by people who like to give cautionary advice to others.

birds of a feather is an allusion cliché used to refer to people who are very similar in character, tastes, attitudes, etc, often in a derogatory way, as *I'm not surprised they go everywhere together. They're birds of a feather*, and *The two older boys are birds of a feather and have both been in prison but the youngest one is honest and hard-working.* As a cliché it has been common since the nineteenth century and is still popular today. It is an allusion to the proverb **birds of a feather flock together** meaning that people of like tastes and character tend to stick together. The proverb has been popular since the seventeenth century but the sentiment is much older, having been used in Greek and Roman times.

bite off more than one can chew is an idiom cliché meaning to undertake more than one is likely to be able to deal with effectively, as *She is trying to save for her holiday but she has bitten off more than she can chew. She cleans offices in the morning, serves in a shop in the afternoon and babysits in the evening*, and *I think the student has bitten off more than he can chew by taking on five subjects in his first year.* As a cliché it dates from the late nineteenth century but cautionary advice against overburdening oneself dates from the Middle Ages.

bite the bullet is an idiom cliché meaning to steel oneself to accept something distressing, unpleasant, etc, as *I know you hate telling people that they are to be redundant but you'll just have to bite the bullet and get on with it*, and *She was dreading going to see the doctor but we finally persuaded her to bite the bullet and make an appointment.* The expression dates from the twentieth century and is still common today, being used in informal or slang contexts. In origin it probably refers to the days before anaesthesia, when soldiers wounded in battle were given a lead bullet to bite on to brace themselves against the pain of surgery.

bite the dust is an idiom cliché meaning to die or come to an end, as *Many of the gangsters bit the dust in the raid*, and *Our plans to go away for the summer have bitten the dust. We've no money*. It became current in America in the late 1930s and later became common in Britain. As a cliché it is still popular today, being used in very informal or slang contexts. In origin the term comes from Western films in which cowboys and Indians were frequently shot and fell off their horses dead into the dust.

blazing inferno, a is a hackneyed phrase used to describe a fire. It is much used by journalists, especially in headlines, as *man leaps from roof in blazing inferno*. It would properly be used to describe a very large and dangerous fire, but is in fact often used to describe anything bigger than a small garden rubbish fire, the tabloid press having a weakness for exaggeration, which sells more copies of newspapers. As a cliché it dates from the late nineteenth century.

blessing in disguise, a is a hackneyed phrase which described a piece of seemingly bad fortune that turns out to be some form of good fortune, as *His gambling losses were a blessing in disguise. He had become addicted and decided to stop*. The phrase appears in a poem by the eighteenth century poet, James Hervey 'E'en crosses from his sovereign are blessings in disguise', 'cross' here meaning 'burden'. The expression has been a cliché since the late nineteenth century and is still widespread today.

blind leading the blind, the is an allusion cliché used to describe a situation in which the people in charge who are meant to be instructing or guiding others know no more than the people that they are in charge of, as *The courier who was meant to be showing us around the area kept getting lost. Talk about the blind leading the blind*, and *They've put me down to teach geography and I know nothing about it. It's a case of the blind leading the blind*. The allusion is to the Bible, to *Matthew* (15:14): 'Let them alone; they are blind leaders of the blind. And if the blind lead the blind, both shall fall in the ditch.' Much the same sentiment as the latter is contained in a proverb featuring in John Heywood's collection of 1546: 'Where the blind leadeth the blind both fall into the dike.' It is still a widespread cliché today.

blood is thicker than water is a proverb cliché meaning that, however binding the ties of friendship, those of family are stronger, as *My best friend's looking for a place to live, but so is my sister. I've got only one spare room and blood's thicker than water*. The concept dates from the Middle Ages and the term appears in John Ray's collection of proverbs in 1670. As a cliché it is still very common today.

blot on the landscape, a is a hackneyed phrase used to refer to something that is considered a disfigurement on the landscape or environment, as *I'm glad they've demolished those high-rise flats. They were a real blot on the landscape*. As a cliché it dates from the late nineteenth century and is still common today, probably because there are so many blots on the landscape.

blow hot and cold is an idiom cliché meaning to vacillate between being enthusiastic and apathetic about something, as *It's difficult to get a decision out of the planning committee. They seem to be blowing hot and cold on our project*. The expression dates from the sixteenth century and has been a cliché since the eighteenth century. It is still common today. In origin it refers to Aesop's fable in which a centaur assumed that a man must be blowing hot and cold from the same mouth because he blew on his hands to warm them and on his soup to cool it.

blue-rinse brigade, the is a hackneyed phrase used to refer to well-off, middle-aged women with time and money to spare, who as a group tend to play a significant part in the management of local affairs, the running of local branches of political parties, etc. Since they are seen to be interfering as well as formidable, the term is used in a derogatory way, as *Local government around here is full of the blue-rinse brigade*, and *We don't want too many of the blue-rinse brigade on the school board*. The cliché dates from the second part of the twentieth century. In origin the expression refers to the fact that women whose hair is going grey sometimes have a blue-rinse put through it to make it less dingy, although this practice has grown less common as hair colouring techniques have improved.

blushing bride is a hackneyed phrase used to refer to a woman on her wedding day. It is particularly beloved of some journalists, as *The blushing bride was attended by two flower-girls*. As a cliché it dates from the twentieth century and is now rather dated, as indeed is the concept. In origin it refers to the fact that brides were traditionally pure and modest.

bone of contention, a is an idiom cliché meaning a cause of dispute, as *The communal wall has been a bone of contention between the two neighbours for years*. As a cliché the expression dates from the nineteenth century and is still in widespread use today. In origin it refers to a bone which is being fought over by two dogs.

bone to pick, a is an idiom cliché indicating a cause of dispute or complaint that requires discussion, as *I have a bone to pick with you. I gather that you have been going around saying that I'm dishonest*. The expression dates from the sixteenth century and refers to dogs worrying over a bone. In this it bears a resemblance to **a bone of contention**. As a cliché it is still popular in informal contexts. It is often used humorously.

bottom line, the is a vogue cliché with its origins in accountancy, where it refers to the bottom line of a financial statement which indicates the extent of the profit or loss. It is one of several terms that began life in a specialist field and then crossed over to the general language. It began to be used figuratively in the middle of the twentieth century and rapidly became a cliché. In the 1980s it practically reached saturation point, journalists, as always in such a situation, playing a part, but aided and abetted by people in the public eye and people being interviewed on radio and television. With its financial connections it was perhaps the ideal cliché for the 1980s, a decade that seemed obsessed with money, and indeed may be considered to be the linguistic equivalent of the Yuppie. People are often slightly confused as to the exact meaning of specialist expressions that become generalized. The result is that **the bottom line** has a range of meanings, from the final outcome of something (as *The talks went on for days and even then the bottom line was that they agreed to differ*), to the crux or most important point of something (as *The bottom line of the discussion is who is going to provide the money*), to the last straw (as *He always shouted her at her when he came home drunk but the bottom line was when he hit her. She left him*). The popularity of the term perhaps waned in the 1990s but that is mostly because it was difficult for any phrase to sustain the level of coverage which it achieved. It is, however, almost certainly one of those rather annoying clichés that will keep popping up.

box of tricks see *bag of tricks*

breath of fresh air, like a is a simile cliché used to indicate someone or something new and refreshing, as *The young members who have just joined the club have been like a breath of fresh air. It was getting so fuddy-duddy*, and *The ideas which the new members have brought to the committee are like a breath of fresh air*. The term became current in the middle of the nineteenth century and is still widespread today. Earlier forms of the expression were **like a breath of heaven** and **like a breath of spring**.

bright-eyed and bushy-tailed is an idiom cliché meaning lively and alert. The expression is used in informal, and often in humorous, contexts, as *How can you look so bright-eyed and bushy-tailed this morning when we've all got a hangover?* In origin it refers to the alert aspect and bushy tail of the squirrel and probably came to Britain from America, where it dates from the 1930s.

brother's keeper, I am not my see *keeper, I am not . . .*

brownie points is an idiom cliché meaning credit for doing something right or for doing a good deed, as *I'll get brownie points from my mother if I clean my room without being asked*. It is often used humorously or ironically and sometimes carries a suggestion that the person getting the brownie points is something of a self-seeker, as *He gets a lot of brownie points from the boss for doing unpaid overtime*. As a cliché it dates from the later part of the twentieth century. There is some dispute over the origin. The obvious origin would appear to be to the

Brownie guides, who received awards or badges, but more for levels of proficiency in various fields, rather than for the good deeds which they were expected to perform without reward. An alternative suggestion is that the expression refers to a points system for employees operated by American railway companies. Yet another suggestion is that **brownie points** shares an origin with brown-nosing which means sucking up to someone in authority and is synonymous with arse-licking.

buck stops here, the see *pass the buck*

bury the hatchet is an idiom cliché meaning to make peace, to end a quarrel or argument, as *He and his brother quarrelled and hadn't spoken to each other for years, but they buried the hatchet when their mother died*. As a cliché the expression dates from the beginning of the twentieth century and is still popular today in informal contexts. In origin it refers to some North American Indian tribes who buried a hatchet on declaring peace.

business, do the is the hackneyed phrase used to mean to accomplish something. As a cliché the expression dates from the second part of the twentieth century and is still common today in informal or slang contexts. It is particularly common in sporting contexts, being exceptionally popular with football commentators to describe scoring a goal or achieving victory, as *They can still win if their striker can do the business in the second half.*

business is business is a catchphrase cliché indicating that the profit motive takes precedence over all other considerations, as *He says that he would like to rent his cousin one of his holiday cottages free of charge but business is business*. As a cliché it dates from the twentieth century.

Nowadays the motivation of the expression is more common than the expression itself.

buy a pig in a poke is an idiom cliché meaning to buy or accept something without examining its quality with the implication that an apparent bargain may deceive, as *He bought a pig in a poke with that car. It was cheap but it kept breaking down.* As a cliché the term dates from the nineteenth century but the idea is much older. The cliché is still common today. In origin it supposedly refers to an old fairground trick when a trader would sell a piglet in a poke (a bag) so that the purchaser could not see it before paying for it. It shares this origin with **let the cat out of the bag**.

by the same token is a hackneyed phrase, often used simply as a filler cliché. As a hackneyed phrase it means in the same way, for the same, or an associated, reason, as *Conditions are so bad that many of the staff are leaving and by the same token those who remain are demoralized.* This is a phrase to which some people become addicted and they use it without thinking and almost without meaning. As a cliché it dates from the late eighteenth century.

C

call a spade a spade is a hackneyed phrase meaning to be direct and blunt, as *They call it giving me early retirement. I call it sacking me. I prefer to call a spade a spade.* Although there is much to be lauded in straightforward talking as opposed to euphemism, there is no doubt that many people who are fond of this expression pride themselves on being blunt to the extent of rudeness or tactlessness, as *They say he has learning disabilities but I prefer to say that he is mentally handicapped. I call a spade a spade.* The expression has been current in English since the sixteenth century but common enough to be called a cliché only since the nineteenth century. The concept, and possibly the wording, is much older, going back to Greek and Roman times. Those for whom directness is not enough were wont to rephrase the expression as **call a spade a bloody shovel** but this version, if not the thinking behind it, is now not so common.

call it a day is a hackneyed phrase meaning to stop work or to stop doing something either for a time or permanently, as *We've run out of paint and so we might as well call it a day*, and *After forty years as caretaker he has decided to call it a day.* As a cliché it dates from the twentieth century and it is still common, being used in informal or slang contexts. In origin it means that those concerned are treating a particular time as though it were the end of the working day, irrespective of what the time actually is. The end referred to does not in fact have to do with work, the cliché being wider in

its application, as *They have not been getting on well for years, so they've decided to call it a day and get a divorce.*

call me old-fashioned is a hackeneyed phrase used as an introduction to a thought or attitude that is no longer fashionable, as *Call me old-fashioned but I don't like the idea of men and women being together in the same hospital ward.* It is often used virtually meaninglessly by those to whom it has become an annoying habit, or in humorous contexts.

calm before the storm, the is an idiom cliché used to describe a period of quiet before the onset of violence, protest, quarrelling, etc. It is usually used by someone predicting, often on the basis of experience, that some form of outburst is about to take place, as *I haven't heard from my mother since I wrote and said I was giving up my job and travelling round the world. This is just the calm before the storm.* The phrase was much used by statesmen in 1938–39 with reference to the period before World War 2 broke out, and was later used in a wider variety of contexts. It has been a cliché since the late nineteenth century. In origin it refers to the period of rather eerie stillness that often precedes a storm.

can of worms, a is an idiom cliché used to refer to a problematic and involved situation that is very difficult to deal with and the full extent of which is hard to estimate, as *I wish that I'd never got involved in this project. It's a real can of worms. All the other* *organizers are quarrelling with each other and most of them are related.* In origin it refers to a container of wriggling worms to be used as bait for anglers. The worms form a tangle and are practically impossible to separate. The expression often includes the word 'open', as *If you try to sort out the quarrel between your neighbours you'll really be opening a can of worms.* It is American in origin and in Britain dates from the later part of the twentieth century. It is found in informal or slang contexts.

cards on the table, lay one's see *lay one's cards on the table*

carry the can is an idiom cliché meaning to take responsibility or blame where that properly lies with, or should be shared by, someone else, as *He can't complain about having to carry the can for his department's mistake. That's part of the manager's job*, and *The rest of the robbers ran away and left the get-away driver to carry the can.* As a cliché the expression dates from the second part of the twentieth century and is still a popular cliché today, being used in informal and slang contexts. In origin it is probably a military expression which was used to refer to the man selected to carry the beer for a group and to carry the can back when it was empty.

cart before the horse, put the is an idiom cliché meaning to reverse the correct or usual order of things, as *He has painted the walls before the ceiling. Trust him to put the cart before the horse.* It became a cliché in the eighteenth century although the expression is considerably older and the concept even older still, going back to Greek and Roman times. It is still a common cliché today.

castles in the air is a hackneyed phrase used to refer to dreams of future happiness, wealth, etc that are unrealistic and so very unlikely to come true, as *She talks of buying a house in the South of France but it's just castles in the air.* The expression **build castles in the air** has been a semi-proverbial saying for some considerable time and **castles in the air** has been a cliché since the nineteenth century. It is still common today. An expression that conveys the same sentiment is **castles in Spain**, although this is now rare.

cat got your tongue? see *has the cat got your tongue*?

catch one's death is a hackneyed phrase that exaggerated the danger of getting cold or wet, as *Surely you're not going out without a coat in that rain. You'll catch your death.* The expression has been popular since the late nineteenth century. It is still used today, but often by older people, in informal or dialectal contexts.

catch redhanded is an idiom cliché which means to find someone in the very act of committing a crime or misdeed, as *He was taking the money from the till when the boss came in and caught him redhanded.* Originally the crime concerned was murder, the image being of a murderer caught with blood on his or her hands. The expression was later extended to cover other crimes. It has been common since the nineteenth century and is still common today, often being used in humorous contexts, as *Ah, caught you redhanded eating chocolates. I thought you were supposed to be on a diet.*

Catch 22 is an allusion cliché used to describe a situation in which one cannot possibly win, as *It's a Catch 22 situation for young people today. They cannot get jobs without experience but they cannot gain experience without jobs.* It is an allusion to the title of a book by Joseph Heller

Catch 22 (1961). The catch refers to the plight of Captain Yossarian, an American bombardier. He wanted out of taking part in any more bombing missions since he did not wish to be killed. The best way to bring this about was to be declared crazy and so he tried to become so categorized. However he was told that if someone wanted to be grounded out of concern for his life that was clearly the thought of a sane mind and he could not be declared crazy. The phrase became a cliché in Britain in the 1970s and is still popular today.

caught napping is an idiom cliché used to indicate that someone has been caught unawares or offguard, as *The first snow of winter caught the roads department napping. They had not enough grit.* As a cliché it dates from the twentieth century and is still popular today in informal contexts. The sentiment was used by Shakespeare in *The Taming of the Shrew* (4:2) 'Nay, I have Ta'en you napping, gentle love.' In origin it refers to finding someone having a nap or short sleep. It is also found in the active form **catch someone napping**

caught with one's trousers down is an idiom cliché meaning discovered in an embarrassing or compromising position, as *He was really caught with his trousers down. He was sitting in the boss's office with his feet up on his desk and smoking a cigar when the boss walked in.* The expression dates from the twentieth century and is still popular, the American equivalent being **caught with one's pants down**. There are two suggested origins. One is that it refers to a man who is having an illicit love affair and is caught in the act by his lover's husband. The other is that it refers to a man who is encountered relieving himself outside, possibly a soldier encountered by one of the enemy. The expression is also found in the active form **catch with one's trousers down**.

cause célèbre (French for 'famous case') is a foreign cliché used to refer to a legal trial or case that attracts a great deal of attention, as *The trial of Ruth Ellis was a cause célèbre because she was the last woman in Britain to be hanged.* As a cliché it dates from the middle of the nineteenth century. It is not so common today as it once was, although it is still used by journalists, often of cases that are in fact quite minor.

chain reaction is a hackneyed phrase and vogue cliché referring to a situation involving a series of events, in which each event causes another, as *When Jack refused to go to school it started a chain reaction among the children in the district. Jim wouldn't go if Jack wasn't going and Jim's sister wouldn't go if Jim wasn't going.* It is one of several clichés which have their origins in technical language, since a **chain reaction** was originally a term used in chemistry and nuclear physics in the 1930s and referred to a reaction that created energy or products that in turn caused further reactions without further energy input from outside. The expression passed into the general language and became popular in the 1970s. As a modern cliché it is still widespread, its technical connections having been largely forgotten by all but specialists. Very often the idea of a series of changes has also been lost and the phrase is used simply to describe any change, often quite minor.

chalk and cheese see *different as chalk and cheese*

chalk it up to experience is an idiom cliché indicating that there is nothing to be done about some setback or piece of misfortune, as *It's annoying that they promised you the job and then turned you down but there's nothing you can do about it. You might as well chalk it up to experience.* The expression **chalk it up** was used to refer to the practice of keeping a record of who owed what in pubs, etc by chalking it on a slate or blackboard. Later, scores in games were chalked on slates. **Chalk it up to experience** dates from around the nineteenth century and today is being used mainly in informal contexts.

champing at the bit is an idiom cliché meaning showing signs of great impatience, as *I wish my husband would hurry up with the car. The children are champing at the bit to go to the seaside.* It has been in use as a figurative expression since the beginning of the twentieth century. It is a popular cliché today, being used in informal contexts. In origin it refers to a racehorse chewing at its bit at the start of a race while waiting impatiently to be off.

change of scene, a is a hackneyed phrase used to indicate a move from one place or situation to another, often temporary and often regarded as being beneficial in some way, as *She was ill and has gone to spend a few days by the sea for a change of scene*, and *He thinks that he's been in the computing industry too long and he's looking for a change of scene.* As a cliché the expression dates from the late nineteenth century and it is still extremely common in all but the most formal of contexts. In origin it refers to the changing of a scene in the theatre.

chapter of accidents, a is a hackneyed phrase meaning a series of misfortunes, as *Don't mention our holiday. It was a chapter of accidents from beginning to end*, and *The car got a flat tyre, I broke the heel of my shoe and I got caught in a thunderstorm. Talk about a chapter of accidents!*

charmed life, lead a is a hackneyed phrase meaning to be extremely lucky, to be involved in a great many risky or dangerous situations but always to remain unscathed, as *The mountaineer has taken part in many dangerous expeditions but he's never even had a minor injury. He leads a charmed life*, and *He's been involved in a great many shady deals but the police never catch up with him. He seems to lead a charmed life.* The expression was used by Shakespeare in *Macbeth* (5:8) in which Macbeth says 'I bear a charmed life which must not yield to one of woman born.' It has been a cliché since the middle of the nineteenth century and is still common today. It literally means to lead a life that is protected in some way by magic.

cheap and cheerful is a catchphrase cliché used to refer to furniture or clothes with the implication that to have spent more would not have been justified. It is sometimes used in a deliberately deprecatory way, just as one might say 'This old thing!' of a dress, as *Oh do you like it? We just wanted something cheap and cheerful for the children's rooms.* It is also sometimes used as a not very subtle way of criticizing someone else's taste, often in rather a bitchy way, as *That's a nice dress you're wearing – something cheap and cheerful for the summer.* As a cliché it dates from around the 1960s.

cheek by jowl is a doublet cliché, cheek and jowl being more or less synonymous. It is used to mean very close, often excessively, uncomfortably or inappropriately close, as *He is such a snob that he objects to going on buses and standing cheek by jowl with what he calls the rabble*, and *In that part of town historic old buildings stand cheek by jowl with ghastly concrete office blocks.* The expression has been current since the sixteenth century. It has been a cliché since the middle of the eighteenth century and is still widespread today.

cheque is in the post, the is a hackneyed phrase used as a business cliché. It is often, in fact, used as a euphemism for 'It is our intention to put the cheque in the post as soon as we can spare the money but we do not wish to admit that', or even as a downright lie told in the hope that the potential recipient of the cheque will stop harassing the potential payer. To those whose salary is paid into a bank automatically at the end of the month this cliché may sound amusing. To those who work freelance it has an all too familiar and depressing ring. As a cliché it dates from the twentieth century and is rampant today.

chiefs and no Indians, all see *all chiefs and no Indians*

children of all ages is a hackneyed phrase usually used in rather hearty tones when trying to interest people in some form of merchandise or leisure venture, as *This board game is suitable for children of all ages*, and *Children of all ages will enjoy a day out in the theme park*. The implication is that something will appeal not only to actual children but to those who are youthful enough in their attitudes, and fun-loving enough, to enjoy it as adults. As a cliché it dates from the twentieth century and is still found today. It almost always sounds cringe-making.

chip off the old block, a is a hackneyed phrase used to describe someone, often a son, who is very like a parent, often his father, in attitude, talent, character, appearance, etc, as *He is a very talented writer. He's a chip off the old block and no mistake*, and *He is a real chip off the old block. He's just as mean as his father was and never gives a penny to charity*. The expression dates from the seventeenth century, although it originally took the form of a **chip of the old block**. As a cliché it dates from the eighteenth century.

chop and change is a doublet cliché meaning to make constant changes, as *I thought*

that she had finished writing the novel but she keeps chopping and changing it. The expression dates from around the middle of the sixteenth century and as a cliché dates from the eighteenth century. It is still a common cliché today. Literally it means to barter and exchange.

circumstances beyond our control is a hackneyed phrase used as an official excuse for things that have gone wrong, whether or not the circumstances were beyond the control of the person making the excuse. It is used, for example, in letters replying to complaints about late orders, as *We are sorry that you have not received the goods which you ordered. This is due to circumstances beyond our control and we have contacted the manufacturer*. It used to be a favourite of people giving reasons for delays or cancellations on public transport, in reality giving no reason or explanation at all. The cliché dates from the twentieth century. It is still used today, but probably less frequently, perhaps because people have become more inventive about composing excuses, perhaps because the public are now less likely to accept a bland excuse, or perhaps because people are less polite and less likely to answer letters or bother giving excuses. When it is used it is found either in fairly formal contexts or in humorous contexts.

clear the air is an idiom cliché meaning to remove any confusion or misunderstanding from the situation, to make an atmosphere less tense, as *There is such an atmosphere in the office since things started going missing. I wish the police would find the culprit and clear the air*, and *She thinks he is trying to get her job. It's time she had it out with him and cleared the air*. The expression became popular in the late nineteenth century and is still popular in all but the most formal contexts. In origin it refers to the sultry atmosphere before a storm that is dispersed when it starts to rain.

clear the decks is an idiom cliché meaning to get ready for action, sometimes carrying the implication that any obstacles or details that are in the way should be removed, as *Right then, let's clear the decks for the party!* and *We'd better clear the decks for the delivery of new stock.* As a figurative expression it dates from the eighteenth century and as a cliché from the late nineteenth century. It is still common in fairly informal contexts today. In origin the phrase refers to the clearing of the decks of ships in preparation for battle.

close shave, a is an idiom cliché meaning a narrow, and often lucky, escape, as *That was a close shave. I nearly bumped into my teacher and I'm supposed to be off sick.* The expression dates from the nineteenth century and in origin it refers to the fact that if someone shaves very closely he may well cut himself badly, especially when shaving with an old open-style razor. As a cliché it is common today in informal contexts. An alternative form of the expression is **a close thing**.

close your eyes and think of England is a catchphrase cliché, possibly originally given as a piece of advice to someone living abroad in circumstances which were either hard or not to their taste, but becoming more popular in a sexual context as a piece of advice to a woman who did not wish to have sexual intercourse with her husband but who thought that she had to put up with it. The catchphrase dates from the late nineteenth century. As a cliché today it is used in humorous or satirical contexts, as *Her new husband is very rich but he is old and ugly. I don't know how she can bear to be with him but I suppose she must just lie back and think of England.*

coals to Newcastle is an idiom cliché meaning something unnecessary or superfluous, as *It's a kind thought but please don't buy a cake for my mother. It'll be coals to Newcastle. She spends half her time baking,* and *I wouldn't move there to find a job. It would be coals to Newcastle. They have enough unemployed there already.* The extended form of the expression is **carry coals to Newcastle**. It was used figuratively from the seventeenth century and is a common cliché today. Newcastle-upon-Tyne was a centre of the coal-mining industry.

coast is clear, the is an idiom cliché meaning that one can escape or proceed without the likelihood of getting caught because there is no one watching, as *The reporters are waiting to interview her. She has asked us to tell her when they've gone and the coast is clear,* and *He stole the money from the old man's house while his sister kept watch to make sure that the coast was clear.* The expression has been popular since the eighteenth century and is still common today in informal contexts. In origin it may refer to smugglers commenting on the absence of coastguards from the shore.

cold blood, in is a hackneyed phrase used to describe an act carried out with calculation and cruelty, as *She did not kill her husband in a fit of passion. She poisoned him in cold blood.* As a cliché it is very frequently associated with murder and is common today. In origin it refers to an old belief that the blood was very hot when one was excited but very cold when one was calm.

cold feet, get is an idiom cliché meaning to become afraid and decide against taking some form of action that one had hitherto plucked up courage to do, as in *He was going to ask her to marry him but at the last* minute he got cold feet, and *She was going to throw in her job and work her way round the world but she got cold feet*. The expression dates from the nineteenth century and is still a widespread cliché today, being really the only phrase that springs to mind to describe the situation. Its origin is uncertain. It has been suggested that it may derive from soldiers retreating from the battle because their feet were frozen.

cold light of day, in the is a hackneyed phrase referring to a time of calm and careful thought, as *It seemed like a good idea to give up our jobs and go to Greece when we had had a few drinks, but next morning in the cold light of day it seemed a mad scheme.* An earlier form of the expression was **in the cold light of reason**. This is still found but it is less common. The expression dates from the nineteenth century and is a common cliché today, aptly describing the effect that reality has on our wilder enthusiasms.

cold shoulder, give the is an idiom cliché meaning to snub or ostracize someone, as *Her fellow workers all gave her the cold shoulder when they discovered that she had beaten her children.* The expression dates from the nineteenth century and appears in the works of Walter Scott. In origin it may refer historically to giving cold shoulder of mutton to guests, instead of a hot meal of a better cut of meat, thereby indicating that they were not welcome and so snubbing them.

cold water on, pour is an idiom cliché meaning to discourage or lessen enthusiasm for, as *The children wanted to sleep in a tent in the garden overnight but their parents poured cold water on the idea.* The concept dates from Roman times, having been used by Plautus. As a cliché it dates from the nineteenth century and is still widespread.

come back, all is forgiven is a catchphrase cliché used humorously or ironically to refer to someone who has left, or been dismissed from, a job, organization, etc, as *None of us can figure out the filing system. Come back Mary, all is forgiven.* The expression probably dates from the end of the nineteenth century and was a popular military catchphrase. As a cliché it dates from the second part of the twentieth century.

come full circle is a hackneyed phrase used to refer to a situation in which events have run their course and things have returned to their original state, as *His greatgrandfather had to sell the manor house in the nineteenth century but he made a fortune in oil and has bought it back again. Things have come full circle.* The idea is that a cycle has been completed. The expression is often extended to **the wheel has come full circle**, an expression that was probably originated by Shakespeare in *King Lear* (5:3) 'The wheel is come full circle.'

come home to roost is an idiom cliché referring to the fact that someone's mistakes, misdeeds, etc have rebounded on him or her, as *He was really horrible to Jim when he was a department manager and Jim was a trainee, but his nastiness has come to roost since Jim was made managing director.* The expression is frequently found in its fuller version **chickens come home to roost**, as *She had been embezzling small amounts of money for years but her chickens only came home to roost when the company was taken over.* The sentiment was referred to by Robert Southey in *The Curse of Kehama* (1809): 'Curses are like young chickens; they always come home to roost.' As a cliché the full expression dates from the middle of the nineteenth century. Both the shortened and full versions are still common today. In origin it refers to chickens returning to their roost at the end of the day, this concept of course predating modern chicken rearing systems in which the birds lack that kind of freedom.

come into the body of the kirk is a hackneyed phrase used to a group of people to encourage them to move closer together, especially to encourage them to sit together in a hall, rather than be spread round it, as *You latecomers needn't sit at the back. Come into the body of the kirk.* In origin it refers to people going to sit in the main part of a church, 'kirk' being the Scots word for church. As a cliché it now tends to sound rather cosy, although it is the kind of expression to which some people, especially now older people, become addicted, often to the annoyance of their listeners.

come out of the closet is an idiom cliché meaning publicly to admit that one indulges in a pastime that others might disapprove of, and that one has hitherto kept secret. It can be used of a wide range of interests and is often used humorously, as *We all thought that she was such an intellectual but she came out of the closet and told us that she reads romantic novels,* and *He is a gourmet chef but he came out of the closet and admits to using tomato ketchup on his own food.* Originally its use was restricted to people revealing that they were homosexual and in this sense it is now usually shortened to **come out**. Closet in American English means a cupboard or wardrobe. **Come out of the closet** in its more general use dates from around the mid 1970s and is still common today in informal contexts.

come to grief is a hackneyed phrase used to mean to end in disaster, to fail, as *Our plans for expansion came to grief when the recession started.* The expression has been popular since around the middle of the nineteenth century. As a cliché it is still common today, being used in all but the most formal contexts. Grief is a rather old-fashioned word for sorrow or unhappiness.

come up and see my etchings is a catchphrase cliché used to ask someone to visit one's flat, ostensibly to admire one's collections of drawings, but really with a view to having a sexual relationship. Although it originally applied only to men inviting women, in these more enlightened days the expression has achieved unisex status. Its early history is uncertain but it is likely that the catchphrase dates from around the beginning of the twentieth century. People who use it today do so in a consciously dated way for humorous effect, as though satirizing an old melodrama. The same kind of sentiment is expressed in **come up some time and see me**, which Mae West uses in the 1933 film *She Done Him Wrong.*

come up to scratch see *up to scratch*

come to the same thing is a hackneyed phrase indicating that one thing or situation is basically much the same as another, that in essence there is no difference between them, as *It comes to the same thing whether you say he was declared redundant or whether you say he was sacked.* A fuller form of the expression is **come to the same thing in the end**. As a cliché it dates from the end of the nineteenth century and is still widespread today.

commanding lead, a is a hackneyed phrase used to indicate the margin by which someone or something is winning. It can apply to a wide range of contexts such as sport, as *Last year's champion has a commanding lead in the marathon event*, and *The favourite had a commanding lead but fell at the last fence*, to elections or political opinion polls, as *In the last published opinion poll the opposition had a commanding lead over the government*. It is a cliché much used by journalists and often the commanding lead referred to is not as substantial as the phrase suggests.

comme il faut (French for 'as it should be') is a foreign cliché used to mean according to etiquette or convention, as *It used not to be comme il faut for a woman to enter a church without wearing a hat*, and *Until fairly recently it was considered comme il faut for men to stand up when a woman came into a room*. The expression was popular in English from the early part of the nineteenth century. It is still found today but its use is often considered rather pompous. It is otherwise used in humorous or ironic contexts.

common or garden is a hackneyed phrase meaning ordinary or common, as *I'm looking for a pair of common or garden sandals. I don't want to spend a fortune on them*, and *We're looking for a common or garden radio for our daughter. We don't want anything hi-tech*. The phrase was originally used of plants that could commonly be found with or in gardens and has been popular since the end of the nineteenth century. It is still a widespread cliché found in a variety of contexts.

conspicuous by his (her or its) absence is a hackneyed phrase indicating that the absence of someone or something is noticeable and likely to be remarked upon, as *The politician was conspicuous by his absence from the dinner. The press are saying that he is going to resign*, and *Any mention of tenants' rights is conspicuous by its absence*

from this agreement. The idea goes back to Roman times, having being used by the historian, Tacitus. The English St Lord John Russell used the expression in an election address in 1859 and it became popular shortly after that. As a cliché it is still used today. It can sound rather pompous but it is also used in a humorous or ironic way, as *Isn't it odd that Jack is always conspicuous by his absence whenever there is any work to be done?*

cool as a cucumber is a simile cliché used to indicate the measure of someone's calmness or composure, as *Everyone else was in a panic when the house went on fire but mother was cool as a cucumber*. The popularity of the phrase probably owes as much to alliteration as it does to the fact that the inside of a cucumber is very cold – hence its almost routine presence in salads. The association of coldness and cucumbers was remarked upon by the English dramatists Beaumont and Fletcher in *Cupid's Revenge* (1615) in which 'young maids' were described as being 'as cool as cucumbers'. The expression is a popular cliché today, as is **cool, calm and collected** which is also used to emphasize someone's self-composure.

corridors of power is a hackneyed phrase used to describe the power invested in government ministries and top civil servants. The expression was first used by the English novelist C P Snow in *Homecomings* (1956) and was the title of one of his later novels (1964). As a modern cliché it is used to refer collectively to the people who make the decisions that govern our lives. Such people are often projected as being more concerned with personal power and internal power struggles than the issues for which they are responsible, as *What do those in the corridors of power care about the plight of old age pensioners?* As a modern cliché it is has a special appeal for political journalists.

cost the earth see *arm and a leg, cost an*

coup de grâce (French for 'blow of mercy') is a foreign cliché used to mean a finishing stroke, something that finishes something off, as *The firm had been struggling for several years and the start of the recession delivered the coup de grâce*. The phrase means literally 'a stroke of grace' as though the event or situation in question was on the whole a good thing, as though it were putting someone or something out of his or its misery. This idea that the finishing stroke is advantageous in some way has not necessarily survived in the modern cliché which frequently simply means that the end has come for someone or something. As an English expression it became popular in the nineteenth century. It is still used today, particularly by people of a literary bent.

cover a multitude of sins is a quotation cliché meaning to be applicable to a wide range of things, especially undesirable things, as *He says that he sells antiques but the term antiques can cover a multitude of sins*. In origin the phrase is a deliberately mis-applied Biblical quotation, from *1 Peter* (3:8) 'Charity shall cover the multitude of sins'.

crazy like a fox is a simile cliché meaning seemingly very foolish but actually very cunning, as *People say that he was crazy to marry a much older woman but he was crazy like a fox. She is very wealthy and he has expensive tastes*. It was the title of a book by the American humorist S J Perelman (1945), although the phrase probably dates in America from the 1930s. Its popularity was increased by being the title of an American TV series (1984). As a cliché in Britain it is more recent, probably dating from the second part of the 1980s.

Foxes are traditionally associated with cunning and so if they appear to be crazy, the implication is that there must be a hidden reason.

crème de la crème (French for 'cream of the cream') is a foreign cliché used to refer to the very best. It was popular in English by the beginning of the nineteenth century. As a modern cliché it is used either by educated people who could be accused of showing off their knowledge and sounding rather pompous, or by people who are using it in a humorous or ironic way. The term was used by Muriel Spark in her novel *The Prime of Miss Jean Brodie* and the popular film version probably led to a renaissance, although mostly in its humorous use.

cross that bridge when one comes to it is an idiom cliché meaning to delay a decision or action until it becomes necessary and so avoid anticipating trouble, as *We have enough problems organizing the concert without worrying about the artists not turning up. We'll just have to cross that bridge when we come to it*. Its ultimate origins are unknown although the phrase is based on a proverb **don't cross the bridge until you come to it**, referred to as an old proverb by Henry Wadsworth Longfellow in *The Golden Legend* (1851). The cliché is still widespread today, but is anathema to those who like to legislate for every possible contingency.

cross the Rubicon is an idiom cliché meaning to take action from which there is no turning back, as *He has left his job and they won't take him back. The Rubicon is crossed*. A popular expression since the eighteenth century, it refers to the crossing of the River Rubicon, which separated Italy and Cisalpine Gaul, by Julius Caesar in 49 BC. This action was carried out with the aim of invading Italy and was done in defiance of Pompey and the Senate. As a modern cliché it is used mainly in either a serious or humorous context by people of a literary bent.

cross to bear, have a is an allusion cliché indicating that someone has to put up with some form of burden or distress. The allusion is to the Biblical account in which Simon the Cyrene had to carry the cross upon which Christ would be crucified at Calvary. The cross symbolized not only the suffering of Christ but the distress of human beings. As a modern cliché the expression tends to be used in a less serious or ironic way to describe something that is relatively trivial, as *Our neighbours have dogs and we don't like dogs. Still they are pleasant people and all of us have a cross to bear*, and *The new job comes with a company car and an expense allowance. Ah well, all of us have a cross to bear.*

cry all the way to the bank see *laugh all the way to the bank*

cry over spilled milk is a proverb cliché which expresses the folly of spending time regretting something that has been done and cannot be undone, as *you threw your money away when you bought that car but there is to use crying over spilled milk*. The idea dates from the seventeenth century and the expression became a cliché towards the end of the nineteenth century. The cliché is one of those rather bracing expressions that tend to irritate the listener rather than offer comfort or encouragement. All of us like to spend some time wallowing in our own misfortune and this cliché represents an attempt to deprive us that pleasure. The origin is obvious. Once milk is spilled one cannot retrieve it for use.

cry wolf is an idiom cliché meaning to give a false alarm, having done it so often that no one any longer takes it seriously, as *She kept claiming to be ill to attract sympathy. When she collapsed, they thought she was crying wolf and ignored her.* The expression has been a cliché since the nineteenth century and is still popular today. In origin it refers to a story about a shepherd boy watching his sheep on a hillside. Because he was lonely and afraid he used to call 'Wolf!' so that people would come to his aid and he would have company. After people had responded to his call several times and found nothing, they ignored his call when a wolf really did attack his sheep.

cup that cheers, the is an allusion cliché referring to tea, and found in Cowper's *The Task* (1783) 'the cups that cheer but not inebriate'. Originally the expression was used to differentiate between tea and alcoholic drinks. As a modern cliché it is dated and is mostly used humorously. Its use is frequently considered pompous.

cut a long story short is a hackneyed phrase which does not always live up to its promise. Although it is a seeming pledge to abbreviate rather than launch into an involved tale, it is sometimes used meaninglessly by people who go right on to tell the full version. The expression has been a cliché since the late nineteenth century and is still commonly used today, particularly by people to whom it has become a habit.

cut and dried is a hackneyed phrase used to describe something that is settled and definite, as *We had hoped to put the idea to the vote but the plans were all cut and dried before we got to the meeting*. The expression dates from the early eighteenth century and is still a widespread cliché today. In origin it probably refers to timber which is cut and dried before being used.

cut both ways is a hackneyed phrase meaning to have an effect on both sides of a question, to have advantages and disadvantages for both parties involved, as *Having a long term of notice on your contract cuts both ways. It means that if they declare you redundant you will have a lot of time to find another job, but if you are offered something better by another company they might not hold the job open that long.*

cut no ice is an idiom cliché meaning to make no impression on, to have no influence on, as *She usually sweet-talks people into doing what she wants but her flattery cut no ice with the headmaster.* The expression is American in origin and dates from the late nineteenth century. Its origin is uncertain, but it is perhaps derived from an icebreaker that fails to break up ice floes as it should.

cut one's coat according to one's cloth is an idiom cliché used to mean to adapt one's expenditure to one's means, as *He is always going to be in debt until he learns to cut his coat according to his cloth.* The expression has been a cliché since the nineteenth century and is still popular today among the ranks of people who like to offer other people advice. The cliché is usually received with irritation by those to whom it is directed since it sounds so smug. In origin the phrase refers to tailoring.

cutting edge, at the is an idiom cliché which is also a vogue cliché. As is the case with several vogue clichés, it has its origins in specialist language, since it was originally used in the field of science and technology. It was used to refer to research that was in the forefront of new developments, its use being then extended to the general language to cover a wide range of contexts, as *He is a competent enough modern artist but no-one could say that he was at the cutting edge*, and *As a musician he tends to play traditional pieces. His programme never contains any material at the cutting edge.*

cynosure of all eyes is an allusion cliché used to refer to someone who is certain of attention, as *When she entered the room in that dress she was the cynosure of all eyes.* The expression has been a cliché since the nineteenth century. As a modern cliché it is mostly found in formal contexts. It is an allusion to John Milton's *L'Allegro* (1632) 'the cynosure of neighb'ring eyes.'

D

daddy of them all, the is a hackneyed phrase, found in informal contexts, and meaning the finest, greatest, most extreme, etc example of something, whether pleasant or unpleasant, as *He's caught big fish before, but that's the daddy of them all*, and *They've had rows before but this one's the daddy of them all.*

daggers drawn, at is an idiom cliché. It describes people who are very hostile towards each other, as *It is difficult working in a firm where the two partners are at daggers drawn.* In origin the allusion is to two enemies with unsheathed daggers who are about to fight.

damage, what's the see *what's the damage*?

damned clever, these Chinese is a catchphrase cliché used in 'The Goon Show', a zany BBC comedy radio show, featuring Peter Sellers, Harry Secombe and Spike Milligan, which was first broadcast between 1952 and 1960. It was an extremely popular series which became a cult, and its devotees still use this phrase, as do some younger people who have been attracted to the series from hearing recordings of it. The Chinese were popularly supposed to be clever and wily, in the way that other races are supposed to have other characteristics. The term is used in describing something exceptionally clever or cunning, with or without Chinese connections. Thus a piece of labour-saving electrical or electronic equipment might elicit the remark.

damn with faint praise is a quotation cliché meaning to compliment with so little enthusiasm that the supposed compliment creates the opposite effect, suggesting at best a lukewarm approval or at worst an understated disapproval, as *When the music critic said that her playing was an interesting interpretation of the piece, the pianist felt that she had been damned by faint praise.* This is a long established cliché, being originally a quotation from Alexander Pope's *Epistle to Dr Arbuthnot* (1733) 'Damn with faint praise, assent with civil leer, and, without sneering, teach the rest to sneer.'

damp squib, a is an idiom cliché meaning something which turns out to be a complete failure or flop, especially when it has promised to be very successful, exciting, etc, as *The protest meeting about the new road was a damp squib. Hardly anyone turned up.* The expression is usually found in rather informal contexts. Originally it refers to a small firework which, if damp, would fail to explode.

dance attendance on is a hackneyed phrase meaning to carry out someone's every wish and obey every whim. It has been in the language since the sixteenth century, at first in the sense of waiting for someone in authority, such as a monarch or noble, to grant one an audience. As a modern cliché it is used in a derogatory way, as *Her lazy husband expects her to dance attendance on him all weekend.* The term has its origins in the old custom of a bride having to dance with all the wedding guests at the wedding feast.

dancing in the streets tonight see *there'll be dancing in the streets tonight*

Daniel come to judgement, a is a quotation cliché from Shakespeare's *Merchant of Venice* (4:1), being the phrase with which Shylock first greets Portia in her role as judge. In his opinion she, like Daniel in the Bible, she is displaying wisdom beyond her years. As a cliché, now usually used by people of literary tastes, either in formal or ironical contexts, it is used to refer to someone in a decision-making role whom one considers to be exceptionally effective, largely because his/her judgement coincides with one's own.

Darby and Joan is a quotation cliché which is used to refer to an old couple who have been happily married for a long time, as *All their friends seem to be divorced but Mr and Mrs Jones are a real Darby and Joan*. The phrase was coined by Henry Woodfall, who used it in a ballad he wrote about the long-lasting and loyal relationship of his employer, John Darby, and his wife, Joan. In modern usage it may refer to any elderly couple, whether happy or not, and is sometimes used ironically of young people, as *they've been going out for six months now – a real Darby and Joan*.

darken someone's door is a hackneyed phrase which is always used in the negative, as *The delinquent son was told never to darken his father's door again*, and *'Get out and don't dare darken my door again,' he shouted in fury*. It indicates that someone should go away and not return and is used nowadays in rather literary or formal contexts by older rather than younger people. As a cliché the expression dates from the nineteenth century, while the origin is a reference to someone's doorway being darkened by a visitor's shadow.

dark horse, a is an idiom cliché meaning a person who may have unexpected qualities or abilities but tends to keep them secret, as *The shy new girl turned out to be a bit of a dark horse and was the life and soul of the office party*, and *In training he didn't look very good but he proved to be rather a dark horse and won the race*. As a cliché the term dates from the nineteenth century and has it origins in horse-racing, referring to a horse about whose previous record little was known. It is still widespread today.

darkest hour is just before the dawn, the is a hackneyed phrase dating as a cliché from the twentieth century and used as an annoying platitude to encourage someone to believe that things are about to improve, as *I know that things are going badly for you but the darkest hour is just before the dawn*.

dawn on is a hackneyed phrase dating from the nineteenth century and indicating that a person has suddenly begun to understand something, as *It suddenly dawned on him that he had been made a fool of*. The origin is a metaphorical reference to the coming of dawn and so light. This is such a common cliché that many will simply regard it as part of the language.

day in, day out is a hackneyed phrase meaning constantly, with the sense of unrelieved, relentless monotony, as *It rained day in, day out, throughout the whole holiday*, and *Day in, day out, we had to listen to her complaints*.

day of reckoning is a hackneyed phrase meaning the time at which one will be called upon to justify one's actions and when the consequences of said actions will have to be faced, as *The student had a good time going to many parties but he knew the* day of reckoning would come in exam week. The term is Biblical in origin referring to the Day of Judgement, when God will pass judgement on all people.

days are numbered used mostly in informal contexts, is a hackneyed phrase indicating that the life, career, usefulness, etc. of someone or something is over, the implication being that that is going to be so short that it can be counted in days. It appears in such contexts, as *We better all look for other jobs. The company's days are numbered,* and *This machine's days are numbered. It's too expensive to run.* The cliché dates from the nineteenth century.

D-day is a hackneyed phrase referring to a day when something important is scheduled to take place, as *The children have been preparing for the exams all term. Tomorrow is D-day.* Historically D-day refers to June 6 1944, the day on which the Allies began their landings in Northern France to stop the advance of the German forces during World War 2. 'D' means day and is simply a military convention used for emphasis, although it is often popularly but wrongly taken to mean 'designated'. As a cliché, D-day now tends to be used by older people who lived through the war.

dead and gone is a doublet cliché which simply emphasizes the fact that someone or something has died or perished, as *They did not appreciate his genius until he was dead and gone,* and *Most of the old village customs are dead and gone.*

dead as a dodo is a simile cliché which simply emphasizes that something is extinct or no longer fashionable or popular. It is used of customs, ideas, attitudes, plans, etc, but not usually of people, as *The tennis club has no active members anymore. It's dead as a dodo,* and *All the old country*

traditions are dead as a dodo in the villages near the city. The dodo was a flightless bird discovered on the island of Mauritius in the early seventeenth century and was extinct by 1700 because it was very easy to catch. The dodo has long been gone but the cliché is still generally popular.

dead body, over my see *over my dead body*

dead but won't lie down is a catchphrase cliché meaning that someone or something has no chance of success but will not recognize the fact and give up, as *He's standing again for president of the club, although he's failed three times already. He's dead but he won't lie down.*

dead duck, a is an idiom cliché, used mostly in informal contexts, meaning someone or something with no hope of success or survival, as *His plan to expand the restaurant is a dead duck without planning permission,* and *If the farmer catches the girl trespassing, she's a dead duck.*

dead from the neck up is an idiom cliché, used in informal or slang contexts to indicate that someone is extremely stupid, as though he/she had no brain, as *Don't expect him to come up with any ideas. He's dead from the neck up.*

dead horse, flog a see *flog a dead horse*

dead in the water is an idiom cliché which is used to describe something which has no hope of success, as *During the recession any plans for expansion are dead in the water.* It is frequently used in business jargon to refer to a company that is ripe for takeover since it is simply drifting rather than making any progress. The cliché dates from the twentieth century and in origin the allusion is to dead fish.

dead loss, a is a hackneyed phrase used in informal contexts to mean someone or something completely useless, ineffective, etc, as *She's very clever but she's a dead loss as a teacher*, and *This holiday resort was a dead loss for young people. There was nothing to do.*

dead men's shoes is an idiom cliché referring to the job or position of someone who has either died or has left under unfortunate circumstances, as *There are few opportunities for promotion in the firm. It's a case of waiting for dead men's shoes.* The cliché dates from the nineteenth century. The origin is a reference to someone waiting for someone to die so that he/she can inherit his/her shoes or other goods.

dead of night is a hackneyed phrase meaning the middle of the night. The expression is most commonly found in rather literary or formal contexts, as *The children were found wandering at dead of night in the forest.* In origin the phrase compares the most silent, darkest part of the night to the silence and darkness of death.

dead to the world is a hackneyed phrase meaning very deeply asleep, so as to be completely oblivious of one's surroundings, as if one were dead, as *We tiptoed so as not to wake the children but they were dead to the world.* The cliché dates from the twentieth century.

dead, wouldn't be seen is a hackneyed phrase indicating a complete disinclination or aversion to doing something, as *I wouldn't be seen dead wearing that school uniform*, and *She wouldn't be seen dead going out with him.* It is always used in an informal or slang context.

deaf as a post is a simile cliché meaning extremely deaf. The simile dates from the sixteenth century but as a modern cliché the expression tends to be used in a derogatory way, for example by someone irritated at not being able to make himself/herself heard, as *There's no point in asking that old man for directions. He's deaf as a post.*

Dear John letter, a is a hackneyed phrase which refers to a letter or message from a wife, girlfriend or partner to indicate to the recipient that the relationship with the sender is at an end, as *The prospective bridegroom received a Dear John letter on the eve of the wedding.* Originally an American expression, it originated during World War 2, when many servicemen received such letters because of the strain of prolonged separation.

dear life, for is a hackneyed phrase meaning to the best of one's ability, as fast, hard, etc as one can, as *We'll have to run for dear life to catch that bus.* The implication of the phrase is that one is going as fast as possible, etc. as though one's life depended on it. It is usually used in an informal context.

death by a thousand cuts is a catchphrase cliché meaning destruction by a series of minor blows rather by one major one, as *The company gradually went bankrupt as many of their small customers failed to reorder. It was death by a thousand cuts.* The expression is an allusion to the English translation of the phrase 'He who is not afraid of death by a thousand cuts dares to unhorse the emperor' which appears in the Chinese Leader Mao Tse-tung's *Little Red Book* (1966).

death, catch one's see *catch one's death*

deathless prose is a hackneyed phrase used nowadays ironically to mean not, as literally, unforgettable prose, but very bad, talentless writing or a piece of unimportant writing, as *'Fourth form essays,'* sighed the teacher, *'another lot of deathless prose.'*

death's door, at is an idiom cliché meaning extremely, or terminally, ill, as *The old man has recovered although they thought he was at death's door.* The origin of the phrase lies in the idea that death was a place that departed souls went to. The expression was used in the sixteenth century and has been considered a cliché since the nineteenth century. It is still common today.

death trap, a is a hackneyed phrase used to indicate something that is dangerous, as *They should do something about the fire precautions in these old buildings. They are real death traps.* The expression is apt to be used in an exaggerated way to indicate something that is only mildly unsafe and is frequently used by journalists.

death warmed up, like is a simile cliché always used in a derogatory and informal context, as *Were you out all night? You look like death warmed up!* It dates from the twentieth century.

delicate condition a is a euphemism cliché for pregnancy. Nowadays people tend to be more frank about pregnancy and the expression tends now to be used by older women, not used to this frankness, as *You should not carry heavy bags in your delicate condition.* It is sometimes used satirically by younger women.

deliver an ultimatum is a hackneyed phrase popular among journalists as well as others to indicate that someone has given someone else a final warning of some kind, as *The terrorists delivered an ultimatum that they would shoot the hostages if their demands were not met immediately.* As is common in journalism, the expression is sometimes considerably more dramatic than the event referred to requires.

de rigueur (French for 'of strictness') a cliché meaning required by etiquette, rules, fashion etc, as *School uniform is absolutely de rigueur on official outings.* It is used in English rather formally, often pompously.

desert a sinking ship is an idiom cliché referring to the fact that people show a distinct tendency to abandon organizations or people that are showing signs that they are about to fail, become bankrupt, etc, as *Most of the firm's employees are looking for new jobs. They are like rats deserting a sinking ship.* The origin of the phrase lies in the fact that rats were said to desert a ship when it was about to founder or run aground.

des res is a hackneyed phrase with its origins in the jargon of twentieth century estate agents. Short for 'desirable residence', it is often used mockingly or ironically, as in *Now that they are married they have moved into a des res on the new estate.*

deus ex machina (Latin for 'god out of a machine') is a foreign cliché only used nowadays in literary or formal and rather pompous contexts. It refers to a person or event that offers unexpected and fortuitous assistance in a difficult or dangerous situation, as *The theatre company thought that they would have to disperse but salvation came in the form of a deus ex machina, John Richards, a wealthy industrialist, who wanted to invest money in the arts.* The origin of the expression lies in ancient Greek theatre where a god appeared on the stage from a machine or mechanical contrivance to resolve some aspect of the plot.

dice with death is an idiom cliché meaning to do something very risky or dangerous, as *That young man is dicing with death driving at that speed.* Its origin refers to playing a game of chance in which dice are thrown.

didn't he do well? a catchphrase cliché having its origins in a remark always made by Bruce Forsyth, the presenter of a late twentieth-century television game show, called 'The Generation Game', at the end of the final game, which involved the winning competitor memorizing as many objects as possible which have passed on a conveyor belt. The cliché is sometimes used ironically to indicate that someone has done badly, as *She just lost us the match. Didn't she do well?*

die in harness is an idiom cliché meaning to die while one is still actively engaged in work, as *The old man was forced to retire although he wanted to die in harness.* The expression is a reference to working horses which died working and so in harness. The expression is still common today although the concept of early retirement has made the practice less common.

die is cast, the is an idiom cliché indicating that a step has been taken from which there is no turning back, as *The die is cast. I've sold the house and now I'll have to move.* It is a translation of the Latin *alea jacta est*, traditionally said to be the comment made by Julius Caesar on crossing the River Rubicon into Italy with his army in 49 BC, thus effectively declaring war on the Roman administration. It is a very common cliché and although it sounds very dramatic it is used in quite ordinary situations. See also **cross the Rubicon**.

die the death is a hackneyed phrase meaning to be completely unsuccessful or in-effective. It is often used of theatrical productions or players, as *The new comedy act died the death in the local club*, but is also widely used more generally, for example by journalists, as *The politician's speech on education died the death in a hall full of teachers.*

different as chalk and cheese is a simile cliché meaning totally unlike. Obviously chalk and cheese are completely different both in appearance and taste. The cliché is most usually applied to people who are utterly dissimilar, as *You wouldn't believe that they're twins. They're like chalk and cheese.*

different ballgame see *ballgame, a different*

dig one's own grave is an idiom cliché meaning that someone is in the process of bringing about his/her own downfall, as *The employees dug their own grave when they conspired to get rid of their manager. The new manager sacked them all.* A more modern, and more informal, form is **dig a hole for oneself**.

dim and distant past, the is a hackneyed phrase which is also a doublet cliché, dim and distant being near synonyms in this case. Although the phrase originally referred to the distant past, as a cliché it is usually used humorously to refer to the fairly recent past, as *I knew him in the dim and distant past when I was at school.* The cliché dates from the late nineteenth century. An alternative, more informal, form is **the dim and distant**.

dinners, more – than you've etc had hot see *more – than you've etc had hot dinners*

dirty old man, a is a hackneyed phrase used to describe a middle-aged or elderly lecherous man, usually one showing a sexual interest in young women or girls or in pornographic material, as *There were a lot of dirty old men watching a blue move*. The expression is sometimes abbreviated to **DOM**. Dirty old men are typically depicted as wearing raincoats.

dirty tricks campaign, a is a hackneyed phrase used to describe a sustained and underhand attempt to discredit someone or something. Originally the term was used mainly in connection with politics, as *The articles on MPs' private lives were thought to be a dirty tricks campaign to bring down the government*, but it has now become more generally used. The expression is one that frequently appeals to journalists.

dirty work at the crossroads is an idiom cliché meaning dishonest or underhand activity, as in *Some valuable documents have disappeared. We suspect there's been some dirty work at the crossroads*. There is doubt over the origin of the expression although it has been suggested that it derives from the historical practice of burying at crossroads the bodies of people not entitled to a Christian burial in a churchyard.

do someone proud is a hackneyed phrase meaning to treat someone exceptionally well. The expression is frequently used of hospitality, as *The bride's parents certainly did us proud at the wedding reception.*

does your mother know you're out? is a catchphrase cliché used derogatorily to indicate that the user thinks that the person addressed is very naive, inexperienced or is younger than he/she is trying to make out, as *When the young man asked her to dance she said, 'Does your mother know you're out?'* It is always used to convey scorn.

dog eat dog is an idiom cliché meaning extremely ruthless competition, as *The young candidates are all good friends but when it comes to getting a job these days it's a case of dog eat dog*. In origin the expression refers to the fact that if it is the only method of survival then a dog will eat another dog, as indeed humans have been known to eat humans in a similar situation. The expression is widely used. Although it is subject to overuse it remains quite a useful phrase since it captures a situation in very few words.

dog in the manger is an idiom cliché referring to someone who keeps something that is wanted by someone else simply out of selfishness or spite, not because he/she has any wish to have it, as *The child has outgrown all those toys but he's too much of a dog in the manger to lend them to his young cousin*. Its origin lies in a fable about a dog who prevented other animals from going near the hay to eat it although the dog did not want it himself. The expression has been a cliché since the middle of the nineteenth century.

dog's life, a is an idiom cliché meaning a miserable way of life, as *He leads a dog's life with that nagging wife of his*, the wretchedness of a dog's life having been recognized since the sixteenth century. However, given the fact that dogs in Britain at least usually lead a very comfortable existence, the term is now frequently used ironically, as in *'Ah, it's a dog's life,' he said, smoking a cigar and putting his feet up on the coffee table*. The expression dates from the sixteenth century and has been a cliché since the middle of the nineteenth century.

dolce vita, la (Italian for 'the sweet life') is a foreign cliché meaning a life of luxury or indulgence, as *The tired mother sometimes envied the dolce vita of her highly paid single friends.*

donkey's years is an idiom cliché which means a very long time, but in fact it is mostly used as an exaggeration, as *I haven't seen him in donkey's years*. This probably refers to the week before last. Its origin is uncertain but it is possible that the term refers to the fact that the donkey is a comparatively long-lived animal. Alternatively it is a pun on a donkey's ears which are very long. An alternative and common form is **donkey's ages**. The expression dates from the late nineteenth century and is still common today in informal contexts.

don't call us, we'll call you is a catch-phrase cliché with its origins in the twentieth-century American entertainment industry. Traditionally, it is said to aspiring actors to whom it is not intended to award park for which they have auditioned. As a cliché it is more generally used as an indication of likely rejection, as *I got an interview for the job but I think it's a case of 'Don't call us, we'll call you,'* and *He said he would phone her but I think he meant 'Don't call us, we'll call you.'*

don't count your chickens before they're hatched is a proverb cliché, still very commonly used as a warning to people not to put faith in things which they don't yet have, as *You'd better not leave your job until you receive an official offer for the other one. Don't count your chickens before they're hatched*. The expression appears in various negative forms, as *It would be unwise to count your chickens before they are hatched*.

don't do anything I wouldn't do! is a twentieth-century catchphrase cliché used to someone going to some social occasion, on holiday, etc. It frequently carries sexual overtones, as *Enjoy the date with your new girlfriend and don't do anything I wouldn't do*. See also **be good**!

don't just stand there is a hackneyed phrase used to incite someone to action, as *Don't just stand there! We have to finish this work today*. It is sometimes lengthened to **don't just stand there, do something** or facetiously to **don't just stand there growing in the carpet**.

don't tell anyone, but . . . is a filler cliché used supposedly to exhort the listener to treat the following statement with confidentiality, but actually as a signpost to indicate that what is to come is a juicy piece of gossip that is too good to keep to oneself. A typical example is *Don't tell anyone but I saw our neighbour with another woman last night*.

do one's own thing is a hackneyed phrase with its origins in the 1960s when such an attitude was part of the Hippie culture. It suggests that individuals should do what they want to, regardless of circumstances. Much of the slang of this era has become dated but this expression has survived as a cliché, as *I don't like joining clubs. I like to do my own thing*. However, it is now frequently used satirically.

do the honours is a hackneyed phrase used when inviting someone to act as host or hostess in some way, such as pouring tea, cutting a cake, opening wine or carving poultry. The expression is still common in certain circles, especially among older and better-off people. Younger people would consider it rather pompous, unless it was being used facetiously. See also **be mother**.

dot, on the see *on the dot*

dot the i's and cross the t's is an idiom cliché meaning to put the finishing touches to something or to take great care over the details of something, as *I have more or less* *finished the proposal but I want to dot the i's and cross the t's before presenting it to the committee.* People who use this expression are often themselves very meticulous and tend to be ridiculed by more slapdash people. In origin the expression refers to the fact that careful writers will take time to dot the i's and cross the t's, a feature of handwriting that can easily be omitted when one is writing quickly or carelessly.

doubting Thomas is an allusion cliché referring to Thomas, one of Christ's apostles, who refused to believe that He had risen from the dead. It has become the standard expression for someone who displays incredulity, as *It is possible that your friend is a changed character. Don't be such a doubting Thomas.*

down-and-out is a twentieth century hackneyed phrase meaning destitute, utterly poverty-stricken. It is used as an adjective, as *down-and-out people without homes* and as a noun, as *the part of the city where the down-and-outs hang out.* The expression, which is frequently, but by no means always, used derogatorily has its origins in boxing, referring to a boxer who gets knocked down and stays down for long enough to be counted out.

down the hatch is a hackneyed phrase used as a toast. The cliché dates from the twentieth century but it is now rather dated. It refers to a hatch or opening in a ship's deck through which cargo and people pass below, the implication being that this resembles the human throat

do you come here often? is a twentieth-century catchphrase cliché traditionally used as a conversation starter at public dances. Now that such dances are no longer a major part of the social scene, apart from discos, the cliché is more com-

monly used facetiously. It might, for example, be said to someone met regularly at the job centre.

draw a blank is an idiom cliché meaning to be unsuccessful, to make no progress, as *The police thought they had a new lead in the murder hunt but they drew a blank.* In origin the expression refers to drawing a blank ticket in a lottery or raffle.

draw in one's horns is an idiom cliché meaning to spend less money, as *Now that I am working only part time I have to draw in my horns.* Although common before that, the phrase became something of a vogue phrase in the recession of the late 1980s and the 1990s. The origin is an allusion to the fact that a snail can withdraw the soft projecting parts of its body, which resemble horns, inside its shell if it feels itself to be in danger. The expression has been considered a cliché since the nineteenth century although it entered the language around the fourteenth century. It is still common today

draw the line at is an idiom cliché meaning to set a limit in one's behaviour, etc that stops short of something, as *The tradesman is not completely honest but he draws the line at breaking the law.* The cliché dates from the nineteenth century and is still common today. In origin it refers to the drawing of lines to indicate boundaries, as in some kinds of games.

dressed to kill is a hackneyed phrase meaning dressed in one's best and most eye-catching clothes, as *The two girls were dressed to kill as they left for the party.* The expression is American in origin and dates from the nineteenth century. It may be an allusion to warriors getting painted up before going to meet the enemy and making a conquest.

dribs and drabs is a doublet cliché meaning very small quantities, as *They expected crowds of people at the opening of the store but the customers came in dribs and drabs*. It is used in informal contexts.

drink like a fish is a simile cliché. Although not particularly apt as a simile it is the standard cliché to describe the act of one who regularly consumes too much alcoholic drink, as *You'll find him in the pub every night. He drinks like a fish*. Fish are open-mouthed most of the time, supposedly giving the appearance of constantly drinking. The expression dates from the seventeenth century.

drive a hard bargain is a hackneyed phrase meaning to make sure that one gets the best deal possible from a transaction, as *We sold the house but the buyers drove a hard bargain and we got less than we hoped*. The association of drive and bargain is a long established one, being used by the English poet, Sir Philip Sidney, who wrote 'there never was bargain better driven' in *My True Love Hath My Heart* (1583).

drop dead is a vogue cliché of the 1990s meaning exceptionally. It is colloquial and most likely to be used by the young and trendy. It is invariably used with a term that flatters, as *Did you see her new boyfriend? He's drop dead gorgeous*.

drop in the bucket, a is an idiom cliché meaning a very small proportion of the actual amount required for something, as *Dad's lending me some money but it's a drop in the bucket compared with what I need for a deposit on the house*. A more formal version of this cliché is **a drop in the ocean**. A very early, slightly different form of the expression is found in *Isaiah* (40:15) in the Bible: 'behold the nations are like a drop of a bucket and are counted as the small dust of the balance.'

drop of a hat, at the is a hackneyed phrase meaning at once, without delay, without much encouragement or excuse, as *His ex-wife made him very unhappy but he would have her back at the drop of a hat*. The cliché dates from the twentieth century and in origin refers to the fact that historically a hat was often dropped as the signal to start a race.

drown one's sorrows is an idiom cliché dating from the twentieth century and meaning to take a great deal of alcoholic drink so that one becomes oblivious of one's troubles. A typical example is *When his marriage was in difficulties he used to go to the pub every night to drown his sorrows*.

dry as a bone is a simile cliché used to indicate extreme dryness, usually of the soil, as *No wonder these plants are dying. The garden is as dry as a bone*. It refers to the dry bones of dead creatures.

dry as dust is a simile cliché meaning extremely dull or boring, as *We stopped going to the lectures because they were dry as dust*. As a cliché it dates from the eighteenth century and is still popular today.

ducking and diving is a hackneyed phrase, almost a doublet cliché since the words are closely related, used to descibe someone who is being evasive, as *You'll never get him to give a straight answer. He's one of those politicians who's always ducking and diving*. As a cliché the expression dates from the later part of the twentieth century. It is very popular today in informal contexts. In origin it refers to someone who is always trying to avoid being seen by ducking or diving out of sight.

Dutch courage is a hackneyed phrase used to refer to courage induced by alcohol in situations in which one might otherwise be afraid to act, as *We'd better go to the pub. We'll need a bit of Dutch courage if we're going to ask the boss for a rise.* The expression has its origins either in the fact that the Dutch historically had a reputation for heavy drinking or to the fact that gin was introduced into England in the seventeenth century by the followers of the Dutch-born William III.

dyed-in-the-wool is a hackneyed phrase used in a derogatory way to describe someone who is of very firmly fixed opinions, as *It was the usual contest between dyed-in-the-wool Tories and dyed-in-the-wool Socialists.* The origin of this twentieth-century cliché lies in the fact that dyed-in-the-wool was once a technical description of yarn which was dyed before it was spun, the implication being that dyed-in-the-wool opinions and attitudes are acquired when one is very young.

✿ E ✿

each and everyone of us is a filler cliché, dating from the nineteenth century, which is used rather pompously simply to mean all of us, as *Each and everyone of us must contribute to this worthy cause.* At best it is used for emphasis but it is frequently simply meaninglessly repetitive.

eager beaver is a hackneyed phrase which is an allusion to the simile **work like a beaver**, the beaver being traditionally famed for its industriousness. The cliché **eager beaver** is used to refer to a person who is particularly enthusiastic or industrious. It is frequently used as a term of disapproval, as *He always wants to go on working when we are ready to go home. He's such an eager beaver!* As a cliché it dates from the twentieth century.

eager for the fray is a quotation cliché, taken from Colley Cibber's version of Shakespeare's *Richard 111* (5:3) 'My soul's in arms and eager for the fray.' It means that one is ready for battle, and as a cliché indicates that one is anxious to get on with whatever challenge awaits one, as *At the start of every new term one of their teaching colleagues always says, 'Well, are you eager for the fray?'* The cliché dates from the nineteenth century and is still used today but often in a satirical context. An alternative, and now slightly more common form, is **ready for the fray**.

eagle eye is a hackneyed phrase which is a metaphorical reference to the fact that the eagle, in common with other birds of prey

is very sharp-eyed. The cliché, which dates from the middle of the nineteenth century can either be a reference to someone's sharp eyesight, as *The pupil smuggled her friend a note but she was spotted by the eagle eye of the headmistress* or to someone's general vigilance, as *The crime rate is quite low here. The area is under the eagle eye of Chief Superintendent Robinson.*

ear to the ground, an is an idiom cliché indicating an ability to keep well-informed. Dating from the late nineteenth century, the expression mostly appears in such phrases as **keep one's ear to the ground**, to make sure that one is well-informed about what is going on around one, as *I hear that there are going to be some changes in the company. Keep your ear to the ground.* The origin is said to lie in the reputed American Indian technique of putting an ear to the ground to hear sounds, such as that of horses, far away.

early bird catches the worm, the is a proverb cliché which is used to recommend or justify an early arrival at an event, etc, as *Get there when the jumble sale opens if you want the best bargains. The early bird catches the worm.* Frequently only part of the proverb is used as an allusion, as *I thought I would be first to arrive. You are an early bird.* The proverb dates from the early seventeenth century.

early days, it's is a hackneyed phrase dating from the twentieth century and indicating that it is too soon in any project, etc to be able to have any results or draw any conclusions, as *The patient doesn't seem to be responding to treatment but it's early days*. The expression is frequently used as an excuse for lack of progress.

early to bed and early to rise (makes a man healthy, wealthy and wise) is a proverb cliché, although only the first part is usually quoted and this usually in the form of allusion as *I want to be in bed before midnight. You know what they say about early to bed, early to rise*. The cliché is mostly used rather pompously or facetiously.

earnest consideration is a hackneyed phrase, often a business cliché, dating from the late nineteenth century and now used mainly in formal contexts, as *We are in receipt of your complaint and will give the matter our earnest consideration*. This is rather a meaningless phrase since the consideration given is likely to be no less perfunctory than any other, only holding out the promise of this as a placatory gesture.

earnest desire is a hackneyed phrase used to suggest that someone is exceptionally anxious to do something. Frequently, however, it is used as an exaggeration of the degree of desire to do something good, or even as a cover-up for a non-desire to do something, simply because it is in the interests of the person supposedly expressing the desire so to do. A typical example would be *The barrister said that his client expressed an earnest desire to lead an honest life in the future*.

earth moved, the is a twentieth century catchphrase cliché usually found in the form of a question **did the earth move for you?** The cliche indicates intensity of sexual satisfaction and is often used humorously in comedy sketches. A form 'Did

thee feel the earth move?' was used by the American novelist Ernest Hemingway in *For Whom the Bell Tolls* (1940).

easier said than done is a hackneyed phrase pointing out the obvious fact that it is easier to talk about doing something than actually to accomplish it. The expression is common in contexts such as *'If you aren't happy in your job', she said, 'you should look for another one.' 'Given the high rate of unemployment, that's easier said than done'*, he replied. The expression dates from the fifteenth century and is still a common cliché today.

easy come, easy go is a hackneyed phrase indicating something, usually money, that is acquired without effort and which therefore can be spent or dispensed with in a casual manner without causing any concern, as *He won £300 on a horse and lost it at cards. Easy come, easy go.* and *She has had three husbands in the course of seven years. Easy come, easy go.* The concept is a very old one but the cliché in its current wording dates from the nineteenth century. It is found in informal contexts

easy, easy is rather an unusual cliché in that it is a slogan that has become a hackneyed phrase uttered in hopeful anticipation of victory. As a kind of slogan, it is most usually heard as a chant shouted by football supporters. As a cliché, it has extended its area of influence and is to be found in other areas of competition such as politics, as *We've got the best candidate. It will be easy, easy.* Unfortunately neither the slogan chant nor the cliché, both dating from the twentieth century, always live up to their expectations and they are often simply examples of bravado.

eat, drink and be merry, for tomorrow we die is an allusion cliché, being a Biblical reference to *Isaiah* (22:13) 'Let us eat, drink and be merry, for tomorrow we die'. Brewer in his *Dictionary of Phrase and Fable* comments that this was a traditional saying of the Egyptians who often exhibited a skeleton at their banquet to remind guests of the shortness of life. As a modern cliché it is usually used as an interjection on happy occasions which occur just before the impending arrival of some stressful or unwanted event, as *Last night out before the final exams, lads! Eat drink and be merry, for tomorrow we die!*

eat humble pie is an idiom cliché dating from the late nineteenth century and meaning to acknowledge in a humiliating way that one has been completely wrong, as *She was so adamant that she was right and then she had to eat humble pie in front of everyone when she was proved wrong.* The origin lies in the fact that humble pie is a corruption of 'umble pie', a dish made from the umble or offal of deer and therefore eaten by the servants while the lord and his guests ate the better cuts of meat.

eat like a horse is a simile cliché dating from the eighteenth century and used of someone who consumes large amounts of food, as *He must be ill, eating so little. He usually eats like a horse.* The cliché is usually used in a derogatory way suggesting over-consumption of food. The opposite of this is **eat like a bird** which dates from the twentieth century.

eat one's hat is a hackneyed phrase used to indicate that the speaker is convinced that something is unlikely to be true, etc, as *I'll eat my hat if he gets here in time.* It first appeared in print in *Pickwick Papers* by Charles Dickens (1836) 'Well if I knew as little of life as that, I'd eat my hat and swallow the buckle whole.'

eat out of house and home is a hackneyed phrase meaning that a person eats so much that the host or provider of the food cannot afford the food bills, as *Her children always ask their friends home for meals and they are eating her out of house and home.* The expression is found in Shakespeare's *Henry IV, Part 2* (2:1) when Falstaff is said by Mistress Quickly to have 'eaten me out of house and home'. The cliché is often used in a humorous context.

eat your heart out! is a catchphrase cliché used nowadays to refer to someone who has cause to be jealous of one, especially when this was not always the case, as *Now that he has a beautiful girlfriend of his own he can say 'Eat your heart out!' to all those Romeos who used to tease him for being womanless.* The cliché used to be a catchphrase popular in show business directed by someone who had just done something particularly well at someone who was famous for this skill, such as an unknown singer saying, *Frank Sinatra, eat your heart out!* As an idiom, **eat one's heart out** means to worry excessively or to pine for something or someone, as if consuming one's heart in grief, as *Ever since her fiancé went to war she's been eating her heart out for him.*

economical with the truth is a euphemism cliché meaning lying or being less than totally truthful, as *He hesitated to be absolutely forthright and call his boss a liar, but he certainly suggested that she was being economical with the truth.* The cliché became popular in the mid 1980s when Sir Robert Armstrong, the British Cabinet Secretary, used the phrase when representing the British government in its attempt to prevent publication of Peter Wright's book *Spycatcher* in the Supreme Court of New South Wales. It became regarded as a kind of symbol of the civil servant's and politician's reluctance to be open, but in fact the expression was not originated by Armstrong or by the civil service. Mark Twain is quoted as having said, 'Truth is a valuable commodity, we need to be economical with it.' And Edmund Burke is said to have commented, 'We practise economy of truth, that we may live to tell it longer.'

egg on one's face, have/be left with is an idiom cliché popular in Britain in the late twentieth century. It means to be left looking a complete fool, as *Our neighbour is always telling us about how efficient and organized she is, but she was left with egg on her face when her car ran out of petrol just after she left home*. It has two possible origins. One is the obvious one, that one has forgotten to wipe the remains of an egg which one has eaten from one's face. The other suggestion is that the egg on one's face is a reference to raw eggs with which a hostile audience might pelt a performer or speaker.

elbow grease is a hackneyed phrase meaning hard physical effort, as *You don't need an expensive polish to bring a shine to that table. You just need elbow grease*. This cliché is based on an old phrase which goes back to the seventeenth century and is still popular today.

elementary, my dear Watson is a catchphrase cliché which refers to Dr Watson, who was the friend and helper of Sherlock Holmes in the Arthur Conan Doyle detective stories, and indicates that something is very simple and obvious. This is not strictly a quotation cliché, since Conan Doyle himself did not actually use the expression, although his son, Adrian, in conjunction with John Dickson, used the phrase in some of the follow-up stories, and adaptors of the stories for films and television also

used it. It is used usually humorously, in such contexts as *Of course I found out the name of her new boyfriend. It was elementary, my dear Watson.*

elephant never forgets, the is a proverb cliché indicating that someone has a good memory and is unlikely to forget something, as *Don't expect the headmistress to forget about your punishment exercise. The elephant never forgets*. The expression is usually used in a light-hearted or humorous context. As to origin it is obviously difficult to assess the extent of an elephant's memory but it has a reputation for having a good memory because it supposedly long remembers trainers or people who worked with it or were kind to it.

eleventh hour, the is a hackneyed phrase meaning the last possible moment, only just in time, as *When the band called off we thought that we would have to cancel the dance, but we found a replacement at the eleventh hour*. It has been suggested that in origin the expression is an allusion to the Biblical parable of the labourers in *Matthew* (20:9) 'And when they came that were hired about the eleventh hour they received every man a denarius.' – a reference to the fact that workers taken on at the eleventh hour of a twelve-hour day received as much pay as those who started work at the beginning of the period. If this is taken as the origin, then the cliché would be categorized as an allusion cliché, but Partridge rejects this as the source and certainly there is no obvious connection apart from the actual wording of the phrase.

embarras de richesses (French for 'embarrassment of riches') is a foreign cliché meaning an overabundance of something. It is used in formal contexts, as *It was felt by the people that for the king to have ten palaces* *was an embarras de richesses* or by someone rather pompous who is showing off his/ her knowledge or education. As is the case with many formal or pompous phrases the expression is sometimes used facetiously, as *We knew they wanted children but six seems to be an embarras de richesses.* The phrase is sometimes used in its English translation as *I do not mind the odd visitor but five is an embarrassment of riches.*

empty nest is a twentieth century hackneyed phrase meaning a household from which all the children have left, leaving either the mother or parents lonely. It is frequently found in the expression **the empty nest syndrome,** as *She should get a job to get her out of the house. She's depressed because she's suffering from the empty nest syndrome.* In origin the expression refers to a bird's nest from which all the fledglings have flown.

end of an era, the is a hackneyed phrase meaning the end of some aspect or stage of something. The phrase suggests that it refers to the end of something important, as *When the last steam train was taken out of regular service it was the end of an era.* In fact the cliché is often used to refer to something fairly trivial, as *It was the end of an era when they left the street.* The expression dates from the late nineteenth century and is much used today, especially by journalists, politicians and those making public speeches.

end of one's tether, the is an idiom cliché meaning the limit of what one can endure, the very limit of one's resources, as *I am worried that she may have a nervous breakdown. She is at the end of her tether looking after the children and her elderly parents.* As a cliché the expression dates from the nineteenth century while its origin lies in the tether or rope that ties up an animal

to allow it to move or graze only as far as the length of the tether allows. The cliché, in common with the state it describes, is common today.

end of the road, the is an idiom cliché used to refer to the end of something, such as a business, career, life, etc, as *The recession was the end of the road for a lot of small businesses.* The origin is the obvious one of the end of a stretch of roadway or the end of a journey.

ends of the earth, the is an allusion cliché meaning the remotest parts of the world. The Biblical allusion is to *Psalms* (98:3) 'All the ends of the earth have seen the salvation of our God.' When the earth was thought to be flat, it could be said to have 'ends'. As a cliché the expression dates from the late nineteenth century and nowadays is often used in an exaggerated way for emphasis, as *He would go to the ends of the earth to find something that would make her happy.*

enfant terrible (French for 'terrible child') is a foreign cliché meaning a person, often a young person, with new and unconventional or startling ideas, who embarrasses older or more conventional people by his/ her behaviour, remarks or attitude, as *The managing director is now captain of the golf club and an elder of the church but I remember him when he was the enfant terrible of the firm and shocked all the older employees.* It is difficult to find an appropriate English translation of this phrase which is one of the reasons why it is so commonly used.

English as she is spoke is a deliberately ungrammatical hackneyed phrase used to mimic the English of someone who is either not very fluent or is speaking ungrammatically. It is sometimes applied to uneducated native speakers and sometimes to speakers of English as a foreign language. Despite the fact that the British are notoriously bad at foreign languages, this does not stop them ridiculing foreigners trying to speak English, as *Oxford Street is full of tourists. Talk about English as she is spoke.*

English disease, the is a catchphrase cliché used to describe industrial strikes, a common phenomenon in the 1960s and early 1970s in Britain, when the trade unions were very powerful. The phrase has also been used to describe other social ills, such as class conflict and economic stagnation. It has even referred to some physical diseases, such as bronchitis or syphilis and also to sexual activity, such as whipping, which involves physical punishment. As a modern cliché, however, it commonly refers to industrial disputes, although the expression has lost prominence with the decrease in the incidence of the phenomenon it describes.

enjoy! is a vogue cliché of the twentieth century which first invited people to sample and enjoy food, as *Mum has cooked us one of her special casseroles. Enjoy!* and was then extended to other commodities such as books. The expression is Yiddish in origin and has come to Britain from America.

enough is enough is a hackneyed phrase used to indicate that it is time something was brought to an end, as *'All right children,' said the teacher, 'enough is enough. You've all had a good laugh and now it's time to get back to work'.* It frequently takes the form of quite a stern warning that no more will be tolerated. The expression appears as a proverb in John Heywood's 1546 collection of proverbs.

enough said is a hackneyed phrase indicating that no more need be said on a parti-

cular subject. The implication is that the rest is obvious or could be readily deduced at least by people in the know, as *I saw him coming out of her flat this morning. Enough said!* Gertrude Stein wrote a poem entitled *Enough Said* (1935) which consists solely of the expression repeated five times. The cliché also exists in a shortened humorous form, **nuff said**, which is found, for example, in comics and cartoons.

envy of the world, the is a hackneyed phrase used to describe an aspect of life in a country that is thought to be of an exceptionally high standard. It is frequently used to describe aspects of life in Britain, although the statement so used is often at least debatable and is frequently just wishful thinking, as *I can safely say that our education system is the envy of the world.* As a cliché it dates from the twentieth century. It is used today chiefly by journalists and old-fashioned optimists.

'er indoors is a catchphrase cliché meaning wife, the implication being although supposedly indoors a lot and so not often visible, wives nevertheless have a great deal of influence. The catchphrase was popularized by the television series *Minder*, first screened in 1979, in which the chief character, Arthur Daley, played by George Cole, referred to his wife in this way. This is one of several clichés used to refer to a wife. See also **better half**.

err on the side of is a hackneyed phrase meaning to indulge in what might be seen as a fault, in order to avoid the opposite, and even greater, fault, as *They decided to err on the side of caution and not buy a house when the market was so uncertain.*

esprit de corps (French for 'team spirit') is a foreign cliché used to describe a sense of unity or common purpose within a group.

It is mostly found in literary or formal contexts where it is thought to sound better than 'team spirit', as *In his retirement speech the chairman spoke of the esprit de corps that had always existed among his board members.* It has been used by English speakers for some considerable time. Jane Austen used it in *Mansfield Park* (1814), although she misspelled it as *esprit du corps*.

eternal triangle, the is an idiom cliché referring to three people who are involved in some kind of romantic intrigue. It can consist of two men and one woman with both men having love affairs with the woman. Alternatively, it can consist of two women and one man with the two women both having love affairs with the man. Sometimes the members of the triangle are all aware of the situation which they are in, and sometimes only one of them is. The expression is frequently used by someone when he/she finds out that a married, or otherwise attached, friend is having an affair. *Ah, a case of the eternal triangle,* he/she might well say, probably either pompously or ironically. The phrase was coined by a book reviewer in the *London Daily Chronicle* in 1907 and is still very common today.

et tu Brute (Latin for 'and you Brutus') is a quotation cliché from Shakespeare's *Julius Caesar* and are the words with which Caesar recognizes the fact that his friend, Brutus, is one of the conspirators in his murder. As a cliché it is used to a friend who has let one down, perhaps because he/she has taken some form of action against one. For example, if all the cabinet ministers passed a vote of no confidence in a prime minister he/she might say to a colleague who was thought to be exceptionally loyal, 'Et tu Brute!' Nowadays the expression is sometimes used in humorous contexts also.

eureka! (Greek for 'I have found it') is a quotation cliché used to announce one's delight at having made a discovery or at having found something, as *Eureka! I've just discovered how to work the video machine.* The expression is often now used in a humorous context. The exclamation was first made by Archimedes in his bath when he discovered that a body displaces its own bulk in water when immersed.

even his/her etc best friends won't tell him/her etc. is a catchphrase cliché originally indicating that someone has a problem relating to personal hygiene, such as an unpleasant body odour or bad breath. It is sometimes now also used to indicate a fault or habit in someone that people might be aware of but not comment on. The catchphrase probably originated in an advertising campaign relating to personal hygiene.

every cloud has a silver lining is an idiom cliché indicating that there is some redeeming quality in even the worst situation, as *At least now you don't have a job you'll have more time to spend with your family. Every cloud has a silver lining.* People to whom such a remark is addressed can find it very annoying, feeling that the users of it are being platitudinous. As a cliché it dates from the early twentieth century. In the 1930s Noel Coward reversed the concept to form **every silver lining has a cloud** in one of his songs.

every dog has/will have his day is a proverb cliché meaning that everyone will have a period of success, happiness in life at some stage. As a cliché it is usually used as a consoling phrase when times are bad or as a remark to inspire optimism, as *It's* *too bad you didn't get that job, but I'm sure you'll get one soon. Every dog has his day.* The cliché is sometimes contracted simply as an allusion to the whole phrase, as *He's going through a bad patch just now, but you know what they say about every dog.* Frequently people who are at the receiving end of the cliché find it annoying and even patronizing.

every effort is being made is a twentieth century hackneyed phrase usually used to reassure people who fear that very little is being done or who feel that very few results of any effort are in evidence. It appears in such official statements as *A police spokesman said that every effort is being made to trace anyone who may have witnessed the attack.*

every inch a/the is a hackneyed phrase used to indicate that someone is the perfect example or epitome of something, as *She would not swear. She is every inch a lady.* It is usually found in complimentary expressions and is mostly used by older, rather conventional people who value the attributes with which it usually comes accompanied. Sometimes the expression is altered slightly to **every other inch a**, indicating either that someone is not quite the perfect example of something or that someone is not in any way a good example of something. The title of the autobiography of the actress Beatrice Lillie is *Every Other Inch a Lady* (1973).

every little helps is a proverb cliché indicating that every contribution to a collection, cause, task, etc, no matter how small, is valuable since a whole is frequently made up of many parts. It is a cliché much used by people who are collecting for charity, indicating that ever the smallest contribution is welcome. In common with other such stock responses, the expression can be very irritating in its predictability. The saying is said to be based on the old proverb, 'Everything helps', quoth the wren, when she pissed in the sea.

every man jack is a hackneyed phrase meaning absolutely everyone, as *I shall see to it that the boys are punished, every man jack of them.* It was used by Charles Dickens in *Barnaby Rudge* (1841) and has been a cliché since the late nineteenth century.

everything but the kitchen sink is a hackneyed phrase used to refer to a great deal of luggage, etc, as *When we go on motoring holidays we seem to take everything but the kitchen sink.* Its use implies that much of the luggage taken is unnecessary or inappropriate. The expression became popular in World War 2 although it was in use earlier in the twentieth century.

everything in the garden's lovely is a catchphrase cliché indicating that everything is going well and that things could not be better, as *Their marriage hit a bad patch last year but now everything in the garden's lovely.* The expression comes from the title of a song popularized by Marie Lloyd, a music hall singer who died in 1922. It is sometimes used to suggest that there is something rather smug and unexciting about someone's way of life, that it resembles a well-kept suburban garden.

everything you always wanted to know about (something) but were afraid to ask is a quotation cliché which has become a catchphrase. The expression refers to the title of a book, *Everything You Always Wanted To Know About Sex But Were Afraid To Ask*, written by David Reuben and published in 1970. It owes its popularity to the fact that Woody Allen used it as a film title in 1972. Several books have been published bearing similar titles but the expression is also frequently used in conversation to indicate a very large quantity of material or information, as in *There you are! A whole section on photography. All you ever wanted to know about cameras but were afraid to ask!* The expression is sometimes used in the negative for humorous effect to suggest too much information often of a boring nature, as *I thought the speaker would never shut up. Her talk was everything you never wanted to know about feminism and were afraid to ask.*

explore every avenue is a hackneyed phrase used to indicate that a subject will be looked into extremely carefully and thoroughly with a view to finding the best means of doing something, etc. It is usually regarded as a pompous and roundabout way of saying that very little will in fact be done, although it will be made to appear that this is not the case. It is apt to appear in such contexts as a formal reply to a letter of complaint or in a promise from a politician or civil servant, as *You may be assured that we shall explore every avenue to find a plan for the town centre that is acceptable to everyone.*

express our appreciation is a hackneyed phrase used to mean either to applaud a speaker or performer by clapping one's hands or to make a financial contribution towards a gift for someone in acknowledgement of services rendered. It is a formal and often rather pompous expression, often lengthened to **express our appreciation in the usual way**, as in *Now ladies and gentlemen, after that excellent talk, I am sure that you will wish to express your appreciation in the usual way by putting your hands together.*

F

face that launched a thousand ships, the is an allusion cliché referring to Helen of Troy whose beauty was a contributory factor in the launching of the Greek fleet which sailed for Troy to avenge Menelaus, husband of Helen, who had gone off with Paris, the son of the king of Troy, and started the siege of Troy. The actual phrase is a quotation from Marlowe's play *Faustus* (Circa 1588) As a modern cliché it is often used not to refer to great beauty but to great ugliness, as *He's very handsome but have you seen his wife? Talk about the face that launched a thousand ships!*

face the facts is a hackneyed phrase meaning to force oneself to accept and deal with the actual reality of a situation instead of ignoring it, putting it to the back of one's mind or taking a romantic or unrealistic view of it, as *I know you think that a baby won't change your lifestyle, but you have to face the facts. Someone will have to look after it.* The expression is an analogy with **face the music**.

face the music is an idiom cliché meaning either to confront a difficult situation boldly or bravely, or to meet the consequences of one's behaviour boldly, as *The boys played truant yesterday and had fun at the seaside. Now they'll have to face the music in the headmaster's study.* There is some dispute about the origin of this expression. At least three possible explanations have been put forward. One suggests that it comes from the fact that a singer faces the orchestra when he/she sings in opera or a musical show, while another suggests that it refers to a theatre performer having to face the members of the orchestra in the orchestra pit as well as the audience. The idea of facing a punishment is perhaps best accounted for by the suggestion that the expression refers to the military practice of playing drums when a soldier was dismissed from the service as a punishment or that it refers to a military band playing The Rogue's March at a similar event.

fact of the matter, the is a filler cliché which is simply an unnecessarily long way of saying fact or truth, as *I am sorry to pull out of the trip at the last minute, but the fact of the matter is that I simply can't afford the fare.*

factor is a vogue cliché which became popular in Britain in the 1980s to indicate something that has an effect on an issue, event, etc, as in Falklands factor, that is the effect that the Falklands War had on the standing of the government of the day. It is used in a variety of situations and is particularly popular with journalists. A recent example, is **the feel-good factor**.

fair and square is a doublet cliché since square here means the same as fair. The expression has been recorded since the early seventeenth century and still appears in a wide variety of contexts, as *I am sorry that I lost the election but I was beaten fair and square by an excellent candidate.*

fair game is an idiom cliché indicating that someone or something is a legitimate or fair target for attack, criticism, mockery, etc, as *The film star objects to intrusions into her private life, but journalists regard everybody famous as being fair game in their investigations.*

fair sex, the is a hackneyed phrase used to describe women. It is rather dated but is still used, especially by older men. Women tend to object to its use on the grounds that it is patronizing, suggesting that all that matters in a woman is her looks. It is used in such contexts as *the fair sex, bless them. Where would we be without them?*

fairweather friend is a hackneyed phrase used to describe someone who is a friend and companion while things are going well, but who disappears when things start to go wrong, as *Jane always seemed very popular but when she was dismissed very few of her colleagues stood by her. They were just fair-weather friends.*

fait accompli (French for 'accomplished fact') is a foreign cliché meaning something that has already been accomplished or carried out, as *They would have tried to stop their daughter's marriage but it was a fait accompli by the time they found out about it.* It is widely used, although mostly in fairly formal contexts, there being no common native English phrase used in the same context.

fall between two stools is an idiom cliché meaning to be unsuccessful with regard to two courses of action, categories, etc because of being unable to decide which to opt for or because of trying to achieve both, when these are not compatible, as *He tried to make the same product fit the domestic and the export market but it fell between two stools and didn't do well in either.* The cliché is the standard way of describing something that does not suc-

cessfully and convincingly fit into a category. The origin of the expression is a reference to someone who cannot decide which of two stools to sit on and falls between them while hesitating.

fall by the wayside is an allusion cliché referring to the Biblical parable about the sower of seeds, some of which fell by the wayside and were devoured by fowls and did not grow (*Luke* 8:5). In the parable, the seed was the word of God and the seeds that fell by the wayside represented people who heard the word but were led astray by the Devil. As far as the cliché is concerned, it means to fail to continue to the end, to fail to see something through, as *A large number of runners started the marathon but several fell by the wayside,* and *She keeps beginning new diets but she always falls by the wayside.* Although the expression has rather a literary sound, the cliché is still fairly widely used.

fall on deaf ears is a hackneyed phrase meaning to be totally ignored or disregarded. As a cliché it implies the person concerned does not wish to hear what is being said, as *Her parents tried to warn her that he was a rogue but their warnings fell on deaf ears.* The phrase dates from the fifteenth century and has been a cliché since the nineteenth century.

fall (or land) on one's feet is a hackneyed phrase meaning to come out well from a situation that could have proved disastrous. It is particularly applied to someone who has a habit of doing this, as *People thought that Jack had made a terrible mistake buying that old house, but he sold it to a developer at a profit. He always falls on his feet.* The origin lies in the fact that the cat has the unusual ability to land on its paws, when it jumps, falls or is thrown from a height.

famous last words is a hackneyed phrase used as a remark to someone who has just said something that is likely to be disproved or is likely to prove inappropriate, as *'At least I got rid of him easily,' said Mary as she closed the door on the double-glazing salesman. 'Famous last words,' said Joan. 'He's just coming up the path again. He must have been at his car collecting leaflets'.* It is thought to have become popular in World War 2.

In origin it is a reference to the dying words of famous people, which are often noted for posterity.

far and away is a doublet cliché used to indicate the degree to which something or someone exceeds others, as *She is far and away the best candidate for the post* and *This car is far and away the most reliable we've had.* It is usually found in a complimentary context but is also found in critical or condemnatory contexts, as *This is far and away the worst food I've ever eaten.* It has been a cliché since the nineteenth century.

far and wide is a doublet cliché meaning extensively. It is used for emphasis to describe how far-reaching, thorough, etc something has been, as *We searched far and wide before we found a cottage we liked.* It has been a stock phrase in the language from earliest times.

far be it from me is a hackneyed phrase which suggests that the speaker is too modest or discreet to, but is going to anyway, as *Far be it from me to tell you how to run your life, but I really don't think that you should marry him.* The expression dates from the late fourteenth century and has been common since the late eighteenth century. It is still commonly used today by people who like to interfere and also by people who use it meaninglessly as a linguistic habit.

far cry, a is a hackneyed phrase used to indicate a great difference, as *Her present lifestyle is a far cry from the one she used to enjoy.* The expression used to be used literally as well as figuratively but as a current cliché it is used only in figurative contexts. In origin it is thought to refer to the measuring of one's distance from one's enemy by the estimation of the shouting distance.

far from the madding crowd is a quotation cliché from *Elegy Written in a Country Churchyard* (1751) by Thomas Gray. It is also the title of a novel by Thomas Hardy (1874). The expression is used to refer to noisy hordes of people and is always found in contexts suggesting a desire to get away from these, as *They love walking in the hills, far from the madding crowd.* Madding is obsolete except in this phrase.

fast and furious is a doublet cliché meaning hectic. It is usually applied to fun or some form of game or sport, as *The fun was fast and furious at the children's Christmas party.* Nowadays it is not commonly used in informal English but would still be commonly found, for example, in reports of social events in local newspapers. Its association with fun has its origins in Robert Burns' poem, *Tam o' Shanter (1793)* 'The mirth and fun grew fast and furious.'

fast lane, the is a vogue cliché which became popular in Britain in the 1970s meaning a high-pressure, swift-moving career or lifestyle. It is found in such statements as *He couldn't take life in the fast lane any more. He's left the city and gone to the country to write books.* and *She loves being in the fast lane. She got bored looking after the children.* In origin the expression refers to the outside lane of a motorway which people use to overtake others.

59

fat chance is a hackneyed phrase said by someone to stress the unlikelihood of something, as *You want tickets for tonight's performance? Fat chance. They've been sold out for weeks.* The cliché originated in America but is now widely used in informal contexts in Britain.

fate is sealed, his/her is a hackneyed phrase indicating that it is quite inevitable that something, usually something bad, is going to happen to someone, as *We don't know the result of Peter's trial yet but his fate is sealed. The jury have just returned to their seats.* It is more usually found nowadays in a jocular or facetious context, as *Ah well, John's fate is sealed. Anne has started going out with him and she's looking for a husband.* The origin of the expression is an allusion to the fact that the edict of a monarch directing someone to be hanged, etc would bear the royal seal.

fate worse than death, a is a hackneyed phrase meaning rape or seduction and refers to the days when the loss of virginity was a great disgrace to a young woman and would seriously affect her chances of marrying. As a modern cliché it may be used in a humorous context of a sexual encounter that is quite welcome, as *He's asked you to stay the night at last. Oh, a fate worse than death.* It is also used facetiously or ironically, as *to have to listen to her talking all day would be a fate worse than death.*

feather in one's cap, a is an idiom cliché indicating a special achievement or honour that one has reason to be proud of, as *Getting a representative into the national team is a real feather in the cap of our local athletics club* and *It's a feather in her cap to get such a famous writer to speak to the women's group.* The term was a cliché by

the eighteenth century and is still common nowadays.

The origin of the phrase lies in the fact that it was the custom among North American Indians to place a feather in a warrior's headdress or cap for every member of the enemy he killed.

feather one's nest is an idiom cliché meaning to provide for oneself or make a profit for oneself while engaged in some activity where one was not meant to be doing this, as *The local organizer has been accused of feathering her own nest at the expense of the charity and has been dismissed* and *The sales manager has been feathering his own nest for years by overclaiming on his expenses.* The expression is still common and has its origin in the habit of birds of making their nests soft and comfortable to hatch their eggs in. It has been a cliché since the eighteenth century.

feel a different person is a hackneyed phrase meaning to feel much better in terms of health or general wellbeing, as *Since he started taking those pills he has felt a different person* and *She feels a different person since she's been able to get out a bit more.* The expression is most likely to be used in informal contents.

the feel-good factor is a vogue cliché which became popular in the 1980s and 1990s to indicate an effect caused by people feeling pleased with their lot. It is particularly used of the influence of perceived affluence on people, on how they vote in opinion polls and elections and on their spending patterns, as *The government hopes that the fall in interest rates will create a feel-good factor among the electorate* and *The department stores think that their increase in sales is due to a feel-good factor in the country.*

feel it in one's bones is an idiom cliché meaning to feel intuitively that something is the case, to have a premonition about something. The something in question can be either good or bad, as *I feel it in my bones that he is going to get the job* and *I feel it in my bones that there is something not right with the firm.* The origin probably lies in the fact that people with rheumatism or arthritis sometimes claim to be able to predict when it's going to rain because of the ache in their bones or joints.

feel one's age is a hackneyed phrase indicating that one is becoming aware of the effects of advancing age, as *Old Jack is still working at the age of 70 but he's talking of retiring. He says he's feeling his age.* It is sometimes used facetiously as *I was going to do so many things when the twins started school but I don't have the energy. I think I'm feeling my age!* The expression has been a cliché since the late nineteenth century.

feet of clay, have is an allusion cliché. It indicates that a person who is held in high regard has an unexpected fault or failing, as *She used to regard her father as some kind of god but she realized that he had feet of clay when she discovered that he mistreated his employees,* and *After her death he discovered that his adored wife had feet of clay. She had been having an affair with a neighbour for years.* The Biblical allusion is to the *Book of Daniel* (2:33) in which an idol is described as being made of gold, silver and bronze with legs of iron, and with feet of iron and clay. The cliché is currently found in quite informal contexts as well as more literary ones.

festive occasion is a hackneyed phrase used to describe a celebratory or special social occasion, as *We like to dress up at Christmas and on other festive occasions.* The expression which is still widely used, partly because it is difficult to think of an alternative, has been a cliché since the late nineteenth century.

few and far between is a doublet cliché which simply reinforces the idea of seldomness. The things that are described as being seldom or widely spaced-out may be pleasant or unpleasant, as *Since the baby was born our nights out have been few and far between,* and *Fortunately his asthmatic attacks are few and far between now.* The expression is used by the poet, Thomas Campbell in *The Pleasures of Hope* (1799) 'What though my winged hours have been, like angel-visits, few and far between.'

fiddle while Rome burns is an allusion cliché indicating that someone is occupying himself/herself with trivialities or minor pursuits while something important required urgent attention, as *When the men walked out on strike in the middle of a rush export order, the production manager went out to lunch. Is that not fiddling while Rome burns?* The allusion is to the legend that Nero, Emperor of Rome, played his lyre and watched the flames from a tower when Rome was on fire (AD64). It has been a cliché since the nineteenth century and is still common.

field day, a is an idiom cliché meaning great activity or great success, as *The press will have a field day when they find out that the politician has left his wife for a young girl.* The expression has its origin in a special day that was set aside for military manoeuvres and exercises. It was later transferred to civilian occasions, such as school outings or other enjoyable events. Nowadays, however, the activity is usually centred on someone else's misfortune, as in *The local gossips had a field day when the bailiffs arrived at his house.*

fighting chance, a is a hackneyed phrase used to indicate that there is a possibility of success if every effort is made, as *He didn't run very well today but he still has a fighting chance of getting into the team if he trains hard*. This an extremely common expression in a variety of contexts and is frequently used to describe someone who is very ill but who has a chance of survival. The origin is an allusion to a physical fight or battle that one might win if one tries one's very hardest.

fighting fit is a hackneyed phrase meaning very well or healthy, in good physical condition, as *Her father was very ill for a while but he is fighting fit now*. The origin is an allusion to a boxer being in good enough condition to fight.

fight tooth and nail is a hackneyed phrase meaning to struggle with all one's strength and resources, as *They fought tooth and nail to stop the new road being built but they lost*. The origin lies in the fact that animals and people will use all the physical means at their disposal, such as teeth and nails, in order to win a fight if there is a lot at stake. As a phrase it has been in the language since the sixteenth century and it is thought to have been a cliché since the mid nineteenth century. It is still commonly used, often as a declaration of intent, as *'We shall fight tooth and nail to prevent the closure of the school,'* . . . *declared the chairman of the protest group*.

figment of one's imagination, a is a hackneyed phrase meaning something which one has imagined and which has no reality, as *She said that she saw a man in the garden but I'm sure that it was just a figment of her imagination*. The word 'figment' on its own refers to something that is a fantastic notion or fabrication, and so there is a tautological element in the expression. The phrase appears in *Jane Eyre* (1847) by Charlotte Brontë 'The long dishevelled hair, the swelled black face, the exaggerated stature, were figments of imagination.'

filthy lucre is an allusion cliché meaning money, as *I detest the man but I wish I had his filthy lucre*. It is found in an informal or slang context and is frequently used in a critical or condemnatory sense, as *All she cares about is filthy lucre*. The expression originally meant money acquired by dishonourable means and before that base profit. It is a Biblical allusion to 1 Timothy (3:3) 'Not given to wine, not greedy of filthy lucre, but patient, not a brawler, not covetous.'

fill the bill is an idiom cliché meaning to be exactly what is required, to be suitable, as *I couldn't decide what to wear to the wedding but this dress will fill the bill*. Although American in origin, it is now commonly used in British English, though not in formal contexts. In origin it refers to the practice of first listing the leading performers on a theatre advertising bill and then filling it up by adding the back-up, lesser known and minor performers.

find one's feet is a hackneyed phrase meaning to become able to cope with a new situation, as if finding out where to place one's feet. It is used in rather informal contexts, as *It's too soon to tell how good the new receptionist is. She's still finding her feet*.

fine tooth comb see *go through with a fine tooth comb*.

finger in every pie, a is an idiom cliché meaning involved in many activities at once, as *I don't know how he keeps track of his business interests. He has a finger in every pie*, and *If you want to know anything* *about village life, ask the vicar's wife. She's got a finger in every pie*. The implication is not a flattering one, since the phrase usually suggests either that something vaguely dishonest is involved or that someone is interfering. The origin is an allusion to someone in a kitchen tasting several pies.

finishing touches is a hackneyed phrase meaning the last details that make something complete or perfect. It is found in a variety of contexts, as *I have iced the birthday cake. It just needs a few finishing touches.* and *My brother is just putting the finishing touches to the speech he is giving to tomorrow's conference*. The origin of the expression lies in the the last strokes that an artist marked in a painting.

fire away! is an idiom cliché used as an informal interjection telling someone to go ahead and say what he or she wants to say, as *OK, I've found a pen, fire away and I'll try to get all the message down,* and *I don't mind answering the questions on your questionnaire. Fire away!* In origin the expression refers to an instruction to begin firing a gun.

firing on all cylinders is an idiom cliché referring to an internal combustion engine, as in a car, which is working effectively at full strength. As a cliché it is commonly used in the negative to indicate that something or someone is not working at full strength or with maximum effort, as *You'll have to excuse me. I have a cold and I'm just not firing on all cylinders today*. The expression is, however, not always used in the negative and is found in such contexts as *The factory will have to be firing on all cylinders to get these orders out on time*

first and foremost is a doublet cliché, first and foremost in this context being more or less synonymous, meaning most impor-

tantly, as *We need many things for the new house, but first and foremost we need a new bed. He had many good qualities but first and foremost he was a good friend.* It is found in a variety of contexts and has been used as a cliché since the mid nineteenth century.

first come, first served is a hackneyed phrase indicating that if something is limited, those who come first will obtain it at the expense of those who follow. *You can't book tickets. They are on sale on the night of the performance and it will be a case of first come, first served.* It is a widespread cliché being used in all but the most formal contexts, As a saying it has been in the language since the middle of the sixteenth century.

first see (the) light of day is an idiom cliché meaning to be born, be first invented, have its first performance, be first in evidence, etc, as *The team have spent years researching a new drug but I don't think it will ever see the light of day,* and *His new opera first saw the light of day in Milan.* The cliché dates from the mid nineteenth century. It is now more frequently used of things than of people.

first thing is a hackneyed phrase meaning early in the day, as *The teacher says that she wants all the essays on her desk first thing,* and *She can never eat anything first thing.* So successful is the phrase as a cliché that it is difficult to think of a suitable alternative. To some extent it is an imprecise term since its timing depends on how early one starts one's day.

first things first is a hackneyed phrase stressing that the most important things should be dealt with first. It seems to state the obvious, as *The homeless family have a lot of problems, but first things first. We must find them somewhere to live,* and can be a very irritating cliché. Sometimes it is used facetiously or ironically, as *We have a lot to get through at the meeting this morning but first things first. Let's have a cup of tea.* The expression dates from the nineteenth century.

first water, of the is an idiom cliché now usually meaning out-and-out, of the very worst kind as *He is a villain of the first water* and *She is married to a bastard of the first water.* The term was originally used in a more complimentary way as *He is an artist of the first water,* but this use is now considerably less common than its condemnatory equivalent. In origin the expression alludes to a system of grading diamonds by which they were classified into three waters, according to their colour or lustre, the latter being likened to the clarity and shininess of water.

the first ... years are the worst is a hackneyed phrase suggesting that the initial period of anything is the worst and if you can tolerate that, you can tolerate the rest that is to come. The number of years cited varies from a relatively small number, such as 5, to an exaggerated total, such as 100, as *So you're just married. Never mind, the first ten years are the worst,* and *Welcome to the workforce. You'll find the first hundred years are the worst.* The cliché is always used in a humorous or ironical context and probably has its origin in a military catchphrase from about the time of World War 2 – 'Cheer up, the first seven years are the worst', seven years referring to a regular soldier's length of service.

fish out of water, a is an idiom cliché referring to someone who is completely out of his/her element or feels uncomfortable or ill-suited to a particular environment or situation, as *The young man is very shy and is a fish out of water at parties.* It can also be used as a simile cliché as **like a fish out of water** as in *As an older woman she feels like a fish out of water in an office full of young people.* It is found in a wide variety of contexts. The origin is the obvious one that a fish cannot survive long out of water. The expression has been a cliché since the mid nineteenth century but as a phrase has been in the language much longer.

fit as a fiddle is a simile cliché indicating extremely heathy, in very good physical condition, as *My mother has been ill but she is fit as a fiddle after her holiday.* The origin is uncertain, there being no obvious reason why a fiddle should be a model of fitness.

fit for a king is a hackneyed phrase meaning of exceptionally high quality, as *That was a meal fit for a king.* The origin is obvious, that only the best was good enough for a royal personage. It has been a cliché since the eighteenth century but in modern times the expression is usually associated with food.

fits and starts, by is a doublet cliché since fits and starts are virtually synonymous in this context. The expression means at irregular intervals, spasmodically, as *The students are meant to be working hard for their exams but they tend to work by fits and starts.* The phrase has been in the English language since the early seventeenth century and is such a well-established cliché that any synonym for it sounds less appropriate.

fit to hold a candle to, not is an idiom cliché meaning not able to be compared with, utterly inferior to, as *Not only is he less qualified than his predecessor but he is not fit to hold a candle to him.* The expression is also found in the form **cannot/can't hold a candle to** which has the same meaning but tends to be used in less formal contexts, as in *Most of the modern pop stars couldn't hold a candle to Elvis*. In origin the expression refers to the menial task of holding a candle for someone so that he/she might see to do something. The phrase has been in the language since the middle of the seventeenth century and has been a cliché since the nineteenth century. Lord Byron used a version of it in *On the Feud between Handel and Bononcini* 'Others aver that he to Handel is scarcely fit to hold the candle.' The cliché is always used in the negative.

flash in the pan, a is an idiom cliché which refers to a brief and unexpected success which is not sustained, as *The student did brilliantly in his first exam, but it proved to be a flash in the pan*. The origin of the expression refers to a seventeenth century flintlock musket. In this a spark from the flint ignited a pinch of gunpowder in the priming pan, from which the flash travelled to the main charge in the barrel. If the charge failed to go off there was only a flash in the pan. The idiom originally meant an abortive effort but has had its present meaning since the 1920s.

flash through one's mind is a hackneyed phrase meaning to occur to one suddenly and possibly briefly, as *It flashed through my mind that he was lying*. The origin of the expression is an allusion to lightning flashing and it has been a cliché since the late nineteenth century.

flat as a pancake is a simile cliché meaning completely flat, as *When he got to his car one of the tyres was flat as a pancake*. As a simile the expression has been in the language since the sixteenth century but its status as a cliché is considerably more recent. Nowadays its use tends to be restricted to tyres or terrain, as *He misses the hills. The land around here is flat as a pancake*. It is also

sometimes used to describe the bust of a woman when it is less than generous, but in this sense it is usually a derogatory term.

flat denial is a hackneyed phrase used to indicate a complete and unconditional denial, as *The politician has issued a flat denial that he has in any way been involved in the fraud*. This cliché is usually found in journalists' reports. It frequently has an effect opposite to the one intended, in that people often take a flat denial to be an admission of guilt. The expression has been in the language since the early eighteenth century.

flat out is a hackneyed phrase meaning as hard, fast, energetically, etc as possible, as *The staff are working flat out to get the orders out on time*. and *I can't go any faster. The car's going flat out as it is*.

flattery will get you nowhere is a hackneyed phrase originating in the middle of the twentieth century and indicating that there is no point in saying good or admiring things about someone or something just to get one's own way as this will be unsuccessful. It occurs in such contexts as *You can stop paying me compliments. Flattery will get you nowhere and I'm still not going out with you*. The expression is sometimes turned around to mean the opposite, as **Flattery will get you everywhere**. This is used in humorous contexts, as *Well I could try and get you a ticket for tonight's performance. Flattery will get you everywhere*.

flavour of the month is an idiom cliché referring to someone or something that is very popular for a very short period of time, as *You're flavour of the month. Why don't you ask the boss if we can leave early?* and *This week the headmaster is backing more freedom for the pupils, but that's just the flavour of the month. By the end of the month he'll be back* *to expelling everyone for the least thing.* The cliché originates in the latter part of the twentieth century and is derived from attempts by ice cream shops in America to get their customers to try a different flavour each month.

flesh and blood has two cliché meanings. One refers to family and relatives, as *My brother hardly ever visits us. He seems to prefer his friends to his own flesh and blood.* This has been a cliché since the nineteenth century but appeared in the language much earlier. For example it occurs in Shakespeare's *Merchant of Venice* (2:2) 'If thou be Launcelot, thou art mine own flesh and blood.' Nowadays the expression is often used in rather sentimental contexts. The second cliché means more or less human nature, usually with an emphasis on the frailty of human nature, especially when sexual matters are involved, as in *He said that seeing his wife in another man's arms was more than flesh and blood could stand,* and *You can't blame young people for wanting to live together. They're only flesh and blood.*

flog a dead horse is an idiom cliché meaning to pursue a futile aim, especially to go on trying to arouse interest in a subject which has already been fully discussed, but which is no longer interesting, relevant or topical, or which has already proved a failure, as in *He's flogging a dead horse trying to get money for his new business. He's already tried all the banks.* It was used in the 1860s to describe Lord John Russell's attempt to bring a new reform bill into Parliament, when the members were totally apathetic towards the issue. The most obvious origin of the expression is an allusion to someone fruitlessly whipping a dead horse to get it to work or run a race.

flotsam and jetsam is a doublet cliché meaning odds and ends or articles of little worth, as *It's not really an antique shop. It's full of flotsam and jetsam.* Sometimes it is used in a derogatory way of people meaning the down-and-outs, as *It's the area of town where the flotsam and jetsam hang out.* Although flotsam and jetsam are connected, they were not originally synonyms. Both were connected with wreckage found on the sea. Flotsam technically referred to articles found floating in the sea, formed from Old French *floter*, to float. Jetsam technically referred to articles thrown overboard to lighten a ship when it was in trouble and is a shortened form of 'jettison'. The expression has been a cliché since the nineteenth century.

fly in the face of danger is an idiom cliché meaning to oppose or defy something dangerous in a seemingly foolhardy way, as *We advised him not to compete in the race when he was unused to the car, but he insisted on flying in the face of danger,* and *She wanted to tell the headmaster that he had made a mistake but she decided not to fly in the face of danger.* In origin the expression is thought to allude to a frightened or angry hen flying in the face of a threatened enemy, such as a dog. The expression is not restricted to danger. **Fly in the face of providence** is common, as *I told him to check his fuel supply but he would fly in the face of providence and ignored my advice.* The cliché is also found in such expressions as **fly in the face of public opinion**, as *The government might have been re-elected but it flew in the face of public opinion and did nothing about unemployment.* It is a general, widespread cliché used in both written and spoken English.

flying colours, with is an idiom cliché meaning very successfully, as *She thought she might have failed the exam but she passed* *with flying colours.* This cliché is found in a variety of contexts and has its origin in the fact that sailing ships which were victorious in battle sailed with their flags, or colours, hoisted high.

fly in the ointment, the is an allusion cliché from the Bible. It refers to *Ecclesiastes* (10:1) 'Dead flies cause the ointment of the apothecary to send forth a stinking savour; so doth a little folly him that is in reputation for wisdom and honour.' As a cliché the expression is used to refer to something that detracts from the pleasing, enjoyable or attractive nature of something, as *It's a wonderful holiday spot. The fly in the ointment is the time it takes to get there.* It is a widely used cliché in all but the most formal contexts.

fly off the handle is an idiom cliché meaning to lose one's temper. Originally American, the expression has its origin in an axe or hammer, the handle of which becomes loosened and flies off after it has struck a blow. It is widely used, but only in more informal contexts, as *I tried to tell her that I didn't break the window but she flew off the handle before I could explain.*

follow in the footsteps of is an idiom cliché meaning either to be someone's successor, as *The professor is looking for a young man of talent to follow in his footsteps,* or, more commonly, to do the same kind of work as, or lead the same kind of life as, someone, as *I think he's going to follow in his father's footsteps and be a doctor,* and *We're worried that he may be a good-for-nothing and follow in his father's footsteps.* The origin alludes to someone following the footsteps or footprints of a guide.

followed suit is an idiom cliché with its origin in card games, such as whist or bridge. It literally means to play a card of the same suit as the previous player. As a cliché it means to do as someone else has just done, as *When the shop steward walked out of the meeting the rest of the workers followed suit.* It is widely used but tends to be commoner in more formal contexts. The expression has been used in a non-literal sense since the middle of the nineteenth century.

follow that cab /taxi/car is a catchphrase cliché used humorously, for example, when a party has to split up into two or more taxis or private cars, as *Follow that car. We don't know where the restaurant is.* In origin the phrase refers to a line popular among film scriptwriters and used in the course of an exciting chase. There is no specific source.

food for thought is a hackneyed cliché meaning something worth thinking about, as *That was an interesting speech. I am sure that it has given us all food for thought.* The expression dates from the early nineteenth century and is a popular cliché today.

fool's paradise a is a hackneyed phrase meaning great happiness that is based on an illusion, as *She's so much in love with him that she's living in a fool's paradise. He's married and still living with his wife.* The expression has been a cliché since the nineteenth century but it has been part of the language since the fifteenth century.

fools rush in is an allusion cliché to the proverb **fools rush in where angels fear to tread** which is itself used as a cliché. Both the shorter and longer versions are used to describe impetuous or insensitive people who do not stop to consider the effects of their actions or words, as *Trust Mary to ask Jane where her engagement ring is. Talk about fools rushing in. Jim and Mary have just split up.* The expression has been popular since the nineteenth century. As a cliché it is still common today as indeed are the fools so described.

foot in it, put one's see *put one's foot in it*

footloose and fancy free is a hackneyed phrase meaning without any commitments or ties. It is frequently used of someone who is not involved in any romantic attachment of a binding nature, as *There's nothing to stop you working abroad. You're footloose and fancy free,* and *She would like to marry some day but just now she's footloose and fancy free.* The word footloose suggests that one is free to go anywhere that one chooses. Fancy free in the sense of not romantically involved occurs in Shakespeare's *A Midsummer Night's Dream* (2:1) 'The imperial votaress passed on, in maiden meditation, fancy-free.'

for better or worse is a quotation cliché, being a slight misquotation from the marriage service in *The Book of Common Prayer,* in which the bride and groom exchange vows 'for better, for worse, for richer, for poorer, in sickness or in health.' It is now used more generally meaning in whatever circumstance, good or bad as *Well, I made the decision to emigrate and I'll have to go through with it, for better or worse.*

forbidden fruit is an allusion cliché to the Bible. It refers to the story of Eve in *Genesis* in which she eats the forbidden fruit from the tree of knowledge and is consequently expelled by God with Adam from the Garden of Eden. It is now used to refer to any illicit pleasure, as *They're under age but they try to get into the nightclub because it's forbidden fruit,* and *He knows she's engaged but he's asked her out. You know what he's like with forbidden fruit.*

foregone conclusion, a is a quotation cliché from Shakespeare's *Othello* (3:3) 'But this denoted a foregone conclusion.' As a cliché it means a result that is either known already or is entirely predictable and so can be taken for granted, as *There's* very little point in their bothering to play the match. Peter's so much the stronger player that it's a foregone conclusion. As a modern cliché it is used in a variety of contexts.

forewarned is forearmed is a proverb cliché indicating that prior knowledge of an impending event enables one to be prepared for it. It occurs in a variety of contexts, as *I'm glad you told me that she is going to ask me for a loan. Forewarned is forearmed,* and *Thanks for telling me that they're planning a surprise visit. That gives me time to get ready. Forewarned is forearmed.* In origin the expression is a translation of a Latin proverb *praemonitus, praemunitus.*

forlorn hope, a is a hackneyed phrase meaning an enterprise that has little chance of success, as *They've applied for time to pay back the loan but it's a forlorn hope.* It also means a very faint hope, as *We are praying that they're still alive but it's a forlorn hope. The coastguards have found an empty boat.* In origin it is a mistranslation of the Dutch *verloren hoop,* meaning a lost troop of soldiers, *hoop* having been taken wrongly to mean hope.

for this relief much thanks is a quotation cliché from Shakespeare's *Hamlet* (1:1). It originally referred to military relief, but as a cliché it is used humorously, as *You've come to take over the babysitting? For this relief much thanks!* It tends to be used by people of rather literary tastes.

forty winks is a hackneyed phrase meaning a short sleep, as *Father always has forty winks after lunch.* It is widely used in informal contexts but its origin is uncertain. The expression has been used since the early part of the nineteenth century.

free, gratis and for nothing is a hackneyed phrase simply meaning free, without charge. It is used for emphasis, free, gratis and for nothing all being synonyms, in informal, often humorous, contexts as *You don't need a ticket for the match. You'll get it free, gratis and for nothing.*

-free zone is a hackneyed phrase used to indicate that a place or situation is free from the thing specified, as *Please put your cigarette out. This is smoke-free zone.* It is often used humorously or satirically, as *Thank goodness this department is still a woman-free zone.* As a cliché the expression dates from the twentieth century and is probably based originally on **war-free zone**. It is extremely common today.

fresh fields and pastures is a quotation cliché which is in fact a misquotation from Milton's *Lycidas*, the correct quotation being 'fresh woods, and pastures new'. Despite its literary connections it is a widely used cliché in both informal and formal contexts, as *I've been in this job for several years. I think it's time for fresh fields and pastures new.*

from the cradle to the grave is a hackneyed phrase meaning all one's life, at all stages in one's life, as *They expect the state to provide for them from the cradle to the grave.* It has been in the language for some considerable time, having been used by the essayist Richard Steele in 1706 'From the cradle to the grave he never had a day's illness.' It has been a cliché since the nineteenth century. Churchill used it in a radio broadcast in 1943 'National compulsory insurance for all classes for all purposes from the cradle to the grave.'

from the sublime to the ridiculous is a hackneyed phrase indicating that there has been a drastic reduction in the scale, importance, quality, etc of the subjects being discussed, as *We've really gone from the sublime to the ridiculous. A minute ago we were talking about the reduction in the*

defence budget. Now we're talking about cake recipes. Napoleon is said to have used it, in French, to describe the retreat of his army from Moscow, but the idea is thought to have come from Tom Paine's *The Age of Reason* (1794) 'One step above the sublime makes the ridiculous, and one step above the ridiculous makes the sublime again.'

from the word go is a hackneyed phrase meaning right from the very beginning. It is mainly used in informal contexts, as *That pupil has been nothing but trouble from the word go,* and *The holiday was a disaster from the word go.* In origin it refers to the call at the beginning of a race, etc.

from time immemorial is a hackneyed phrase meaning from earliest times, beyond anyone's recall, as *There has been a standing stone there since time immemorial.* The cliché is sometimes used in humorous, informal contexts to mean quite a long time, as *Those curtains have been up in her front room since time immemorial.* The term may derive from English law where it meant beyond legal memory, i.e. before the reign of Richard I (1189–1199).

fullness of time, **in the** is an allusion cliché referring to the Bible, *Galatians* (4:4) 'But when the fullness of time was come, God sent forth His son.' As a cliché it is used in formal contexts, frequently rather pompously. It is often used when conveying a reproach to someone who is considered to be impatient, as *We shall consider your request in the fullness of time, but we have a large number of applications to deal with.*

full steam ahead is an idiom cliché meaning as fast as possible, as *Now that have the go-ahead for the order it will be full steam ahead to get it done on time.* In origin the expression refers to a steam engine as used in trains and steam ships, 'full steam' indicating that a boiler had developed maximum pressure and so was able to go at maximum speed. In its figurative context the expression became popular in the late nineteenth century.

funny ha ha is a hackneyed phrase meaning funny in the sense of amusing. It is found in informal contexts, as *When she said that her father was funny I thought she meant funny ha ha.* The expression is often used in conjunction with its converse, funny peculiar, as *His stories are funny peculiar, rather than funny ha ha.*

F-word, the is a hackneyed phrase which could also be regarded as a euphemism cliché used as a substitute for 'fuck', a word which is supposedly still taboo but which is widely used in ordinary speech and in modern novels and plays, although not yet officially in newspapers or radio or television. **The F-word** is used in situations where fuck is supposedly taboo but is in many ways less acceptable than the word for which it is substituted, since it sounds so ridiculous. Because of this latter fact it is often used satirically and people often send it up by coining other words in analogy with it where there is no suggestion of anything taboo, as the M-word for money or the S-word for sex. The analogy is also extended to other words that are taboo, as the C-word for 'cunt'.

G

gainful employment is a hackneyed phrase meaning paid employment, a job. It is used nowadays in formal or rather pompous contexts, as *The judge asked if the accused was in gainful employment*, although it is also used in humorous or ironic contexts.

game is not worth the candle, the is a proverb cliché indicating that the project, etc involved is too troublesome, difficult, etc for the advantages it would bring, as *I gave up having a weekend job. I was paying so much tax that the game wasn't worth the candle.* It is a translation of the French *le jeu n'en vaut la chandelle* which meant literally that the card game being played was not worth the cost of the candles required to provide light for it, the amount of money at stake being so low. The English version appeared in John Ray's collection proverbs of 1678 and it is still popular today.

game of two halves, a is a hackneyed phrase much used by sports commentators or those involved in a sport to remind people of the obvious fact that football matches, etc are divided into two halves. It is usually used to indicate that there could be a complete turnaround of fortunes in the second half, especially if tactics are changed. Frequently it is used almost meaninglessly, it being the fate of sports commentators to have to make comments when there is nothing meaningful to say.

gameplan is a vogue cliché popular from the 1980s and referring to a series of tactics by which it is hoped to attain an objective, as *She says that taking a shorthand and typing course is just part of her gameplan to become a journalist.* Basically it means simply plan but it is used in an attempt to make a statement sound grander. The term originates in American football.

gather ye rosebuds while ye may is a quotation cliché used as a recommendation to make the most of a good opportunity or a good period of one's life while one can, as it probably will not last, as *Gather ye rosebuds while ye may. You're not getting any younger,* and *I have a feeling that the future for the industry's not too good. Gather ye rosebuds while ye may.* As a cliché it tends to be used by people who have rather literary tastes. The expression is a quotation from the English poet Robert Herrick's *To the Virgins, to Make Much of Time* (1648).

a gay Lothario, is an allusion cliché, being a reference to *The Fair Penitent* (1703) by Nicholas Rowe, in which it is used of a character 'Is that haughty, gallant, gay Lothario?' The expression is used to refer to a man who is a habitual womanizer, as *He's always chatting up the women in the hotel bar. He's a real gay Lothario.* As a modern cliché it tends to be used mainly by older people or people with literary tastes. Nowadays, when gay most frequently means homosexual, rather than merry, the term might be misinterpreted. In any case the word gay is frequently omitted, as *He's quite a Lothario.*

general exodus, a is a hackneyed phrase meaning a general movement of people from a room, building, area, etc, as *At lunchtime there is a general exodus of office workers from the tower block,* and *There is a general exodus of the inhabitants from the city during August.* The expression has been a cliché since the late nineteenth century.

generation gap, the is a vogue cliché referring to the differences in attitudes, social values, lifestyle, etc that exist between one generation and another, especially those between parents and their adolescent children, as *Their plans for Christmas night say it all about the generation gap. The parents want a quiet family night in playing Scrabble. The teenage children want to go to an all-night disco.* Although this phenomenon existed before the later part of the twentieth century it was then that young people sought to assert their identity and acquired more freedom. Thus the differences between the generations became more marked and were given a name.

gentleman's agreement, a is a hackneyed phrase used to refer to a non-written agreement, such as might be sealed by the handshake of two gentleman, as *We had a gentleman's agreement about the division of our relative's property but my brother broke his word.* Nowadays it is a unisex term, women as well as men being able to strike such agreements. In these times of hard-nosed business deals, people tend to view a gentleman's agreement with cynicism, agreeing with A J P Taylor in *English History 1914–45* (1965) 'much used hereafter for an agreement with anyone who was obviously not a gentleman and who would obviously not keep his agreement.'

get a life! is a hackneyed phrase used as general term of abuse, as *Of course I'm going to get there on time. Get a life!* It dates from the later part of the twentieth century and is much used by young people, having overtaken most other forms of abuse. The expression suggests that the person to whom the remark is directed is rather a sad case who has no life worth speaking of.

get a result is a hackneyed phrase used by sports commentators and those involved in sport. It is a curious phrase since by the very nature of things a result will be achieved, whatever its nature. As a cliché the expression dates from the later part of the twentieth century and is used to refer to the fact that it is important for a particular team to win or score a goal in a football match.

get away from it all is a hackneyed phrase dating from the second part of the twentieth century and meaning to get away from one's usual daily routine, usually by taking a holiday. It is much used by holiday firms and travel journalists, as *So if you fancy getting away from it all on a winter break, this could be the place for you.*

get down to brass tacks is an idiom cliché meaning to begin to deal with basic principles or issues, as *We shall allow some time for initial pleasantries and then get down to brass tacks,* and *During the meeting on the economy it was almost impossible to get the politician to get down to brass tacks and stop talking about theories.* It is a late nineteenth century expression which is thought to have its origin in the brass tacks marked at one-yard intervals on a shop counter, for measuring cloth, etc. Thus, getting down to brass tacks literally meant measuring precisely. As a modem cliché it is used in all but the most formal contexts.

get in on the act is an idiom cliché meaning to get involved in an undertaking, usually when one is unwanted, as *We had enough people on the committee but Mrs Jones just had to get in on the act*. In origin the expression is an allusion to an act in the theatre, the implication being that someone has succeeded in getting involved in someone else's act and so will get some of the applause. The likelihood is that the cliché originates from the days of music hall. The American comedian, Jimmy Durante, popularized it in the 1930s. As a modern cliché it is used mainly in informal contexts.

get into trouble is a euphemism cliché meaning to get pregnant while one is unmarried, as *In those days girls who got into trouble were automatically expelled from school*. It is no longer generally considered a social disgrace to be pregnant and unmarried and so the cliché is rather inapt nowadays. However the expression is still widely used by some older people whose attitudes may not accord with modern thinking.

get more than one bargained for is a hackneyed phrase meaning to be confronted with a greater problem, etc than one had expected, as *The boxer thought that he would defeat the local champion easily but he got more than he bargained for*. The expression has been a cliché since the late nineteenth century.

get off one's chest is a hackneyed phrase commonly used in fairly informal contexts and meaning to disclose something that has been worrying, upsetting, annoying, etc one, as *If I've said something to annoy you I wish you'd get it off your chest*. It is as though one has removed a burden from one's bosom or heart. The *London Daily Chronicle* of 1902 described the expression as 'a horrid vulgar phrase'.

get one's act together is a hackneyed phrase dating from the second half of the

twentieth century and meaning to get oneself organized, as *If you don't get your act together and start applying for university places you'll be too late*. It is used in informal or slang contexts.

get one's money's worth is a hackneyed phrase used mainly in fairly informal contexts indicating that one has obtained full value, as *We certainly got our money's worth at the concert. There were three encores.* The term 'money's worth' appears in Shakespeare's *Love's Labour's Lost* (2:1) 'One part of Aquitaine is bound to us, Although not valued to the money's worth.' The current expression dates only from the nineteenth century.

get one's teeth into is an idiom cliché meaning to begin to tackle something in a determined manner, as *He's bored. He needs a job that he can get his teeth into*. The origin is an allusion to teeth sinking into something substantial. The expression has been a cliché since the early twentieth century and is still common in fairly informal contexts.

get out of bed on the wrong side is an idiom cliché meaning to get up in the morning in a bad temper, as *What a mood the boss is in this morning! He certainly must have got out of bed on the wrong side*. The expression is an allusion to the legendary superstition that it was bad luck to put the left foot down first. If someone had a day of exceptional ill luck it was put down to rising from the wrong side of the bed. By the nineteenth century the concept of ill-luck had changed to bad temper. As a modern cliché it is found mainly in informal contexts.

get out while the going's good is a hackneyed phrase meaning to leave at an opportune time before things take a turn for the worse, as *Mother hasn't found out about your school report yet. I would get out while the going is good.* The cliché dates from the early part of the twentieth century and is used mainly in informal, often humorous, contexts. In origin the expression may be a reference to the 'going' or state of the ground in horse racing.

get the message is a hackneyed phrase meaning to understand, especially to understand the significance of something that had previously escaped one, as *It wasn't until she put in ear plugs that he got the message and realized how loudly he was snoring.* The cliché is used only in informal or slang contexts.

getting on is a hackneyed phrase meaning growing old or elderly, as *No wonder her memory's getting bad. She's getting on you know.* Frequently the expression is modified to **getting on a bit**. The expression **getting on** is also used to mean getting quite late, as *I think we'd better start dinner without him. It's getting on.* In both meanings the expression is used in fairly informal contexts.

gift of the gab, the is a hackneyed phrase meaning the ability to talk fluently and eloquently, as *He should get a job as a salesman. He's really got the gift of the gab.* 'Gab' here means mouth, being related to the slang word 'gob'. The expression is usually said with light criticism or grudging admiration and is found in informal contexts. It became popular in the eighteenth century.

gild the lily is an allusion cliché, being a reference, although not an exact one, to Shakespeare's *King John* (4:2) 'To gild refined gold, to paint the lily, To throw a perfume on the violet . . . Is wasteful and ridiculous excess.' It means to add

unnecessary ornament or decoration, as *I don't know why she wears so much make-up. She's so pretty that it's gilding the lily.* It can also mean to exaggerate, as *He won't have told her the truth about his holiday cottage. He'll have gilded the lily a bit.*

gird up one's loins is an allusion cliché meaning to prepare for action, as *We have guests coming for dinner. We'd better gird up our loins and start cooking.* It an allusion to several passages in the Bible, as in *1 Kings* (18:46). 'He girded up his loins, and ran.' In Biblical times the Jews wore loose clothing and tied it up with a girdle only when they were going to work or be active. The apostle Peter used the expression figuratively 'gird up the loins of your mind' (*Peter* 1:13) and it has been a cliché since the nineteenth century. Nowadays it is usually mostly found in a humorous or ironical context.

girl Friday is a hackneyed phrase indicating a female personal assistant, as *The boss has advertised for a girl Friday to do his secretarial work.* The term is analogous with **man Friday**, a general assistant, but is considered sexist.

give a dog a bad name is an allusion cliché to an old proverb **give a dog an ill name and hang him**. It means to damage the reputation of someone by speaking ill of him/her, as *It just takes a few dissatisfied customers to affect business. Give a dog a bad name, as they say.* The expression has been a cliché since the early nineteenth century.

give and take is a hackneyed phrase meaning mutual concessions, a willingness to grant or allow a person something in return for being granted something oneself, as *In marriage there has to be some give and take,* and *If there is going to be a new wages agreement there will have to be* *some give and take between the management and the union.* The expression can also be used as a verb, as *It's difficult to fit into a new school. You have to learn to give and take.* The phrase has been in the language since the eighteenth century and it has been a cliché since the middle of the nineteenth century.

give an inch is an idiom cliché, an abbreviated version of **give someone an inch and he/she will take a mile**. It indicates that it is inadvisable to make any concession at all to a person because he/she will take advantage of the concession to try to obtain even more, as *If you let her start work late one morning she'll try to do it every morning. Give her an inch and she'll take a mile.* An earlier version of the expression was **give him an inch and he will take an ell**. This appeared in John Heywood's collection of proverbs in 1546.

give a wide berth to is an idiom cliché meaning to avoid, as *If I were you I'd give your father a wide berth. He's furious with you for damaging the car.* Literally the expression meant to give a ship plenty of space to manoeuvre safely. The phrase has been a cliché since the second part of the nineteenth century.

give it a miss is a hackneyed phrase used in informal and slang contexts and meaning not to go to something, as *We usually go to the village fête every year but this year we'll be away and so we'll have to give it a miss.* The expression is used in informal contexts.

give one's back teeth is an idiom cliché meaning to do absolutely anything to obtain something that one wants very badly, as *I would give my back teeth to live in a house like that.* The expression was previously **give one's eye teeth**, eye teeth being the upper canine teeth so called since they are

situated under the eyes. Originally the expression was **to give one's eyes,** as in *Barchester Towers 1857* by Anthony Trollope 'Bertie would give his eyes to go with you.' The modern cliché is used in informal or slang contexts.

give the old heave-ho to is a hackneyed phrase meaning to get rid of someone, to ask someone to leave, as *She was so inefficient that the boss gave her the old heave-ho after a week.* The cliché is used only in informal or slang contexts.

give up the ghost is a hackneyed phrase originally meaning to die, being found in the Bible in the *Book of Job 14:10* 'Man dieth, and wasteth away: yea man giveth up the ghost.' The 'ghost' referred to is the soul which is thought to be separated from the body on death. As a modern cliché it means to give up, to stop trying, as *He has been turned down for so many jobs that he's given up the ghost.* It is also applied to machinery, etc which breaks down, as *This car won't get us any farther. It's given up the ghost.* As a modern cliché the expression is used in informal contexts.

glutton for punishment, a is a hackneyed phrase referring to someone who seems to seek out or actively enjoy unpleasant or burdensome tasks, as *The new teacher has actually volunteered to take his third year class on a weekend trip. He must be a glutton for punishment.* The cliché is usually used in humorous or ironic contexts. An earlier form of the expression was a **glutton for work** which dates from the latter part of the nineteenth century.

go against the grain is an idiom cliché meaning to be contrary to a person's principles, feelings, wishes, etc, as *It goes against the grain for her to have to ask her father for money. She's so independent.* In origin the expression is a reference to the grain of wood. It is easier to cut or plane wood with the grain rather than across or against it.

go by the board is an idiom cliché meaning to be abandoned, as *Her resolution to diet went by the board when she was given a box of chocolates*. The board referred to is the side of a ship and the expression originally meant to fall overboard and so be lost. The modern cliché is used in informal contexts and was common by the late nineteenth century.

God's gift is a hackneyed phrase which is used to indicate someone marvellous, very handsome or beautiful, indispensable, etc as though he/she had been heaven-sent. The phrase is always now used ironically of someone who has an over-rated opinion of himself/herself, as *He thinks he's God's gift to women but all the girls in the office laugh at him*.

goes without saying, it/that is a filler cliché used to indicate that something need not be said since it is so generally well known or accepted, as *It goes without saying that pupils are expected to arrive on time*. The expression is often followed by the very statement that supposedly need not be said and is frequently virtually meaningless. Sometimes, indeed, what follows is not at all obvious or generally accepted and may not even be true, as *It goes without saying that we have the best education system in the world*. Some authorities state that the cliché is a translation of the French *cela va sans dire* and dates from the late nineteenth century.

go from strength to strength is an allusion cliché, being a Biblical allusion to *Psalms 84:7* 'They go from strength to strength, everyone of them in Zion appeareth before God.' The expression means to improve markedly and progressively and is found in such contexts as *Setting up the business took a long time but it's going from strength to strength now*. It has been a cliché since the middle of the nineteenth century.

go haywire is a hackneyed phrase meaning to go hopelessly wrong, to start behaving or working totally erratically, as *Our computing system has gone completely haywire*. Originating in America, the actual origin of the expression is uncertain. It is probably an allusion to the fact that the coils of wire used for tying bundles of hay easily became entangled.

go in one ear and out the other is a hackneyed phrase meaning to make no impression on a hearer or listener, as *His mother kept telling him to clean his teeth after meals but her advice went in one ear and out the other*. The expression is commonly used in informal or humorous situations.

golden boy/girl is a hackneyed phrase meaning a young man or woman of great talent, popularity, etc, as *She is the golden girl of British athletics*. The expression is much used by journalists, particularly in a sporting context.

golden opportunity, a is a hackneyed phrase meaning an exceptionally good or favourable chance, as *Being invited to give a talk at the conference is a golden opportunity to get your name known in the profession*. The expression has been a common cliché since the middle of the nineteenth century.

golden rule, the is a hackneyed phrase meaning the rule or principle which is the most important in a particular situation, as *When dealing with customers the golden rule* *is always to be polite.* It is often used in rather a dogmatic or patronizing way. Originally the term indicated the principle that one should always do to others as one would wish them to do to oneself.

gone for a burton/Burton is a hackneyed phrase meaning lost, ruined, dead, etc. The expression is found in informal or slang contexts, as *I thought I might get my stolen car back but it seems to have gone for a burton.* In origin the phrase was an RAF expression during World War 2 meaning missing, presumed dead or drowned. The origin of this is uncertain but it has been suggested that Burton was short for Burton ale, several ales being produced at Burton-on-Trent, and that to go for a burton was to go for a drink, i.e. to be in the drink, 'drink' being slang for sea.

good as gold is a simile cliché meaning extremely good when referring to behaviour, particularly that of children, as *The baby was good as gold when her parents were out.* The cliché dates from the nineteenth century.

good clean fun is a hackneyed phrase meaning harmless or innocent entertainment or activities, as *The school party may usually be just good clean fun but the staff are worried about drink and drugs being brought in.* As a cliché the expression dates from the 1930s and now tends to be used either by older people or in an ironical context.

good in parts is an allusion cliché indicating that there are some good points or aspects about something, but generally conveying a critical rather than a complimentary opinion, as *The play was good in parts but it needs a lot of rewriting.* The expression refers to a saying 'good in parts, like the curate's egg' which first appeared in the illustrated satirical magazine *Punch* 1895. An illustration showed a young curate being asked by his bishop if his breakfast egg was to his liking. Too nervous to say that it was not, the young man replied that 'Parts of it are excellent!' As a cliché the phrase dates from the twentieth century and now tends mostly to be used by older or rather literary people.

good old days, the is a hackneyed phrase meaning the past, especially when looked upon with nostalgia by someone who remembers it, as *In the good old days we could have got there by train but they closed the line.* As a cliché the expression dates from the twentieth century and is sometimes used ironically. The sentiment goes back to ancient times.

goods and chattels is a hackneyed phrase meaning all one's belongings, as *She left her husband and appeared on our doorstep with all her goods and chattels.* As a cliché the expression is commonly used in a humorous or ironical context. In origin the phrase was a legal term referring to all a person's movable property. The expression dates from the sixteenth century and has been a cliché since the eighteenth century.

go off at half-cock is an idiom cliché meaning to act or start prematurely or without sufficient preparation and so be unsuccessful, as *The council's new traffic scheme has gone off at half-cock. It needed more research.* In origin the expression refers to the firing mechanism of a matchlock gun. This could be set, supposedly securely, half-way between the firing and the retracted positions. However, if the mechanism slipped, the gun went off unexpectedly and the shot was obviously wasted. The cliché is frequently used by journalists among others.

go overboard is an idiom cliché meaning to display a great deal of enthusiasm, often excessive enthusiasm, for something or someone, as *She's certainly gone overboard for that shade of green. She wears it all the time.* The expression which is found in informal contexts, has its origins in going to the extreme act of jumping off a ship. As a cliché it has been popular since the first half of the twentieth century.

go round in circles is an idiom cliché meaning to make no progress although frequently putting in a lot of effort, as *We've discussed ways to deal with the company's financial problems all day and we're just going round in circles.* In origin the expression refers to a person who is lost going round in circles without ever reaching his/her destination. An alternative form is **run round in circles**.

gory details the, is a hackneyed phrase meaning the unpleasant details of something. It derives from the word 'gore', meaning blood which has been shed and has clotted. As a cliché it sometimes retains its connections with blood, as *I'm sorry you had to have an operation but I don't want to know the gory details.* But frequently is more generally applied, as *She's bound to tell me about her marriage break-up, I hope she spares me the gory details.* As a cliché it dates from the twentieth century and is still common in rather informal contexts

go the extra mile is a vogue cliché of the late twentieth century meaning to put in the extra effort, money, etc required to do or achieve something, as *Management and unions are very close now but neither of them will go the extra mile to achieve an agreement.* It is particularly popular among politicians and journalists. In its Biblical origin the phrase refers to *Matthew* (5:41) 'And whosoever compel thee to go a mile go with him two.'

go the whole hog is a hackneyed phrase meaning to do something completely and wholeheartedly, especially with regard to spending money or effort, as *I was going to buy a new dress but I decided to go the whole hog and buy shoes and a bag as well.* The expression, which is used in informal contexts, is American in origin and has been a cliché since the nineteenth century. The ultimate origin of the expression is uncertain but it may be an allusion to the fact that hog was once a slang word for 'shilling'.

go through with a fine tooth comb is an idiom cliché meaning to search or study something very closely and carefully, as *You should always go through legal documents with a fine tooth comb.* The phrase is popular with journalists, for example when describing police searches. Its origin refers to the kind of comb commonly used to find and remove lice from hair.

go to rack and ruin is a doublet cliché since rack is an old variant of wreck and therefore meant much the same as ruin. It means to get into a state of neglect, decay, disorganization etc, as *He says he's emigrating because this country's going to rack and ruin.* It has been a cliché since the late eighteenth century although it has been in the language since the end of the sixteenth century.

go to the dogs is a hackneyed phrase meaning to be ruined. The expression can be used either of institutions, etc, as *That used to be a very good restaurant but recently it's gone to the dogs,* or of people, as *After he got into university he went to the dogs and failed all his exams.* When used of people, the ruination is often of a moral nature and is usually self-induced. The expression has been a cliché since the late nineteenth century although it has been in the language for longer than that. As a cliché it is used mainly in informal contexts. Its origins lie in the fact that dogs were generally considered to be inferior creatures.

go to the other extreme is a hackneyed phrase meaning to adopt a course of action, thought or attitude that is completely the opposite from the one which one has previously held, as *When the child was scolded for being late she went to the other extreme and now arrives at school half-an-hour early*. As a cliché it dates from the late nineteenth century.

go to town is a hackneyed phrase meaning to do something with great thoroughness, enthusiasm or expense, as *She's really gone to town on redecorating the house. She's practically rebuilding it*. It is used mainly in informal contexts. American in origin, the expression dates from the nineteenth century and refers to the fact that country people tended to go to town on special or important occasions.

grand old man, the is a hackneyed phrase used to refer to someone who is eminent and long-serving in a particular field, as *Nelson Mandela is now regarded by many as the grand old man of South African politics.* Prime Minister William Gladstone was referred to as 'the grand old man of British politics'. It does not appear to be one of those terms that have been reformed by feminism, as 'grand old woman' is not much in evidence. The expression dates from the late nineteenth century.

grasp the nettle is an idiom cliché meaning to tackle a problem boldly and firmly, as *If you think that she stole the brooch you must grasp the nettle and accuse her*. The cliché, which dates from the late nineteenth century, is commonly and frequently used by people who like giving others advice. Nettles are popularly held to sting less if one grasps them firmly.

grass grow under one's feet, not to let the see *not to let the grass grow under one's feet*.

grass is always greener, the is an allusion cliché based on the proverb **the grass is always greener on the other side of the fence**, which itself is used as a cliché. Both expressions are used to indicate that someone else's lot in life, or some other situation, often seems preferable to one's own, whether or not this is actually the case, as *I think you would be better staying in your present job. You know nothing about the other firm. You know what they say about the grass being always greener*. As a cliché it dates from the nineteenth century and, in common with the condition it describes, is very common today.

greatest/best thing since sliced bread, the is a hackneyed phrase meaning someone or something marvellous or wonderful, as *To her the new car's the best thing since sliced bread*. It is commonly used ironically of people, as *You'd better not disagree with the new manager. He thinks he's the best thing since sliced bread*. The cliché is always used in informal contexts, often in an ironical or derogatory way. In origin the expression, which dates from the middle of the twentieth century, refers to the fact that sliced bread was regarded as a great labour-saving convenience when it was first introduced.

great unwashed, the is a hackneyed phrase meaning the common people. As a cliché it was popular from the middle of the nineteenth century and is now rather dated. However, it is still used by snobbish people, both old and young, who regard

79

themselves as superior to others, as *I don't think I'll go to the hunt ball this year. They've started letting in the great unwashed*. It is also often used ironically, as *You won't find her at university dances. She's scared of mixing with the great unwashed.*

Greek, all see *all Greek to me*

green-eyed monster, the is an allusion cliché meaning jealousy. It is a reference to Shakespeare's *Othello* (3:3) 'Oh, beware my lord of jealousy, It is the green-eyed monster which doth mock the meat it feed on,' says Iago to Othello. As a cliché it dates from the nineteenth century and is still very commonly used in a wide variety of contexts, as *Bob thinks he fancies his brother's new girlfriend but it's just a case of the green-eyed monster*. The cliché is also used to indicate envy or covetousness as well as jealousy, as *She's just being nasty to you because she wants a car like yours. It's the green-eyed monster.*

green light, the is an idiom cliché meaning permission to proceed, as *As soon as we get the green light from the planning department, we'll start on the extension*. It is frequently used by journalists and headline writers. As a cliché it dates from about the mid nineteenth century and owes its origin to traffic lights where green means go and which were first used on railways.

grim death, like is a hackneyed phrase meaning very firmly and determinedly, as *The child was so scared of traffic that she clung to my hand like grim death*. The cliché dates from the middle of the nineteenth century and in origin refers to the unbreakable grip that death has on people.

grim reaper, the is an idiom cliché meaning death. It refers to the representation of death as an old man with a scythe. As a

modern cliché its use tends to be restricted to people of rather a literary bent, who often use it in ironical or humorous contexts, as *I think I'll retire soon. I want to do some travelling before the grim reaper catches up with me.*

grin and bear it is a hackneyed phrase meaning to put up with something unpleasant without complaining, as *I know you don't like studying when your friends are out playing, but your exam's tomorrow. You'll just have to grin and bear it*. As a cliché the expression dates from the late nineteenth century.

grind to a halt is an idiom cliché meaning slowly to come to a standstill, as *Work on our new house has always been slow but now it has ground to a halt completely*. The cliché, which in origin refers to an engine that gradually ceases to function, is widespread and is frequently used by journalists and headline writers. It dates from the twentieth century.

grin like a Cheshire cat is a hackneyed phrase meaning to smile broadly, as *He stood there grinning like a Cheshire cat while we tried to push the car*. It is often used in a derogatory way, the user being annoyed by the smile which is often of a triumphant, smug, etc nature. The ultimate origin of the expression is unknown, but it has been suggested that Cheshire cheese was once sold moulded like the face of a smiling cat. Although the expression was popularized by Lewis Carroll in *Alice's Adventures in Wonderland* (1865), it has been in use since the eighteenth century.

grist to the mill is an idiom cliché meaning something which brings profit or advantage, as *Collect as much stuff as possible for the church jumble sale. All is grist to the mill*. The expression has been a cliché since the nineteenth century although it has been used figuratively since the sixteenth century. Grist was corn for grinding which thus kept the mill operating profitably.

guiding light is a hackneyed phrase referring to a person or thing that has helped to shape one's life or career, as *The headmaster of his primary school was the famous scientist's guiding light,* and *Her mother's stand against sexism was the guiding light of the girl's early life.* As a cliché the expression dates from the mid nineteenth century and has its origin in a light from a lantern, etc which shows people the way in the dark.

❧ H ❧

hair of the dog, a is a hackneyed phrase used to refer to an alcoholic drink taken as a supposed cure for a hangover, although it is just as likely to prolong said hangover. It is a common cliché today, as *How about a hair of dog? You look absolutely terrible*, and has been so for a considerable time. It appeared in John Heywood's collection of proverbs (1546) and has its origin in an old remedy for a dogbite which consisted of burning the hair of a dog and placing it on the bite.

halcyon days is an idiom cliché referring to times that are remembered with nostalgia as being happy or perfect, as *The old women were looking at old photographs and talking about the halcyon days of their childhood*. The expression dates from the late sixteenth century and has been a cliché since the middle of the nineteenth century. In origin it refers to the old belief that the kingfisher, whose Greek name is *halcyon*, laid its eggs on the sea during a fourteen-day period of calm and good weather.

half a loaf is better than none is a proverb cliché which urges the advisability of being satisfied with what you have rather than spending time looking for or wishing for more. It is an old proverb, having appeared in John Heywood's collection (1546) and is still a common cliché today, as *Don't be too disappointed about not passing all of your exams. You passed quite a few and half a loaf is better than none*. The cliché conveys rather a smug, self-righteous sentiment

and tends to irritate the person to whom it is directed.

hale and hearty is a doublet cliché, hale being an archaic form of healthy, and hearty meaning much the same in this context. The cliché is used to emphasize how healthy or fit someone is, as *The old man is well over eighty but he is remarkably hale and hearty*. The expression has been a cliché since the middle of the nineteenth century and is still popular today.

half the battle is a hackneyed phrase used to refer to a very successful beginning which will make the rest of an enterprise easier, as *It is going to be difficult getting funding for the new project, but if we get a government grant, that will be half the battle*. The expression became a cliché in the second half of the nineteenth century and is still common. It is a shortened form of the saying **the first blow is half the battle**, an expression dating from the eighteenth century.

hand in glove with is an idiom cliché referring to close association or intimate terms. It often carries a suggestion of dishonesty, as *He was not involved in the corruption investigation, but people think he was in hand in glove with the people who were found guilty of bribery*. The expression has been a cliché since the late nineteenth century and is still common. It is derived from an older expression **hand and glove** which appeared in John Ray's collection of proverbs (1678), and refers to the fact that a glove is very close to the hand.

handle with kid gloves is an idiom cliché meaning to treat extremely carefully or sensitively, as *You had better handle that customer with kid gloves. He has good grounds for complaint and he is absolutely furious*, and *The situation between the two countries is at a very delicate point and must be handled with kid gloves*. It has been a cliché since the late nineteenth century. In origin it refers to the fact that kid gloves are very fine and delicate.

hand over fist is an idiom cliché meaning very quickly or in large amounts, usually with reference to making money, as *They have been making money hand over fist with their food delivery service*. It has been a cliché since the nineteenth century. The expression was originally **hand over hand** and was a nautical term referring to the way sailors climbed a rope.

hands are tied, one's etc is an idiom cliché indicating one's powerlessness to act. It is a favourite let-out of bureaucrats, who use it as an excuse for not taking action. Their argument is that they are so restricted by rules and regulations that they are not free to take the action that someone wishes them to take, as *If it were left to me I would give you permission to have a street collection for your charity but my hands are tied*. The figurative form of the expression has been in existence since the seventeenth century. It is related to **bound hand and foot** or **tied hand and foot** which carry the same connotations. This was a cliché in the earlier part of the twentieth century but is no longer common.

hands down, win see *win hands down*

handwriting is on the wall see *writing is on the wall, the*

hang in the balance see *balance, hang in the*

hanged for a sheep as a lamb, might as well be is a proverb cliché indicating that one might as well commit a major crime, misdeed, etc rather than a minor one if the extent of the punishment is going to be the same, or that one should not indulge in half-measures. The proverb has been in existence since the seventeenth century and has survived to this day as a wide-spread cliché. It is now often used in a humorous context, as *I've broken my diet and had an ice cream and so I might as well be hanged for a sheep as a lamb and have a box of chocolates*. In origin the proverb refers to the days when the theft either of a sheep or a lamb was punishable by death.

happily ever after, live is a hackneyed phrase used to refer to a happy future existence, often in relation to a couple who have just married. The expression has been a cliché since the eighteenth century and is the classic ending of many fairy stories, as *The frog was turned back into a handsome prince. He then married the beautiful princess and they lived happily ever after*. The expression is still common today, but given the rate of marriage break-up, it is often used in ironic or humorous contexts, as *Mary and Jim got married five years ago and lived happily ever after until last year when they got divorced*. In ironic or humorous contexts the cliché is also applied to situations not involving marriage, as *What have the kids to look forward to? They leave school and live happily ever after on the dole*.

happy couple, the is a hackneyed phrase used to refer to a couple who are being married, who are just about to be married, or who have just been married. The cliché has been popular since the middle of the nineteenth century and is still common today, being much used by journalists, as *The happy couple posed for the cameras after the ceremony*. Nowadays it is frequently used in a humorous context. The term is also sometimes extended to include other than bridal couples, as *Here is a picture of the happy couple celebrating their golden wedding.* An alternative form of the expression is **the happy pair**.

happy event, a is a euphemism cliché used to refer to Childbirth. It is still used, even though people are now much more open about referring to pregnancy without euphemism. The users are mainly older people, especially women who have not yet been affected by the new frankness, as *I hear that your granddaughter is looking forward to a happy event.* It is also used humorously by journalists or by younger people.

happy hunting ground is a hackneyed phrase indicating a place where one often goes, especially in order to obtain a great many things that one wants, as *The local market used to be a happy hunting ground for antique dealers but nowadays it just sells rubbish.* As a cliché it dates from the twentieth century and is still in common use today. In origin it refers to the fact that American Indians believed that after death they would go to a kind of heaven which would be very well stocked with game.

happy pair, the see *happy couple, the*

hard act to follow, a is a hackneyed phrase used to describe someone or something that is outstanding that will be difficult to emulate, as *Our chairman has unfortunately retired and we shall have to replace him. It's a pity; he's a hard act to follow,* and *Last year's village fête was such a success that it will be a hard act to follow.* The expression is American in origin and takes its derivation from vaudeville. It expresses the difficulty of following a successful act which has found favour

with the audience in case one cannot achieve a similarly high standard. In Britain the cliché dates from the second part of the twentieth century and is used in informal contexts. An alternative form is **a tough act to follow.**

hard and fast rule is a hackneyed phrase used to refer to rules that cannot be altered or dispensed with whatever the circumstances, as *The pupils can choose whether or not to wear school uniform. There are no hard and fast rules on the subject.* The original form was **hard and fast line** which was first used in political contexts in the late nineteenth century. As a cliché **hard and fast rule** dates from the twentieth century. In origin the expression refers to a nautical term, 'hard and fast' referring to a ship that has run aground.

hard facts is a hackneyed phrase simply meaning facts, 'hard' being used for emphasis to indicate that the facts cannot be denied, as *I am sorry that they are having to leave the flat but the hard facts are that they cannot afford the rent.* It is sometimes simply used meaninglessly by people who hardly ever use simple words without some form of qualification. The expression has been a cliché since the middle of the nineteenth century.

has the cat got your tongue? is a catch-phrase cliché used to someone who has given no reply or comment when one might be expected. It is most often used to children who understandably have nothing to say to the other clichés frequently directed at them by adults, as *What are you going to do when you grow up? Has the cat got your tongue?* The origins of the phrase are obscure, but it has been common since the middle of the nineteenth century, although recently it has become rather dated. Children continue to suffer from it but it is usually directed at them by older people.

have . . . will travel is a catchphrase cliché. The original catchphrase dating from the early part of the twentieth century was **have gun will travel**, supposedly popularized by a personal advertisement in *The Times*. It was further popularized in the 1960s by the Western television series bearing the title and was then used humorously of items other than guns, as *I'm looking for a job anywhere. It's a case of have typewriter, will travel*, and *The lease on my flat is up. Have bed, will travel.*

have a bone to pick see *bone to pick, a*

have a finger in every pie see *finger in every pie, have a*

have a lot on one's plate is an idiom cliché meaning to have many matters which require one's attention. It is used very commonly in informal contexts, many of them involving business, as *I'm sorry that I didn't return your call but I've got a lot on my plate just now*. In origin it refers to a plate of food that is somewhat overfull and so will take a long time to eat.

have a nice day is a catchphrase cliché used as a standard greeting. It is still considerably less common in Britain than it is in America, where it was popularized by truck-drivers on their CB radios, but is sufficiently common to be annoying. It tends to be used by sales assistants and others who really do not care whether you have a nice day or not, but is sometimes used ironically to someone who has been particularly rude to one or who has done one a particularly bad turn, *Oh, you've given me a parking ticket? Have a nice day!* **Have a nice one** is an even more annoying alternative form of the expression.

have I got news for you? is a hackneyed phrase used to try to impress one's listener with what one is about to say, the implication being that the information is either startling or unwelcome to the receiver, *You thought he was the best candidate for the job? Well, have I got news for you? We've discovered that his qualifications are phoney!* and *Were you planning a weekend away? Well, have I got news for you? The boss says that we have to work overtime this weekend to finish the order*. The expression is American in origin and has been popular in Britain from the second part of the twentieth century. Its use tends to be restricted to the kind of person who likes to bring bad news.

have it in for is a hackneyed phrase meaning to have a grudge against someone or to feel spiteful towards someone, as *He's had it in for his neighbour ever since she complained about his dog*. It has been a popular cliché since the first half of the twentieth century and is still widespread today.

have one's hands full is an idiom cliché meaning that one has a great many things to do, as *With two young children to look after she has her hands full*. The expression dates from the fifteenth century and is still very popular today.

have something up one's sleeve see *up one's sleeve*

have the other half is a hackneyed phrase meaning to have another drink. It originally referred to having another half pint of beer, to follow a half pint already drunk. It was then extended to other drinks, as *You've finished your whisky? Will you have the other half?*

have what it takes is a hackneyed phrase indicating that someone is sufficiently talented, hard-working, etc to achieve what he or she is aiming at, as *She wants to be a professional singer but the competition is so great and she really doesn't have what it takes.* The cliché dates from the twentieth century and is still very common today. It is rather a patronizing cliché since the user is sitting in judgement on someone's else's capabilities

have you heard the latest? is a catchphrase cliché used by someone who cannot wait to impart the latest piece of juicy gossip, as *Have you heard the latest? Mary and Jim have split up!* It is a twentieth century cliché and is still popular today.

head and shoulders above is an idiom cliché used to refer to someone who is immeasurably superior to others, as *She is bound to do well in the exams. She is head and shoulders above the other pupils.* It has been a cliché since the middle of the nineteenth century and is still widespread. In origin it refers to someone who is so tall that his head and shoulders are literally above the smaller people in a group.

head over heels is a hackneyed phrase meaning utterly and completely. The cliché in its modern form and in its association with love dates from the nineteenth century and is still popular nowadays, as *He has fallen head over heels in love with his best friend's fiancée.* The implication of the phrase is that one is so much in love that one is turning upside down. It does not seem particularly appropriate and it was originally found in the more appropriate form of **heels over head**, which dates from the fourteenth century.

heads will roll is a catchphrase cliché which carries the threat that someone is going to be in trouble or be punished in

some way, as, *If the boss finds out that the office door was left unlocked overnight, heads will roll!* The expression became popular about the middle of the twentieth century and is still quite common. In origin it refers to heads rolling after they were cut off by the guillotine, used in France for executions.

heart in mouth, with is an idiom cliché used to emphasize the extent of one's fear or alarm, as *With heart in mouth I watched the child balancing on the parapet of the bridge.* The expression dates from the sixteenth century and has been a cliché since the eighteenth century. It also exists in the form **my heart was in my mouth**, as *Our hearts were in our mouths as we watched the police trying to get the man down from the roof.* In origin the expression refers to the choking feeling that is caused by sudden fear or panic, as though one's heart had jumped into one's mouth.

heart in the right place, have one's is an idiom cliché meaning to be well meaning, to have good intentions. The expression has been a cliché since the later part of the nineteenth century. It is still popular today, often carrying the suggestion that the virtue referred to compensates for some other fault, as *He did the wrong thing by taking the child in, but his heart was in the right place,* and *The headmistress seems very stern but her heart is in the right place. She is very understanding if the children have real problems.* In origin it refers to the old belief that the heart was the seat of the emotions.

heart-to-heart is a hackneyed phrase meaning a confidential and intimate conversation, as though people's hearts were close together. It is an abbreviated form of **heart-to-heart talk** which has been a cliché since the beginning of the twentieth century. **Heart-to-heart** is still a popular cliché today and usually carries the suggestion that people are opening up to one another and not hiding their feelings.

helping hand, a is a hackneyed phrase which is rather a tautological way of saying simply help or assistance. The expression dates from the fifteenth century and has been a cliché since the eighteenth century. It is still common today in rather informal contexts, as *We are moving house tomorrow. Could you give us a helping hand?*

helping the police with their inquiries is a hackneyed phrase which is sometimes a euphemism cliché referring to someone who is making a statement to the police, and sometimes is being held by them, in connection with some form of crime, as *A local man is helping police with their inquiries into the disappearance of the child.* It is an expression much used by journalists, probably because they are quoting the guarded statements of the police, who have to be careful what they say for fear of prejudicing the outcome of any future trial. The phrase has become particularly widespread because of the popularity of crime fiction and crime series on television.

here we go! is a twentieth century cliché used to imply repetition, usually the repetition of something which one has already found tedious, as *Here we go! She's going to tell us about her struggle to get to the top again.* The expression is also used in the more obvious sense of 'we are about to start'. When trebled, **here we go!, here we go!, here we go!**, the expression becomes a well-known football supporters' chant.

hide one's light under a bushel is a quotation cliché meaning to be so modest and retiring that one conceals one's talents, as *I didn't know you could sing like that. You must have been hiding your light under a bushel,* and *She is actually a very accomplished pianist but she rarely plays in public. She prefers to hide her light under a bushel.* The expression is a quotation from a Biblical passage, in *Matthew* (5:15) 'Neither do men light a candle, and put it under a bushel, but on a candlestick . . . let your light so shine before men that they may see your good works.' Bushel refers to the container in which was measured the unit of weight also called a bushel. It has been a cliché since the middle of the nineteenth century.

high and dry is an idiom cliché meaning abandoned in a very difficult situation, as *We thought that he was giving us a lift back to town. We were left high and dry when he drove off without us.* The expression has been a cliché since the late nineteenth century and is still common, usually in an informal context. It is nautical in origin, referring to a ship that has run aground.

hit it off is a catchphrase cliché meaning to get along very well, as *I wasn't looking forward to meeting her since we have very little in common, but in fact we hit it off very well.* The expression dates from the late eighteenth century and is still a common cliché, being used in all but the most formal contexts

hit or miss is a hackneyed phrase meaning haphazard or random, as *I've made something for the child to eat but I don't know what she likes and so it's a bit hit or miss.* As a cliché the expression dates from the twentieth century although the concept is much older, dating from the sixteenth century. In origin it refers to the hitting or missing of a target.

hit the nail on the head is an idiom cliché meaning to be absolutely accurate, to say or do exactly the right thing, as *I think you hit the nail on the head when you said that she was naive,* and *You hit the nail on the head when you diagnosed that the child had measles.* The analogy dates from the early sixteenth century and it has been a cliché since the nineteenth century. In origin it refers to hitting a nail right in the middle of its head with a hammer.

hive of industry, a is an idiom cliché used to refer to a place where there is a great deal of activity going on, as *All the children were busy writing a story. The classroom was a real hive of activity,* and *We were all sewing like mad to get her wedding dress finished in time. The room was a hive of industry.* The expression has been a cliché since the late nineteenth century and is still popular today. In origin it refers to the fact that insects which live in hives always seem to be engaged in frantic activity.

hold one's own is a hackneyed phrase meaning to succeed in maintaining one's position against competition or attack, as *She was much the less experienced tennis player but she held her own against the defending champion.* The expression has been in use since the sixteenth century and was a cliché by the nineteenth century. The expression is also used as a medical cliché. In describing a patient's condition, it means that he or she is not getting any worse and is putting up a fight for survival, as *He was very badly injured in the accident but at the moment he is holding his own.*

hold the fort is an idiom cliché, often a business cliché, meaning to look after something while someone is away or until someone arrives, as *I have to go to the dentist this morning. Do you think you could hold the fort to save me closing the shop for the morning?* The phrase is American in origin, dating from the American Civil War, and as a cliché dates from the twentieth century, being still popular today.

hold your horses is an idiom cliché, often found in the imperative, used to urge someone not to move or act so quickly or hastily, as *Hold your horses! You can't book the holiday yet. We haven't all agreed on where we're going.*

holding the baby see *baby, left holding the*

home James! is a catchphrase cliché used to tell the driver of a car or bus to drive off, as *Right! Everyone is back in the bus. Home James!* and *The children are settled in the back seat. Home James!* It is a shortened form of **home James and don't spare the horses!** The expression dates from the late nineteenth century and is still used today in a humorous way, although it is rather dated. In origin it refers to a person telling his coachman to take him home as rapidly as possibly.

honest truth, the is a hackneyed phrase used to emphasize the truth of something, as *I had nothing to do with it and that's the honest truth.* It dates from the late nineteenth century and is still a common cliché. Not infrequently it is used to try to hide the fact that the user is in fact lying.

hope against hope is an allusion cliché meaning to go on hoping or wishing for something when there is little probability of the hope or wish being realized, as *The children were hoping against hope that it would snow on Christmas Day, although they were having a very mild spell of weather.* It has been a cliché from the late nineteenth century and is still common today. The expression is a Biblical allusion to *Romans* (4:18) 'Who against hope believed in hope that he might become the father of many nations.'

horns of the dilemma, on the is an idiom cliché meaning faced with two equally undesirable potential courses of action, as *She was on the horns of a dilemma. She could not decide whether to accept a lift home from him and be bored out of her mind or to wait for the bus and get soaking wet.* In medieval rhetoric a 'dilemma' was a way of arguing which consisted of proving that one of two statements must be true, both being damaging to one's opponent's case. It was likened to a two-horned animal. In choosing which of the two statements he preferred to admit as truth, the opponent was pictured as having to throw himself on to one or other of the 'horns'. As a modern cliché the expression tends to be used by people of a literary bent or by people who use rather formal English.

horses for courses is a catchphrase cliché meaning what is suitable or appropriate for someone or something is not necessarily so for others, as *We like to try to provide a wide range of hobbies for our members to choose from. We know there are horses for courses,* and *This drug worked for your mother but it might not work for you. There are horses for courses in the medical world.* As a general cliché the expression has been popular since the later part of the twentieth century. In origin it refers to horse racing in which some courses suit some horses better than others.

hot dinners, more – than you've etc had see *more – than you've etc had hot dinners*

how long is a piece of string? is a catchphrase given as a reply to a question when one has no idea of even an approximate answer, as *How long will it take to finish this? How long is a piece of string?* The question need not be in any way related to length, as *How much would it cost to renovate that old house? How long is a piece of string?* It started out as a kind of trick question from about the 1920s and developed into its present use later.

how time flies is an idiom cliché used to emphasize how quickly time seems to pass, as *Is it midnight already? How time flies!* The connection between time and flying is an old one, the Romans having had the proverb, *tempus fugit*, meaning time flies, or flees. The modern cliché dates from the twentieth century. It is still common today, sometimes being used ironically, especially when it is extended to **How time flies when you're having fun**, as *This lecture seems to have been going on for hours. How time flies when you're having fun!*

how to win friends and influence people is a catchphrase cliché mostly used nowadays in an ironic way, as *You have just upset the whole office with your tactless remark. How to win friends and influence people!* and *He really knows how to win friends and influence people. He just poured a glass of red wine down the boss's wife's dress.* The expression originated in America and became popular as the title of a book by Dale Carnegie (1936). In its straight version it has been a cliché in Britain since the late 1940s.

how was it for you? is a hackneyed phrase of the second part of the twentieth century used as a stock phrase to inquire after a partner's level of sexual satisfaction during intercourse. It is so hackneyed that is now mostly found in humorous or satirical contexts, such as comedy shows.

hue and cry is a hackneyed phrase used to indicate an uproar or public protest, as in *There was a real hue and cry when they threatened to close our local post office*. It has been a cliché since the middle of the nineteenth century. In origin it refers to an Anglo-Norman legal term, *hu et cri*, for the summons issued to members of the public to join the hunt for someone who had committed a crime. They were required by law to shout and make other noise.

I

if the cap fits, wear it is a proverb cliché meaning if the situation applies to you, you should admit and accept the fact, as *I don't know if she's right when she calls you a womanizer but if the cap fits, wear it*. Sometimes the cliché is shortened to **if the cap fits**, with the second part being understood, as *No one has accused him of getting the job dishonestly, but if the cap fits*. The cap may refer to the cap traditionally worn by the court fool.

if the mountain will not come to Mohammed, Mohammed must go to the mountain is a proverb cliché indicating that if the person or thing that one wishes to see is unwilling or unable to come to one, then one must go to that person or thing. The second part of the saying is often omitted, as *I asked my sister to come and discuss our father's birthday party, but she cannot leave the children. Ah well, if the mountain cannot come to Mohammed*. The cliché is often extended to mean that if one cannot get one's own way then one should accept the fact and adopt an appropriate course of action. The origin of the expression refers to a story in which Mohammed, asked to give proof of his miraculous powers, ordered Mount Sofa to come to him. When this failed to happen, he accepted that he would have to go to it. The cliché is used in a variety of contexts but tends to be restricted to people of a literary or academic bent.

if the worst comes to the worst is a hackneyed phrase meaning if the most disadvantageous circumstances should occur, and is usually followed by some fairly radical expedient, as *If the worst comes to the worst, we can always sell the house and buy a small flat*. The expression dates from the late sixteenth century and has been a widespread cliché since the late nineteenth century.

if you can't beat 'em/them join 'em/them is a catchphrase cliché of American origin dating from the early 1940s, as *If the students upstairs are insisting on having a party you might as well go to it. If you can't beat 'em, join 'em*. The cliché is mostly used in informal contexts.

if you can't stand the heat get/keep/stay out of the kitchen is a catchphrase cliché indicating that a person should not undertake a difficult job unless he/she is prepared and able to cope with the stress and strain of it, as *The young woman burst into tears on her first day as a teacher and was told by a colleague, 'If you can't stand the heat, stay out of the kitchen.'* The cliché is American in origin, dating from the mid 1950s, and is associated with President Truman particularly with reference to the American presidency.

if you've got it flaunt it is a catchphrase cliché dating from the second part of the twentieth century and meaning you should make the most of what you have. It is frequently associated with physical assets and is used in informal contexts, as *Why shouldn't she wear a low-cut dress. She's got the figure for it. If you've got it flaunt it!*

ignorance is bliss is an allusion cliché, being a reference to the closing lines of *Ode on a Distant Prospect of Eton College* (1742) by Thomas Gray. 'Where ignorance is bliss 'tis folly to be wise.' The expression means that sometimes it is better not to know the true facts of a situation for the sake of one's peace of mind, as *She thinks her husband is faithful and don't tell her otherwise. Ignorance is bliss, as they say.* As a cliché the expression dates from the nineteenth century.

I hate to mention it but . . . is a hackneyed phrase used to introduce something that the hearer is not going to want to know. Often it introduces something that the speaker will actually enjoy saying, rather than hating it, as *I hate to mention it but you now owe me over £200.* It is mostly found in informal contexts and dates from the late nineteenth century.

I hope we will always be friends is a hackneyed phrase commonly used when announcing the break-up of a relationship to a girlfriend/boyfriend/partner/spouse, as *I'm moving out because I don't love you anymore and I've found someone else. But I hope we will always be friends.* The statement, originating in the second part of the twentieth century, usually does little to alleviate the situation as the other half of the partnership is not usually in the mood to be disposed to friendship.

I'll be in touch is a hackneyed phrase, dating from the second part of the twentieth century, frequently used informally simply to bring a conversation or informal meeting to an end, with the user often having no serious intention of getting in touch, and sometimes having the definite intention not to do so, as *I'm sorry I can't come to the party with you but I'll be in touch.* An alternative to this expression is

I'll give you a ring or **I'll give you a call**, yet another being **I'll get back to you**.

ill-gotten gains is a hackneyed phrase meaning money or profit obtained in an illegal or bad way, as *He's in prison but his wife and family are living off his ill-gotten gains.* It is often nowadays used ironically or humorously, as *Well, it's pay day. What are you going to do with your ill-gotten gains?* As a cliché it dates from the nineteenth century.

I'm a stranger here myself is a hackneyed phrase, dating from the second part of the twentieth century, and said by someone who is asked for directions in a place which is unfamiliar to him/her, as *I'm sorry I don't know where the post office is. I'm a stranger here myself.* It is the kind of cliché that one often criticizes others for using and then finds oneself automatically using it when faced with the appropriate situation.

in a certain/interesting condition is a euphemism cliché meaning pregnant, as *At one time women were expected to leave work if they were in a certain condition.* Established as a cliché since the mid nineteenth century, it is rather dated now that people are less inhibited about referring to pregnancy frankly and is mostly used by older people in rather formal contexts, or by others in an ironical or humorous way. See also **delicate condition**.

in all conscience is a hackneyed phrase meaning by any reasonable standard, to be fair, as *I cannot in all conscience recommend him as a good worker.* It has become a habit with some people and is often used virtually meaninglessly as a filler cliché. It has been commonly used since the eighteenth century.

in all honesty is a filler cliché which is seemingly used to underline the truth of something but is usually used meaninglessly as a conversation filler and is often used just as a habit, as *In all honesty, I think we should finish work for today.*

in a meeting is a hackneyed phrase used as a business cliché, dating from the second part of the twentieth century, which is often a euphemism cliché for not wishing to be contacted or communicated with, as *I am sorry Mr Jones cannot listen to your complaint in person. He is in a meeting.* It is usually used by a receptionist, secretary, assistant or other member of staff to protect a colleague from an unwanted intrusion, whether he/she is in a meeting or not.

in a nutshell is a hackneyed phrase meaning very briefly, as *In a nutshell they lied.* It is an extremely widespread expression. As a cliché it dates from the mid nineteenth century and refers to the fact that a nutshell holds very little. Pliny, the Roman writer, in his *Natural History* wrote that Homer's epic poem, the *Iliad*, was copied in such tiny writing that the entire text might have been enclosed in a nutshell. It is by no means uncommon for the cliché to be used to introduce a fairly lengthy statement and so to give the hearer false hope of brevity.

in a tick/in two ticks is a hackneyed phrase for a very short time, although this can turn out to be a longer time than the user promises, and is often used simply to give false hope of speediness, as *If you have a seat the doctor will be with you in a tick.* In origin the expression refers to the ticking of a clock. It is more colloquial than **in a minute** and is the kind of cliché that becomes a habit with some people.

in cold blood see *cold blood, in*

inferno, blazing see *blazing inferno.*

in flagrante delicto is a foreign cliché. The English cliché means in the very act of committing an offence, as *She thought her adultery would go unsuspected but her husband came home and found her and her lover in flagrante delicto.* Despite the literal meaning, A P Herbert in *Unholy Matrimony* suggested 'in flagrant delight' as an alternative. As a cliché in English it has been common since the nineteenth century, although nowadays it tends to be used either in formal contexts or by people of an academic or literary bent.

in high dudgeon is a hackneyed phrase meaning resentfully, huffily, as *She went off in high dudgeon when we refused to do what she wanted.* 'Dudgeon' is an archaic word for anger. The expression has been a cliché since the mid nineteenth century.

in less than no time is a hackneyed phrase meaning very quickly. It is used in informal contexts often to try to placate someone who is impatient, as *Don't cry. Your mummy will be here in less than no time.*

inner man, the is a hackneyed phrase meaning one's stomach, as *I'm almost ready to go but the inner man is in need of some sustenance.* Originally the expression applied to the soul but it has had its present meaning since the late eighteenth century. Nowadays it is usually used humorously or pompously.

in no uncertain terms/manner is a hackneyed phrase meaning clearly and frankly, as *I told her in no uncertain terms exactly what I thought of her behaviour.* As a cliché it dates from the twentieth century.

ins and outs, the is a hackneyed phrase meaning all the aspects and details of something, as *I'm not agreeing to the plan until I've had a chance to consider all the ins* *and outs.* In origin the expression refers to the various windings and turnings of a path and thus to the intricacies of a situation. As a cliché it dates from the late nineteenth century and is now used mostly in informal contexts.

in one ear and out the other see *go in one ear and out the other*

in point of fact is a filler cliché meaning the same as **in fact** which is itself often a filler cliché. Both are often used meaninglessly and so unnecessarily, as *In point of fact I haven't seen him for weeks.* **In point of fact** dates from the early eighteenth century but it is still very much used today.

interesting condition see *in a certain condition*

in the bag see *bag, in the*

in the balance, to hang see *balance, hang in the*

in the cold light of day see *cold light of day*

in the dark is an idiom cliché meaning having no or little knowledge about something, ignorant of something, as *The workers are completely in the dark about what's happening to the firm.* The expression has quite a modern ring to it but in fact the equating of darkness with lack of knowledge goes back to Roman times. It is still widespread today in informal contexts.

in the dim and distant (past) is a hackneyed phrase usually used humorously to indicate the near, or the relatively near, past, as *I used to wear shoes like that in the dim and distant when I was a teenager.* As a cliché, the expression dates from the twentieth century.

in the family way is a euphemism cliché meaning pregnant, as *She's taking time off work because she's in the family way.* This is a considerably less formal cliché than **in a certain condition** and has survived the modern, open use of the word "pregnant".

in the final analysis is a hackneyed phrase simply meaning in the end, as *You can make as many suggestions as you like but in the final analysis she will do just as she pleases.* It is a pretentious alternative to **after all is said and done** and is a cliché that some people easily become addicted to.

in the land of Nod is a hackneyed phrase meaning asleep, as *The children were all safely in the land of Nod when we left.* Nod was the name of the land to which Cain was exiled after killing his brother, Abel (*Genesis* 4:16) but the expression more probably has its origin in the association between feeling sleepy and the act of nodding. Jonathan Swift (1667–1745) wrote in *A Complete Collection of Genteel and Ingenious Conversation* that he was 'going into the land of Nod' meaning that he was going to sleep. The cliché is usually used in a rather humorous context nowadays.

in the land of the living meaning alive, in existence, is an allusion cliché, being a Biblical allusion to *Jeremiah* (11:19) 'Let us cut him off from the land of the living, that his name may be no more remembered.' As a modern cliché the expression is often used humorously or in informal contexts, as *I'm lucky to be still in the land of the living after that heavy branch fell on me.*

in the pipeline is a hackneyed phrase which was a vogue expression in the 1960s and 1970s. It means under way, awaiting processing, as *The present figures do not take account of wage increases that are in the pipeline.* Pipeline literally refers to a long pipe for conveying oil, water, etc. If the commodity is still in the pipeline it has not yet come through.

in this day and age is a filler cliché which simply means now, as *Fancy having such dreadful toilet facilities in this day and age.* It is an extremely widespread cliché used in all but the most formal contexts.

iron hand in the velvet glove, the is an idiom cliché indicating severity or mercilessness which is hidden under the guise of kindness or leniency, as *The children thought that they would have an easy time with the smiling young teacher, but they soon discovered that it was a case of the iron hand in the velvet glove.* In *Latter-Day Pamphlets* (1850) Thomas Carlyle ascribes the phrase to Napoleon Bonaparte.

it fell off the back of a lorry is a hackneyed phrase, dating from the mid twentieth century and used informally to describe something that has been acquired cheaply and fortuitously, often by questionable means, as *You won't get a mountain bike as cheaply as Jim's. I'm sure his fell off the back of a lorry.* The expression frequently refers to stolen, or possibly stolen, goods, the implication being that the item in question was taken from the back of a lorry rather than falling off.

it goes without saying see *goes without saying, it/that*

it happens is a hackneyed phrase indicating a philosophical acceptance of some unpleasant event, as *It's sad that they've divorced but it happens.* An alternative form is **these things happen**. Both clichés can be very annoying or upsetting to someone to whom something unpleasant has just happened and is not yet at the philosophical stage.

I think I can safely say is a filler cliché which is a meaningless and rather pretentious introduction to a statement. It is a cliché often adopted by public speakers, as *I think I can safely say that educational standards have never been higher.*

it never rains but it pours is a proverb cliché indicating that when something bad happens it is either very bad or is accompanied by several other bad things, as *The fridge has broken down and now the car won't start. It never rains but it pours.*

it's a far, far, better thing that I do now is an allusion cliché being a reference to a speech by Sydney Carton in *A Tale of Two Cities* (1859) by Charles Dickens 'It is a far, far better thing that I do than I have ever done.' People using the cliché usually wrongly add 'now' to the original speech. As a cliché it is now usually used by people of literary tastes in a humorous or ironical context, suggesting in an exaggerated way that something quite minor is an act of great self sacrifice, as *My sister couldn't get a ticket for the concert and so I gave her mine. It's a far, far, better thing that I do now.*

it's always darkest before the dawn is an idiom cliché used to cheer up people who are in some kind of trouble by people who are not, as *I know you're feeling hurt by your wife's rejection but things will improve. It's always darkest before the dawn.* Nothing brings out clichés in some people like other people's misfortunes. Instead of keeping silent, which would be preferable, they feel obliged to come out with platitudes, which at best is annoying. An alternative form is **the darkest hour is just before the dawn**.

it's a small world is a hackneyed phrase used, for example, when one encounters someone one knows in somewhere unexpected, as *We were climbing in the Himalayas and met our next-door neighbours. It certainly is a small world.* The cliché dates from the twentieth century.

it's for your own good is a hackneyed phrase used when something unpleasant has happened to or been said to someone, often by way of some kind of punishment, and often to a young person, as *We did not want to cut off your allowance but it's for your own good. You must learn the value of money.*

it's not for me to say is a hackneyed phrase which is virtually meaningless since the user goes on to say what he/she thinks, despite the disclaimer, as *It's not for me to say, but he is quite obviously making the biggest mistake of his life.* This is the kind of cliché that easily becomes habit-forming.

it's not the end of the world is a hackneyed phrase indicating that, however bad a situation is, things could be worse. It is used to refer to a wide variety of situations, from the relatively minor, as *I know you have missed the bus but it's not the end of the world*, to the major, as *I've just been declared redundant but I suppose it's not the end of the world.*

it stands to reason is a filler cliché that simply serves as an introduction to something that someone is going to say. Often what is said is not particularly reasonable or obvious. Indeed often the reverse is the case, as *It stands to reason that the staff will do anything to keep their jobs.* The expression has been current since the sixteenth century, becoming a cliché about the nineteenth century.

it takes all sorts (to make a world) is a hackneyed phrase indicating that humankind is made up of many different sorts of people. It is usually used in reply to someone who is complaining about someone else, as *You might think he's got peculiar tastes, but it takes all sorts.* Sometimes the phrase is extended, as *She's not exactly my favourite person but it takes all sorts to make a world.* In its longer version the expression has been current since the seventeenth century and in its shorter version since the late nineteenth century, becoming a cliché in the twentieth century.

it takes one to know one is a catchphrase cliché used informally to indicate that someone who is swift to identify and criticize a wrongdoer of some kind is often guilty of a similar offence, in the way that a thief would be swift to spot the signs that someone had stolen something, as *Mary's husband says that Jim is being unfaithful to his wife. Well, you what they say. It takes one to know one.* The cliché dates from the twentieth century.

it takes two to tango is a catchphrase cliché indicating that some activities involve two people and so both must accept some responsibility for them. The expression, which has been popular since the 1930s, often has sexual connotations, as *You can't put all the blame on your husband's girlfriend. It takes two to tango* and is used in informal contexts. The tango is a dance of Latin American origin for couples.

it will all out come out in the wash is an idiom cliché meaning that everything will work out satisfactorily in the end, as *Try not to worry about your sister's marriage problems. It will all come out in the wash.* The expression dates from the nineteenth century and in origin refers to the removal of dirt and stains from clothes by washing.

I've got a headache is a hackneyed phrase popularly supposed to be used by a woman as an excuse for not having sex, as *Not tonight darling. I've got a headache*. It is now often used in a humorous or ironical context. As a cliché it dates from the twentieth century.

J

jack of all trades, a is a hackneyed phrase used to refer to someone who can turn his or her hand to a wide range of tasks, as *There is no need to get a whole team of tradesmen to do your repairs. The man who lives next door to us is a real jack of all trades.* The expression has been in existence since the early seventeenth century. As a cliché it is becoming rather dated and is frequently used disparagingly. It is sometimes accompanied by the suggestion that someone who tries his or her hand at a wide range of jobs is unlikely to be really skilled at any of them as in the expression **a jack of all trades and master of none.**

jam tomorrow is a hackneyed phrase indicating that prosperity or happiness will come in the future, usually with the suggestion that one will have to put up with a certain amount of hardship, misery, etc until the rosy future arrives. It was exceptionally commonly used in Britain when Margaret Thatcher was Prime Minister in the 1980s, as *There is little point in promising people jam tomorrow when they are losing their jobs because of the recession.* It is still popular as a cliché, being usually used in relation to the economy. In origin the expression is an allusion to *Through the Looking Glass* (1872) by Lewis Carroll, in which the Red Queen offers Alice a job with 'twopence a week, and jam every other day . . . jam tomorrow, jam yesterday, but never jam today.'

jaundiced eye, a is a hackneyed phrase used to mean from a cynical viewpoint as

though looking only for the bad points or disadvantages of something, as *Our neighbours look on anything young people do with a jaundiced eye.* The expression became a cliché in the nineteenth century and is still common today. In origin it refers to the old belief that to someone who was suffering from jaundice, a condition in which the skin and the whites of the eyes turn yellow, everything which he or she looked at seemed to be coloured yellow. The playwright, John Webster, refers to this belief in *The White Devil* (1:2) (1612) 'They that have the yellow jaundice think all objects they look on to be yellow.'

je ne sais quoi French for 'I do not know' is a foreign cliché used to refer to something that one cannot define exactly, as *She was by no means beautiful but she had a certain je ne sais quoi.* As a cliché it was popular from about 1890 but is now dated. It is still used but only by pretentious people who are trying, usually unsuccessfully, to impress others, or by people who are using it in a consciously humorous or ironic way.

jet set, the is a hackneyed phrase used to refer to wealthy and fashionable people who have a great deal of leisure time and travel from one fashionable resort to another, as *It was the time of year in Cannes when the jet set arrived.* The term was originated in the 1950s and rapidly became a cliché. As a cliché it is still used today but it is becoming rather dated as foreign travel becomes more and more common in the lives of ordinary people and is no longer the province only of the rich. It is in fact now used of people who are very wealthy and fashionable, whether or not they engage in continuous travel, although in origin the expression refers to travel by jet-propelled aircraft which began in the 1950s and was very expensive.

jewel in the crown, the is an idiom cliché and also a vogue cliché used to refer to the best part of anything, as *The visitors were attracted by the Highland scenery which is the jewel in the crown of the Scottish tourist industry*, and *Lack of money has forced her to sell the painting which was the jewel in the crown of her private collection*. The popularity of the cliché in recent years is a result of the televising of *The Raj Quartet* by Paul Scott. The first book of the series was entitled *The Jewel in the Crown*, the 'jewel' being India, and the crown being that of Queen Victoria. The origin of the phrase may lie in the title of a painting *The Jewel in Her Crown*, mentioned in the first volume of Scott's quartet and depicting the Queen receiving a large jewel (representing India) from an Indian prince. The application of the expression **jewel in the crown** was commonly used to describe the British colonies in the first part of the twentieth century. It is now frequently subject to overuse in a more general context.

Job's comforter is an allusion cliché used to describe someone who, although pretending to comfort or sympathize with someone who is undergoing some form of misfortune or distress, is in fact exacerbating the distress, as *His friends visited him in hospital to cheer him up but they turned out to be real Job's comforters by telling him how ill he looked and how they knew of someone with his condition who had never walked again*. It has been a cliché since the middle

of the eighteenth century and is still widespread today. The expression is Biblical in origin, being an allusion to *Job* (16:2) where Job refers to his friends as 'miserable comforters.'

jobs for the boys is a catchphrase cliché used to suggest that people are getting jobs or posts because they know someone with influence in the relevant area, as *The foreman on the building site would only take on tradesmen if they knew one of his friends or family. It was an obvious case of jobs for the boys but he got away with it*. The expression became popular in the 1930s and is still popular, as indeed the practice is. It is often used in connection with politics, as *The government were accused of jobs for the boys when it came to selecting members of the various committees*.

jockey for position is an idiom cliché meaning to try to manoeuvre one's way into a position of power, wealth, etc, as *Now they have heard that the managing director is retiring, all the other executives are jockeying for position*. In origin the expression is an allusion to racing where it refers to a jockey trying to manoeuvre his horse into a winning position. It was in existence in its racing meaning in the early part of the twentieth century and began to be used figuratively in the 1950s. It is mostly used in a business context today and usually in a derogatory way.

join the club! is a catchphrase cliché used to express sympathy or solidarity to someone who is experiencing an unfortunate situation which other people present have already experienced, as *Has she stopped speaking to you? Join the club! She has completely ignored us since she met her new smart friends*. The expression began to be popular in the late 1940s and is still used widely today in an informal context.

jolly hockey sticks is a catchphrase cliché used to describe a hearty, robust, games-playing girl, woman, school, club, etc, as *We have decided not to send our daughter to the local girls school. It is too jolly hockey sticks for words and she is very artistic.* The expression, which is used in a derisory way by people who are not themselves the open-air, games-loving types, was used in the BBC radio show, *Educating Archie* by Monica, Archie's girlfriend, the show being broadcast in the late 1940s and the early 1950s. It is thought to have been coined by the actress, Beryl Reid.

jump down someone's throat is an idiom cliché meaning to reply to someone in a very sharp or angry way. It is used in informal contexts and is often considered unnecessarily sharp by the receiver of the remark, as *There is no need to jump down my throat just because I am a few minutes late.* The expression has been in existence since the late nineteenth century, Anthony Trollope having made use of it in *Cousin Henry* (1879) 'Was she to jump down your throat when you asked her?'

jump on the bandwagon is an idiom cliché meaning to associate with something because it is fashionable or because it is going to be advantageous to oneself, as *When the property market was booming in the 1980s many people jumped on the bandwagon and set up as estate agents.* As a cliché the expression is still popular today and has its origin in the fact that in the southern states of America it was common for a band to play on a wagon being driven through the streets to advertise some forthcoming event, political meeting, etc. At election times people would jump on the wagon to show their support for the relevant candidate.

jump the gun is an idiom cliché meaning to act prematurely or impetuously, as *They jumped the gun by starting to build the new house before they had planning permission.* The expression has been popular since the middle of the twentieth century and is still widespread today in an informal context. In origin it refers to competitors who start out before the sounding of the starter's gun that marks the beginning of a race.

just deserts is a hackneyed phrase meaning a deserved reward or punishment, as *Let us hope that the person who committed this horrible crime gets his just deserts.* Nowadays it is used in a formal context. Historically the word 'desert' in this context means what is deserved, commonly used until the middle of the eighteenth century but obsolete since then except for its use in this cliché.

just doing my job is a twentieth century catchphrase cliché usually used by over-zealous people in some form of relatively minor authority to indicate that they are not being deliberately obstructive or obstreperous but are simply obeying the procedure as set down by the rules of their jobs. It is a cliché guaranteed to arouse wrath in those to whom it is addressed and has associations with the ultimate in military disclaimers of all responsibility 'We were just obeying orders', which gives the user licence to do just about anything in the name of authority. The sentiment behind **just doing my job** is timeless and so the cliché is still alive and well in many bureaucratic areas of society.

just for the record is a filler cliché used to emphasize that note should be taken of what is being said. It does not suggest that someone write down, or in any way officially record, the remarks that follow the statement but simply that the speaker wishes to make his or her position clear, as *Just for the record, it was not my suggestion* *that we go to France on holiday*. It became popular from the 1950s and is still extremely common, being used mainly in an informal context. In origin the expression refers to the keeping of official records.

just one of those things, it's is a catchphrase cliché expressing a philosophical view that certain situations or events happen inexplicably and that there is nothing one can do about them, as *There is no point in worrying about the plant dying while you were taking care of the house. It was just one of those things.* It has been popular since the middle of the 1930s, being popularized by a Cole Porter song having the expression as its title.

just the job is a catchphrase cliché indicating that whatever is being referred to is exactly right or what is required or is particularly pleasant, as *Ah, a cold beer after a hard day's work. Just the job!* In origin the expression was military slang and as such has been in use since about 1935. It gradually became more general and was in general civilian use from the 1950s. As a cliché it is still common in an informal or slang context.

just what the doctor ordered is a twentieth century catchphrase cliché indicating that whatever is being referred to is exactly what is required, suitable or relevant, or is particularly pleasant, as *A holiday in the sun with no work worries. Just what the doctor ordered!* In origin the expression refers to a doctor's prescription or recommended treatment for curing an illness.

❧ K ❧

keep a low profile is a hackneyed phrase meaning to remain as unnoticeable as possible, to keep out of the limelight, as *After the scandal involving the politician died down he kept a low profile for the rest of his career.* As a cliché it has been common since the early 1970s and is still widespread, often used by journalists in connection with political or other public figures.

keep a stiff upper lip is an idiom cliché meaning to keep one's true emotions, such as fear, sadness or despair hidden, and to remain stoical, as *I know that you are miserable because your girlfriend has left you but you really must try to keep a stiff upper lip.* Although the term is American in origin, where it first appeared in the early 1880s, it is frequently regarded as a typically English characteristic, the English tending not to show their emotions in the way that, for example, the Latin races do. The expression came to Britain shortly after its appearance in America and has been a cliché since around 1880. It is still popular today with people who regard the practice as being a virtue but it is often used by others in a humorous or ironic context. The origin of the phrase seems rather odd. It presumably refers to the trembling of the lips as an indication of emotion, as though one were about to cry, but in fact it is usually the lower lip that trembles in such a situation, as any parent who has watched the wobbling of a child's lip before the inevitable ensuing flood of tears will testify.

keep a straight face is an idiom cliché meaning not to laugh or smile but to maintain an expression of gravity. It began to be popular in the 1950s and is still in widespread use, as *I could scarcely keep a straight face when he was taken in by the hoax.* In origin it refers to keeping one's facial muscles tight in order to avoid smiling.

keep at arm's length is an idiom cliché meaning to avoid becoming too familiar or friendly with someone, as *Our neighbours are very pleasant but we try to keep them at arm's length. Otherwise they would always be popping in at all hours uninvited.* Originally the expression was **at arm's end** but by the middle of the seventeenth century it had taken its present form, becoming a cliché about the middle of the nineteenth century. It is still widespread today. In origin the phrase refers to the physical act of preventing someone from getting too close to one by extending one's arm to push him or her away.

keep a weather eye on is an idiom cliché meaning to watch closely, as *Keep a weather eye on the new boy's work. He is totally inexperienced.* The phrase sounds rather literary but it is in widespread use, often with the suggestion that one does not altogether trust the person to whom the weather eye should be directed. It is nautical in origin, a reference to a sailor on a sailing ship watching carefully for signs of a change in the weather that might affect the vessel.

keep body and soul together is an idiom cliché meaning to succeed in surviving physically but only just, to live at semi-starvation level, as *It is difficult to keep body and soul together on such a low income.* The expression came into existence in the eighteenth century, becoming a cliché in the nineteenth century. It is still used today but often in a humorous or ironic context. In origin it refers to the belief that the soul leaves the body on death.

keep it dark is a hackneyed phrase used to urge someone to keep something secret, as *Keep it dark but I've heard a rumour that we are getting a pay rise.* It is often now used in a humorous or ironic context. In origin it was underworld slang and has been in existence since about 1830. The expression means the same as → **keep it under your hat**.

keep it under your hat is an idiom cliché used to urge someone to keep something secret, as *Keep it under your hat but I've applied for another job.* The expression dates from the late nineteenth century and is still common today, being used in an informal or slang context. In origin it refers to someone hiding something under his or her headgear.

keep one's ear to the ground see *ear to the ground, an*

keep oneself to oneself is a hackneyed phrase meaning to avoid contact with other people as much as possible, as *We have not yet got to know our new neighbours as they keep themselves to themselves.* An alternative form is **keep to oneself**, as *I have often seen her at meetings but she seems to keep to herself.* It has been a common cliché since the beginning of the twentieth century.

keep one's end up is a twentieth century idiom cliché meaning to maintain equality with others in a venture, to perform one's part in something as well as others involved as *All the others in the quiz game were very well informed but we managed to keep our end up.* It is mainly used in informal contexts and in origin is a cricketing term, meaning not to lose one's wicket. Alternatively it is a reference to people carrying a heavy weight, such as a piece of furniture, where it is important that both people keep the ends off the ground.

keep one's fingers crossed is an idiom cliché dating from the twentieth century and meaning to hope and wish for success, as *We are keeping our fingers crossed that we get a fine day for the children's picnic.* In origin it refers to the making of the sign of the cross to avert bad luck or danger.

keep one's head above water is an idiom cliché meaning to remain financially solvent, as *It was difficult to keep the firm going during the recession but we were just able to keep our heads above water.* The expression dates from the early eighteenth century, becoming a cliché in the nineteenth century. It is still very common and is sometimes used of non-financial situations, meaning to keep up with excessive demands or commitments, as *I have so much work on hand that it is difficult to keep my head above water.* It alludes to the need to keep one's head above water to avoid drowning.

keep one's mouth shut is an idiom cliché meaning to keep silent. It is used in very informal or slang contexts, as *If you have any sense you will keep your mouth shut about witnessing the attack. They are very dangerous people.* The expression has been a cliché since the nineteenth century.

keep one's nose clean is an idiom cliché meaning to keep out of trouble. It is used in very informal or slang contexts, as *The boy has already been in trouble with the police and so he'd better keep his nose clean if he doesn't want to end up in prison.* The expression has been existence since the late nineteenth century and has been a common cliché since the 1940s. In origin it probably refers to keeping one's nose out of something and so not getting it dirty, and may first have been popular among criminals.

keep one's nose to the grindstone is an idiom cliché meaning to keep working very hard, as *I shall have to keep my nose to the grindstone if I am going to finish this work by the end of the week.* The expression is often used of rather monotonous work and in origin refers to a grindstone on which knives are sharpened as it revolves. It has been a cliché since the middle of the eighteenth century. The phrase is not only used reflexively as it is possible to keep the noses of other people to the grindstone, as *His parents try to keep his nose to the grindstone as his exams are coming up soon.*

keep one's powder dry is an idiom cliché meaning to be in a state of readiness for possible action, but not yet to take the action, as *I don't think their campaign will damage our business but we should keep our powder dry in case it does.* The phrase was used by Oliver Cromwell to his men before the battle of Edgehill in 1642 'Put your trust in God, but keep your powder dry.' This was a reference to the importance of keeping gunpowder dry because if it got wet it was ineffective. The expression has been used figuratively since the nineteenth century.

keep the ball rolling is an idiom cliché meaning to maintain an activity without a halt, as *She launched the campaign against the closure of the hospital but she needs a lot of supporters to keep the ball rolling.* The

expression has been a cliché since the late nineteenth century. Its origin may refer to the importance of keeping the ball in play in ball games.

keep the home fires burning is an idiom cliché meaning to keep things running smoothly in the home, as *Most of her friends go out to work but she prefers to stay at home with the children and keep the home fires burning.* The expression, which was popularized by a song at the time of World War 1, is now dated. When it is used it is often in a humorous or ironic context.

keep the wolf from the door is an idiom cliché meaning to succeed in making enough money to provide food or to keep one solvent. The expression dates from the sixteenth century and has been a cliché since the beginning of the nineteenth century. It is still used nowadays but usually in a humorous or ironic context, as *The job is not particularly well paid but I just about manage to keep the wolf from the door.* In origin the phrase refers to the common belief that wolves are always hungry and eager to eat people.

keep up appearances is a hackneyed phrase meaning to maintain an appearance of respectability, relative wealth, etc irrespective of the true situation or how poor one is, as *He lost his job but he thought it was important to keep up appearances so that his neighbours would not find out and he left the house every morning at the same time as he used to leave for work.* It shares the same twentieth-century sentiment as **keep up with the Joneses**. The expression has been a cliché since the second part of the twentieth century, and is mostly used in a derogatory way.

keep up with the Joneses is a hackneyed phrase meaning to attempt to maintain the style of living and level of spending and acquisition of consumer goods of one's neighbours or acquaintances, as *They do not earn nearly as much as their friends and got into very severe debt by trying to keep up with the Joneses.* The expression is used in a derogatory way, and it is always other people who indulge in this materialistic practice. It has been a cliché since the middle of the twentieth century and has its origins in the title of a comic strip by Arthur R Momand published in the *New York Globe* from 1913. Jones was chosen since it is a common name. Momand is said to have rejected the even more common name Smith because it was the name of his own neighbours and he did not wish to give offence.

keep your chin up is an idiom cliché used, usually in the imperative form, to urge someone not to lose heart or courage, as *I know that the person you have to play is very good but keep your chin up and do your best.* The expression has been a cliché since the 1940s, having replaced the older **keep your pecker up** which had the same meaning but was used in more informal or slang contexts.

keeper, I am not my brother's is an allusion cliché, being a Biblical reference to *Genesis* (4:9), when Cain, after murdering his brother, Abel, and being asked where he was, says to God, 'I know not: am I my brother's keeper?' As a cliché it is often found in the form of a statement rather than a question, and indicates that the person concerned is disclaiming responsibility for another person, not necessarily either a brother or a close relative, as *I have no idea why Jack's late. I am not my brother's keeper.* The cliché is most commonly used by people of an academic or literary bent.

kickstart, give a is an idiom cliché which became a vogue cliché in the 1980s, often

used with reference to the British economy, as *The government is looking for ways to kickstart the economy in order to put an end to the recession.* In origin the expression refers to kick-starting an engine. The cliché means to take affirmative action to make something happen.

kick the bucket is a euphemism cliché meaning to die. The expression dates from the eighteenth century and is commonly used as a modern cliché in a very informal or slang context. The origin of the expression is uncertain. One suggested explanation is that the bucket referred to was an East Anglian term for a wooden frame on which pigs were slaughtered and which was kicked by them as they died. Another suggestion is that people who kill themselves by hanging may stand on an up-turned bucket or something similar in order to tie the rope, the bucket then being kicked away.

kick upstairs is an idiom cliché meaning to promote someone to a position that is higher in rank but carries considerably less responsibility. The practice is carried out in order to get rid of someone whom it would be very difficult, expensive or impolitic to sack. The expression was in use in the early nineteenth century. It is still a common cliché today in informal contexts, although modern business methods which are frequently aimed at reducing budgets, and so staff numbers, seem to be more in favour of redundancy than of kicking people upstairs. It has been used to describe the elevation of a member of the British House of Commons to the House of Lords.

kill the fatted calf is an allusion cliché meaning to prepare a splendid homecoming or reception. In origin it is an allusion to the parable of the prodigal son in the Bible (*Luke* 15), in which the father of the son who had returned home after having squandered his inheritance, instead of punishing him, arranges a splendid feast, for which a 'fatted calf' is to be killed. The expression has been a cliché since the nineteenth century. Nowadays it is often used in a humorous or ironic way for a lavish celebration of some kind, as *Given the size of our salary rise I don't think we will be killing any fatted calves.*

kill the goose that lays the golden eggs is a proverb cliché meaning to put an end to a source of wealth or other form of profit or advantage through greed, thoughtlessness or stupidity. The expression has been widely used since the beginning of the nineteenth century and is still in widespread use today, as *They killed the goose that lays the golden eggs when they began to steal from their old aunt. She found out and cut them out of her will,* and *She killed the goose that lays the golden eggs when she kept forgetting to return books. Her friend, who has a huge collection, refused to lend her any more.* In origin the expression refers to one of Aesop's fables, in which a man, who discovers that his goose has begun to lay golden eggs, kills the goose because he thinks that he will get a great many eggs at once by this means and by doing so deprives himself of the source of the golden eggs.

kill two birds with one stone is a proverb cliché meaning to succeed in achieving two goals by means of one action or effort, as *I killed two birds with one stone while I was at the library. I changed my books and I photocopied some documents on their copier.* The expression dates from the beginning of the seventeenth century and comes originally from Latin. It has been a cliché since the nineteenth century. As to the derivation of the phrase it does not seem very likely that two birds

would ever obligingly stay so close together when being attacked that the attacker could hit both of them at once.

kill with kindness is an idiom cliché meaning to spoil someone, to do someone a disservice by treating him or her with too much indulgence or generosity, as *Giving children a lot of sweets as a reward is just killing them with kindness. Think of the damage to their teeth.* The original saying was '**to kill with kindness as fond apes do their young**', a reference to the fact that apes sometimes hug their offspring in affection so tightly that they kill them. **Kill with kindness** was common in the middle of the sixteenth century and has been a cliché since the early nineteenth century. It is still common today. Thomas Heywood wrote a play called *A Woman Killed With Kindness* in 1607.

kindred spirit, is a hackneyed phrase indicating a person who is very like another in temperament, interests, etc, as *When I introduced my friends to each other it was obvious that they were kindred spirits and they have been close friends ever since.* The expression has been in use since the middle of the nineteenth century and has been a cliché since late that century. It is still widespread today.

kiss and tell is a hackneyed phrase and a modern vogue cliché meaning to reveal an intimate secret. The term has been in existence since the late seventeenth century but enjoyed a new lease of life in the 1980s when it became common for people to have illicit affairs with public figures, such as politicians, and then to tell their stories to the tabloid press for widespread publication, as *The politician has resigned his post in the government after the kiss-and-tell revelations by his ex-mistress.* Since the person who does the telling in such a situation is usually well paid by the press for so doing, a variation has arisen on the theme, **kiss and sell.**

kiss of death, is an idiom cliché meaning a destructive effect, as *Losing his licence because of drink-driving was the kiss of death to his career.* In origin the expression refers to the kiss with which Judas Iscariot betrayed Jesus Christ at the Last Supper, Judas having indicated to the enemies of Jesus that he would identify him to them by kissing him (*Matthew* 26: 47–49). As a cliché the phrase is not related to treachery and dates from about the middle of the twentieth century. It is current still.

knotty question, a is an idiom cliché indicating a difficult problem that is hard to solve. The expression has been a cliché since the nineteenth century. In origin it refers to a knot in a piece of wool, etc which is difficult to undo.

know all the answers is a hackneyed phrase used to describe someone who is, or thinks he or she is, very well-informed or knowledgeable. American in origin, the expression has been popular since the 1930s. As a modern cliché it is usually used in a derogatory way, as *There is no point in trying to give him any advice about driving a car. He knows all the answers.*

know a thing or two is a hackneyed phrase used to indicate that one has a good deal of information about something, or that one has a good deal of experience in connection with something, as *The old man knows a thing or two about engines.* The expression often carries the suggestion that it is not given to many to have this kind of knowledge, as *'I know a thing or two about women,' he leered.* As a cliché it dates from the second half of the twentieth century and is still widespread today, especially among

people who like to impress others with their superiority.

know chalk from cheese, not to see *different as chalk and cheese*

know for a fact is a hackneyed phrase sometimes used to emphasize how certain someone is about something, as *I know for a fact that she leaves those children on their own without a babysitter.* It is often used simply as a filler cliché by people who use it out of habit, almost without realizing that they are using it. In such situations 'know' alone would suffice. As a cliché the expression dates from the twentieth century.

know from Adam see *not know from Adam*

know one's onions is an idiom cliché which, like **know the ropes,** means to have a thorough knowledge of one's subject, although in origin it is rural rather than nautical. As a cliché it is still in current use, as *I enjoyed the talk on local history. The speaker certainly knew her onions,* but it is rather dated.

know the ropes is an idiom cliché meaning to be well-informed about or skilled in something, as *We are not looking for a trainee computer operator. We need someone who knows the ropes.* The expression came into figurative use and then became a cliché in the late nineteenth century. It is still widespread today, being used in all but the most formal contexts. The term derives from the days of sailing ships when it was necessary for sailors to know all about the ropes in order to be able to help sail the boat effectively.

know what's what is a hackneyed phrase meaning to be fully informed about what is going on, as *Vague promises are not enough. We want to know exactly what's what.* The expression was used by Samuel Butler in *Hudibras* (1663) 'He knew what's what, and that's as high as metaphysic wit can fly.' It is possible that he coined the term. As modern cliché it is often used by rather precise people who like everything to be straightforward.

know where one stands is a hackneyed phrase meaning to understand exactly the nature of one's position or circumstances, as *There have been rumours about redundancies and the workers would like to know where they stand.* The expression has been a cliché since the late nineteenth century and is still widespread today.

know which side one's bread is buttered is an idiom cliché meaning to have a clear idea of where one's best interests lie, of what situation or course of action will be to one's advantage, as *The young people know which side their bread is buttered. They would never dream of leaving home and moving into a flat.* The expression is quite old, having appeared in John Heywood's collection of proverbs in 1546. It has been a cliché since the nineteenth century and is still common nowadays.

⚹ L ⚹

labour of love, a is a hackneyed phrase indicating a task done, not for money or other reward, but out of affection or regard for the person for whom one is doing it or because of the pleasure or satisfaction which one derives from doing it, as *She hates housework and so it is a real labour of love when she cleans her grandmother's house*, and *Turning that waste site into a rose garden is a real labour of love but they are both keen gardeners*. In origin the expression may be Biblical, being a reference to *1 Thessalonians* (1:3) 'Remembering without ceasing your work of faith, and labour of love, and patience of hope in our Lord Jesus Christ, in the sight of God and our Father', and to *Hebrews* (6:10) 'For God is not unrighteous to forget your work and labour of love, which we have shown towards His name, in that ye have ministered to the saints, and do minister.' Both passages refer to people who do God's work as a labour of love.

lady of the house, the is a hackneyed phrase meaning the woman who is in charge of a house and usually refers to the wife of the owner of a house. It is now dated on two counts. The word 'lady' is now usually disliked by modern women, who prefer 'woman', and most women now have jobs outside the house as well as running the home. The expression, in common with **the woman of the house**, is now considered patronizing. As a cliché it became popular in the nineteenth century and continued to be so until the rise of feminism. It is still used by some people, such as certain salesmen, who have not caught up with the times, and appear on doorsteps saying *Is the lady of the house at home?*

land of milk and honey is an allusion cliché meaning a place providing comfort or luxury. The expression became a cliché in the nineteenth century, and although it is still used today, it is now rather dated, tending to be used by people of a literary bent, as *Some immigrants are disappointed when they arrive in Britain since they are expecting a land of milk and honey and the reality is very different*. The expression is an allusion to a passage in the Bible, to *Exodus* (3:8) in which God tells Moses 'And I am come down to deliver them out of the land of the Egyptians and to bring them out of that land unto a large and good land flowing with milk and honey.' Sometimes the expression appears in a variant form which is closer to the original, **a land flowing with milk and honey**, as *They expected a land flowing with milk and honey, not a land of poverty and unemployment*.

land of the living, in the see *in the land of the living*

land on one's feet see *fall on one's feet*

lap of luxury, the is a hackneyed phrase meaning great ease or affluent circumstances, as *They used to be very poor but since he won the football pools they have been able to live in the lap of luxury*. The expression dates from the late eighteenth century and has been a cliché since the middle of the nineteenth century. It is still in widespread use today.

large as life, as is a simile cliché meaning in person or actually, as *We heard that he had died but he turned up at the reunion dinner large as life*. The expression dates from the late eighteenth century and is still a common cliché today.

larger than life is a hackneyed phrase meaning on a grand scale, as *He was a very insignificant person although his father and grandfather were both larger than life figures*, and sometimes has the extended meaning of dramatically exaggerated. The expression is a development of **(as) large as life**.

last but not least is a hackneyed phrase meaning last in terms of sequence but not in terms of importance. It is frequently used in situations where names or items have to be listed but where there is no obvious order of merit, as *We have a number of people to thank for their contribution to the organization of the reception – Jack Jones, Mary Smith, Fred Brown, Jane Green and last, but not least, John White*. Sometimes the impression is even created that the person or thing mentioned last is not the least in importance but possibly the greatest. The expression dates from the sixteenth century, being used by John Lyly in *Euphues and his England* (1580). It has been a cliché since the nineteenth century and is still extremely common.

last legs, be on one's is an idiom cliché meaning to be near to the end or collapse, as *The firm was on its last legs when it was bought by one of its competitors*. It can also be used to mean close to utter exhaustion, as *She rode the poor horse until it was on its last legs*. As a cliché the expression dates

from the twentieth century and is still very common today.

last of the Mohicans, the is a catchphrase cliché referring to the one remaining in a group, series, etc when all the rest have gone. In origin it refers to a novel by James Fenimore Cooper, *The Last of the Mohicans* (1836). The expression probably became a cliché around the turn of the century. It was formerly more commonly used over a wider set of contexts. For example it was once used of the last cigarette in a packet. Nowadays it tends to be used of a survivor of a group that is dying out, as *All the rest of the women go into the village pub but she is the last of the Mohicans and thinks a pub is no place for a woman*.

last straw, the is an idiom cliché having its derivation in the proverb **it is the last straw that breaks the camel's back**. It refers to an event, fact, etc which, when added to all other events or facts that have gone before, makes a situation finally impossible to bear, as *We had to work late every night that week but it was the last straw when we also had to work on Sunday*. Originally, as the derivation indicates, the suggestion was that the final event or act was rather trivial, it being simply the cumulative effect that proved disastrous, but this is no longer the case. The expression has been a cliché since the nineteenth century and is still widespread. An alternative form of the same theme, **the last feather that breaks the horse's back**, existed in the seventeenth and eighteenth centuries but this is now obsolete.

late in the day is a hackneyed phrase meaning late or overdue, often with the suggestion of being too late, as *It is a bit late in the day to decide to go to university but if you ring around you might just get a place,* and *It is a bit late to start studying for the exam. It begins in an hour.* As a cliché it dates from the twentieth century and is still widespread.

laugh all the way to the bank is a hackneyed phrase referring to someone's joy at having made a substantial profit, as *People said that he was mad to invest in that scheme but he went ahead and he is now laughing all the way to the bank*, and *I knew him when he lived in miserable poverty but now he is laughing all the way to the bank*. It is a variant of **cry all the way to the bank**, an ironic expression which means much the same, except that the latter places more emphasis on the fact that the investment which led to the profit was in some way wrong, ill-advised, or disapproved of, as *The environmentalists tried to stop him building a factory there but he defied their objections and is now crying all the way to the bank*. The expression originated in America in the 1960s and later spread to Britain where **laugh all the way to the bank** is the commoner expression.

laugh: not to know whether to laugh or cry see *not to know whether to laugh or cry*.

laugh on the other side of one's face is an idiom cliché meaning to feel disappointed, miserable, depressed, etc after having felt happy, successful, triumphant, etc, the implication being that one deserved the change in one's fortunes and might even have brought these on oneself, as *He was boasting about having given so little money to the old lady for the car, but he was laughing on the other side of his face when the car would not start*. The expression sometimes takes the form of **laugh on the wrong side of one's face**. As a cliché the expression dates from the eighteenth century, although the concept is older. It is still common today.

laugh out of court is an idiom cliché meaning to treat someone or something with derision, refusing to take the matter seriously, as *Our request for a pay rise of 15% will be laughed out of court*. As a cliché it dates from the late nineteenth century and is still common, although used in rather formal contexts or by people who have rather a formal manner of speaking and writing. In origin it refers to a court of law. The idea of a case being treated derisively is mentioned in Horace's *Satires* (35BC).

laugh up one's sleeve is an idiom cliché meaning to be secretly amused, often at the expense of someone else, as *She pretended to sympathize with his predicament but all the time she was laughing up her sleeve at him*. As a cliché the expression dates from the late eighteenth century and is still widespread today. Historically the expression originally took the form of **laugh in one's sleeve** and had its origin in the fact that people could hide a smile by hiding their faces behind the wide sleeves of earlier fashions. This expression dates from the early sixteenth century, being included in John Heywood's collection of proverbs.

law and order is a hackneyed phrase, indeed almost a doublet cliché, since the two words in this context are virtually interchangeable, used to refer to the enforcement of a country's laws, as *Both political parties are now putting law and order near the top of their agendas*. The expression has been common since the nineteenth century and is still a common cliché today. Since it is very frequently a political issue it tends to enjoy periodic spells of exceptional popularity. Traditionally it is a cliché beloved of the political right wing which advocates tougher laws and penalties and disliked by those on the left who fear that it is associated with a harsh, insensitive regime.

law unto oneself, a is a hackneyed phrase used to refer to someone who always does things his or her way, taking little note of conventions or rules, and tending to be unpredictable, as *I have no idea whether Mary will agree to the plan or not. She is a law unto herself.* The expression has been a cliché since the late nineteenth century. It is still quite common but usually in the slightly less formal form of **a law to oneself**.

lay it on with a trowel is an idiom cliché meaning to exaggerate one's flattery or complimenting of someone, often in order to achieve something of advantage to oneself, as *It is one thing to compliment a girl on her appearance but he lays it on with a trowel*, and *They wanted her to babysit and so they laid it on with a trowel about how much the children loved her.* The expression refers to the kind of trowel that is used to apply plaster and was used by Shakespeare in *As You Like It* (1:2) 'Well said, that was laid on with a trowel.' It has been a cliché since the middle of the nineteenth century and is still popular today. A modern alternative form is **lay it on thick**.

lay one's cards on the table is an idiom cliché meaning to be absolutely truthful about one's role in a situation, to state openly what one is going to do, as *He should lay his cards on the table and give details of his financial interest in the project*, and *They have laid their cards on the table and said that they will sell the property to the highest bidder, irrespective of who that might be.* The cliché dates from the twentieth century and is still common today, although it is often used as a kind of smokescreen by people who are not really being completely honest about their activities or intentions, but who are using the phrase to deceive other people into thinking that they are honest. In origin the

phrase refers to card-playing. An alternative form of the expression is **put one's cards on the table**.

leading light is an idiom cliché referring to someone who is prominent in an organization, as *She is one of the leading lights in the local operatic society.* It has been common since the late nineteenth century, being frequently used by journalists on local papers reporting local events. Nowadays it is sometimes used ironically to describe someone in an organization who thinks too much of himself or herself. In origin the expression is a nautical term for a light used with other marks as a guide to the entrance of a harbour, channel, etc.

lead on, Macduff is an allusion cliché, being a misquotation from Shakespeare's *Macbeth* (5:10). The misquotation dates from the late nineteenth century and is now a common cliché used to urge someone to get going, as *All the people taking part in the search are here now. Lead on, Macduff!* The actual quotation is 'Lay on, Macduff, and damned be him that first cries, "Hold, enough!"' Another expression that is closer to this is **lay on, Macduff**. This was a cliché from the early nineteenth century and was used to incite someone to vigorous action.

lean over backwards see *bend over backwards*

learn something to one's advantage is a hackneyed phrase meaning to hear about something that will result in something advantageous, usually some form of financial profit, for oneself. It originated in the standard legal formula for informing someone about an inheritance, as *If you call at the offices of White, White, White and White, you will learn something to your* *advantage*, and has been a cliché since the late nineteenth century. Nowadays the expression in the general language, as opposed to the language of the law, is usually used in a humorous or ironic context, as *Mary left a message on my answering machine saying that if I called her back I would learn something to my advantage.*

leave in the lurch is an idiom cliché meaning to abandon someone and leave him or her in a difficult situation, as *He promised to lend us his car for our journey but just as we were about to start out he left us in the lurch by saying that he needed it for himself after all.* It is a very old term, dating from the sixteenth century, and has been a cliché since the late eighteenth century. It is still very common today, although it is usually restricted to informal contexts. In origin 'lurch' refers in games such as cribbage to a position in which one player loses by a large margin.

leave no stone unturned is an idiom cliché testifying to the thoroughness of some activity. It is common among journalists and others, such as police officers or politicians, who are anxious to impress on the public that everything that can be done is being done, as *The local police have said that they will leave no stone unturned until the missing child is found.* The expression has been a cliché since the eighteenth century but actually dates back to a Greek legend by Euripides. In it the Theban Polycrates, unsuccessfully looking for the treasure which Mardonius had left in his tent before the battle of Plataea, sought the help of the Delphic oracle who advised him to move every stone. This was later translated as 'turn over every stone'.

leave well alone see *let well alone*

left to one's own devices is a hackneyed phrase meaning left alone to do as one pleases, as *There are some organized trips during the holiday but we'll be left to our own devices most of the time*, and *The child gets home before the rest of the family and she is left to her own devices until they get back.* The expression has been a cliché since the late nineteenth century. The archaic word 'devices', meaning a plan or scheme, appears in the *Book of Common Prayer* 'We have followed too much the devices and desires of our own hearts.'

leg to stand on, not to have a see *not to have a leg to stand on*.

let bygones be bygones is a hackneyed phrase urging someone to forget about the past and the unfortunate things that may be associated with it, such as a quarrel, as *I know your family and his haven't spoken for years, but you should try to let bygones be bygones and write to him.* The word 'bygone' means past or former, as 'in a bygone age' and is archaic. The expression dates from the seventeenth century and is still widespread today. More or less the same sentiment is found in the expression **forgive and forget**.

let me just say is a filler cliché used virtually meaninglessly as there is usually no question of the speaker being prevented from saying what he or she wishes, as *Let me just say how much I admire your work.* It is the kind of phrase that some people use out of sheer habit without realizing it and which is a source of irritation to their regular listeners. It is found in both spoken and written English and is sometimes used for emphasis.

let me tell you is a filler cliché frequently used virtually meaninglessly by people to whom its use has become a habit. Sometimes it is used for emphasis, as *Let me tell you that you will live to regret it.* Unlike → **let me just say** it is usually restricted to spoken English.

113

let's face it is a hackneyed phrase urging someone to accept the reality of a situation, as *Let's face it. He's gone and he's not coming back*. It is also used as a filler cliché virtually meaninglessly by people to whom its use has become a habit. As a cliché it has been common since the middle of the twentieth century. It is found in informal contexts, usually in spoken English.

let's get this show on the road is an idiom cliché urging someone to stop delaying and get started doing something, as *Well, we've had a long enough coffee break. Let's get this show on the road*. As a cliché it dates from the middle of the twentieth century, having its origins in mobile forms of entertainment, such as circuses or fairs.

let sleeping dogs lie is a proverb cliché advising someone not deliberately to look for trouble, not to interfere in a situation with which there is nothing wrong. The expression dates back to the thirteenth century and is still a widespread cliché today, as *I wouldn't mention holidays to the boss. Let sleeping dogs lie; he seems to have forgotten the time you pretended to be off sick*. In origin it refers to a watchdog that has fallen asleep.

let the cat out of the bag is an idiom cliché meaning to reveal a secret, usually carelessly or thoughtlessly, as *Please don't mention the surprise party to Jane. She is bound to let the cat out of the bag*. As a cliché the expression dates from the nineteenth century and is still very common today, particularly in informal contexts. In origin it refers allegedly to a fairground trick by which traders sold unwary buyers a cat in a bag, assuring them that it was a pig. The buyers did not realize their mistake until they let the cat out of the bag by which time it was too late.

let the grass grow under one's feet, not to, see *not to let the grass grow under one's feet*

let well alone is a hackneyed phrase advising someone not to interfere with something if it is all right, in case he or she makes the matter worse, as *I know the picture on her television isn't very good but you should let well alone. She won't thank you if you break it*. The expression has the alternative form **leave well alone**. It was popularized by the eighteenth century prime minister, Sir Robert Walpole, who made it his motto, although the actual expression is considerably older than that. The same idea is found in → **let sleeping dogs lie** and in the modern slang expression of American origin **if it ain't broke don't fix it**.

lick and a promise, a is a hackneyed phrase meaning a superficial wash or clean, as *The boys would never think of washing their necks. They just give their faces a lick and a promise*. The expression dates from the nineteenth century and is still common today in an informal context. In origin it may refer to a cat quickly licking itself clean.

lick into shape is an idiom cliché meaning to get someone or something into a more acceptable form or into the required condition, as *The young runner has great potential but he is not very fit. Never mind, we'll soon get him licked into shape*, and *The house which they've bought is in a terrible state. It'll take a lot of money to get it licked into shape*. The expression dates from the seventeenth century and has been a cliché since the nineteenth century. It is usually used in an informal context. In origin it refers to an old belief that bear cubs are born shapeless and literally have to be licked into shape by their mothers.

lie back and think of England is an alternative form of **close your eyes and think of England**

life and soul of the party, the is an idiom cliché used to describe someone who is very lively and sociable and who helps to make a party or other gathering a success. The expression has been popular since the late nineteenth century and is still common today. It is sometimes used critically by those who do not like vivacious people.

life in the raw is a hackneyed phrase indicating a rough, uncivilized way of life, as *She says that she sees life in the raw being a social worker in a deprived inner city area*. The expression has been a cliché since early in the twentieth century and is still common today.

life is just a bowl of cherries is a catch-phrase cliché meaning that life is absolutely splendid. It is mostly now used ironically, as *I'm late for work, the car won't start, I've got oil on my shirt. Isn't life just a bowl of cherries?* It originated in America, being popularized by a song sung by Ethel Merman in *Scandals* (1931).

life is not worth living is a hackneyed phrase indicating the depression that someone feels, often as a result of someone else going away, as *She felt that life was not worth living after her fiancé broke their engagement*. The expression has been popular since the late nineteenth century and is still common today.

light at the end of the tunnel, the is an idiom cliché used to refer to a time of happiness after a period of misfortune or to a solution to a problem that has long remained unsolved, as *She has been in a state of black depression but she has at last begun to see the light at the end of the tunnel*, and *The firm has been in financial difficulties but there is now light at the end of the tunnel*. The expression was popularized by American President, John F Kennedy who used it in a press conference about the war in Vietnam (1962). It is still common today.

light fantastic, is an allusion cliché meaning dancing. It is now used in a humorous context, as *Do you fancy a bit of the light fantastic?* It is a short version of **trip the light fantastic** which means to dance and is also now used humorously, as *He fell down drunk when tripping the light fantastic at the wedding reception*. As a cliché the expression dates from the late nineteenth century. It is an allusion to a passage from *L'Allegro* (1632) by John Milton 'Come and trip as you go, On the light fantastic toe.'

light of day, first see (the) see *first see (the) light of day*

like a house on fire is a simile cliché meaning very well and usually used to describe people who get on very well together, often just after first meeting, as *I was worried that my daughter would be a bit shy at the party but she got on like a house on fire with the other children*. The expression can also mean very quickly, as *Because he is going to a party later he is getting through his homework like a house on fire*. The expression dates from the nineteenth century and is still very popular today. In origin it refers to the fact that houses made of wood or thatch burn extremely quickly.

like clockwork is a simile cliché which is the standard cliché used to indicate the efficient running of something or to indicate regularity, as *The office runs like clockwork when she's in charge*, and *The public transport there runs like clockwork*. In origin of course the expression refers to the mechanism of a clock.

like death warmed up is a simile cliché meaning very pale or ill, as *How is your hangover? You look like death warmed up.* The expression dates from the early part of the twentieth century and may have first been military slang. It is still common today in an informal, and often humorous, context.

like grim death see *grim death, like*

like I need a hole in the head see *need like a hole in the head*

like it was going out of fashion is a simile cliché and also a catchphrase cliché, meaning very quickly or in great quantities. It is most commonly used in connection with spending money, as *Whenever she goes near a dress shop she spends money like it was going out of fashion*, although it is found in other contexts, as *He smokes cigarettes like they were going out of fashion*. The expression dates from around 1930 and is still common today in informal or slang contexts. An alternative form of the expression is **as though it was going out of fashion**. The same sentiment is expressed in → **like there was no tomorrow**.

like something the cat brought in is a simile cliché dating from the early part of the twentieth century. The phrase is used as an informal comment on the untidy, bedraggled or generally unacceptable appearance of someone, as *You can't go to the party like that. You look like something the cat's brought it.* In origin the cliché refers to some kind of prey, such as a half-eaten mouse or bird, that a cat might bring into the house.

like there was no tomorrow is a catchphrase cliché which, in common with → **like it was going out of fashion**, means

very quickly or in great quantities and is usually used to refer to the spending of money, as *In the January sales everyone seemed to be spending money like there was no tomorrow.* The expression has been popular since the middle of the 1970s and is still common today in informal or slang contexts.

like two peas in a pod is a simile cliché, being a standard cliché to express close physical resemblance, as *The twins are like two peas in a pod.* The expression has been in existence since the sixteenth century and is still widespread today. An alternative form of the expression is **like peas in a pod**.

Lion's share, the is an idiom cliché meaning the largest portion of something, as *All his children were left some money by the old man but the eldest son got the lion's share.* It has been a cliché since the middle of the nineteenth century and is still common today. In origin the expression refers to one of Aesop's fables, in which the lion got either the largest share of, or indeed all of, any prey killed in hunting since the other animals were afraid of him.

lips are sealed, my is an idiom cliché used to indicate that someone will not reveal what he or she has been told. Although the actual concept is an old one, the expression became current in the early part of the twentieth century, being popularized by Stanley Baldwin, British prime minister, who used it (1937) in reply to questions about whether the then King Edward VIII was going to abdicate. It is still common today and is often used humorously.

lip service, pay is a hackneyed phrase meaning to pretend to approve of or support something while not really doing so, as *The teachers pay lip service to the new* *education policy but they go on using the old methods*. The expression **lip service** has been in existence since the seventeenth century and is a common cliché today. The sentiment, although not the wording, is Biblical. It is referred to in *Matthew* (15:8). 'This people draweth unto me with their mouth and honoureth me with their lips, but their heart is far from me.'

little bird told me, a is a hackneyed phrase indicating that one has heard something but does not wish to reveal the source. A version of the saying appeared in John Heywood's collection of proverbs in 1546, and the actual expression has been common since the nineteenth century. It is still common today but sounds rather coy if used seriously, as *A little bird has told me that wedding bells are in the air*, and is often used humorously.

little black book is a hackneyed phrase used to indicate a notebook in which someone carries details of current and past partners and consults it when he or she is partnerless, as *His girlfriend's just walked out on him and so he's going through the phone numbers in his little black book*. Of course the book need neither be black nor little, it being the concept that is important. As a cliché the expression dates from the second part of the twentieth century.

little grey cells is a hackneyed phrase, dating from the second part of the twentieth century, meaning brains or intelligence. It is used humorously or ironically in informal contexts, as *For goodness sake use your little grey cells and think of a way to get us there on time*. The expression came into being because part of the brain is composed of a greyish tissue which contains the nerve endings.

little knowledge is a dangerous thing, a is a quotation cliché being a misquotation of a passage from *An Essay on Criticism* (1711) by Alexander Pope 'A little learning is a dangerous thing.' The expression is used as a warning that a small amount of knowledge about a subject can be more dangerous than knowing nothing at all because the knowledge can be applied wrongly, and because one can think that one knows more than one actually does. Nowadays the misquotation is more common than the actual quotation, as *I should call in an experienced tradesman to do your electrical repairs and not get your DIY friend to do them. A little knowledge is a dangerous thing.*

little pitchers have big ears is a proverb cliché meaning that children may overhear things they should not, since people have a tendency to overlook the presence of children, as *Could we discuss this later. Little pitchers have big ears, you know*. The likening of the largeness of children's ears to the handle of a pitcher or jug dates from the sixteenth century and the expression was a cliché from the late part of the nineteenth century.

little woman is a hackneyed phrase sometimes used by sexist men to refer to someone's wife, as *And what are you going to give the little woman for Christmas?* It is now dated, since women have had more status in the community since the rise of feminism, and tends to be used by older men whose attitudes have not changed with the times.

live and let live is a proverb cliché advising people to get on with their own lives and show tolerance for the way in which other people choose to live theirs, as *You should learn to live and let live. It is no business of yours whether they are married or just living together.*

lock, stock and barrel is a hackneyed phrase meaning absolutely everything, as

The landlord said that he wanted the tenants to leave, lock, stock and barrel. The term has been popular since the early part of the eighteenth century and is still commonly used today for emphasis. In origin the phrase refers to the three parts of a gun – the lock or firing mechanism, the stock or handle, and the barrel.

lone wolf, a is a hackneyed phrase which refers to someone who prefers to spend a great deal of time by himself or herself rather than with other people, as *We asked Jim to come on holiday with us but he refused. He's a bit of a lone wolf.* The expression is American in origin and refers to the fact that wolves usually hunt in packs. It dates from the twentieth century.

long arm of the law, the is a hackneyed phrase used to refer to the police force and the legal process generally, the implication being that its influence is extremely far-reaching. It has been popular since the late nineteenth century and is still used today, although it is dated and is usually used in humorous or ironic contexts, as *You can try to hide but the long arm of the law will get you!*

long in the tooth is an idiom cliché meaning old or ageing, as *He's getting a bit long in the tooth to be playing professional football.* The expression has been popular since the nineteenth century and is still common today in informal, and often humorous contexts. In origin it refers to the fact that the gums of horses recede as they grow old which makes it seem as if their teeth get longer. A horse's age is gauged by examining its teeth.

long shot, a is an idiom cliché meaning a guess or attempt that is unlikely to succeed but that is worth trying, as *It is a bit of a long shot but you could try contacting him at his parents' old address.* In origin the expression refers to the fact that early firearms had to be fired from a position near the target in order to be accurate. A long shot was fired from a distance and so would be likely to miss the target. The expression has been used figuratively since the later part of the nineteenth century and is still a common cliché today.

long time no see is a hackneyed phrase used as an informal greeting to someone whom one has not met for some time, as *Long time no see! Have you been away?* The expression is deliberately ungrammatical and has its origins in pidgin English used by the Chinese in the late nineteenth century and is a translation of a Chinese greeting.

loose end, at a is a hackneyed phrase indicating that one has nothing very much to do and has spare time, as *I don't mind doing your shift this afternoon. I am at a loose end anyhow.* The concept was referred to in John Heywood's collection of proverbs in 1546 and the phrase is still a common cliché today, being used in an informal context. In origin the expression refers to a length of rope that has become unfastened leaving an end dangling and not in use.

love is blind is a hackneyed phrase meaning that people who are in love are often blind to each other's faults. It is an old concept, having been referred to by Plato and the phrase was used by Shakespeare in several of his plays, such as *Romeo and Juliet* (2:1). Both the concept and the phrase are still common today, with the phrase often being used in a humorous or ironic context, as *I cannot imagine what she sees in him. No wonder they say love is blind.*

M

make a clean breast of is an idiom cliché meaning to make a full confession of something, as *When one of the other pupils was accused of the theft he decided to own up and make a clean breast of it*, and *She was afraid that her husband would find out that she had had an affair and decided to make a clean breast of it to him*. The expression has been a cliché since the late nineteenth century and is still widespread today. In origin it refers to the fact that the breast or heart was considered to be the seat of the emotions where one's innermost thoughts were kept.

make a mountain out of a molehill is an idiom cliché meaning to exaggerate the importance or difficulty of something, as *He was just a few minutes late but she got very angry and refused to go out with him. She's always making mountains out of molehills* and *They're causing a scene because their neighbour told off their children. They're just making a mountain out of a molehill*. The expression has been current since the middle of the sixteenth century and has been a cliché since the late eighteenth century. Both the cliché and the practice which it denotes are popular today. It is one of those expressions that are mostly always applied to other people, one's own problems always being viewed with a sense of proportion.

make an honest woman of is a hackneyed phrase meaning to marry someone, as *I'm glad you've finally decided to make an honest woman of Jane. You've been going out with her long enough*. As a cliché it dates from the nineteenth century and is still used today, but in a humorous or ironic way. Originally the term was restricted to a woman who had previously been seduced by the man in question and the sexual connotations sometimes survive to this day, as *They've been living together for years but he's now going to make an honest woman of her*, although this is not necessarily the case. In these days of sexual equality the inverse of the phrase is sometimes found, **make an honest man of**.

make an offer one cannot refuse is a hackneyed phrase meaning to offer such advantageous terms that the person who is offered them would be a complete fool to turn them down. The expression is usually associated with the world of commerce or employment, as *We hadn't really thought of selling the cottage but a young couple made us an offer we couldn't refuse*, and *I was perfectly happy with my previous firm but one of their competitors made me an offer that I couldn't refuse*. It often carries the suggestion that there might have been an ethical reason for turning down the offer, but that the size of the amount was enough to still any qualms about this, as *We felt bad about selling the land to the developers but they made us an offer that we couldn't refuse*.

make ends meet is a hackneyed phrase meaning to live within the limits of one's income, the implication usually being that to do so is something of a struggle, as *They are finding it very difficult to make ends meet since the baby was born*. It has been a cliché since the nineteenth century, although the expression itself is much older. In origin it is thought to refer to the beginning and end of one's financial year, as is suggested by the French form *joindre deux bouts de l'annee*, to join the two ends of the year. Another suggestion is that it simply refers to the opening and closing lines of a statement of income and expenditure. The cliché is still widespread today, as is the struggle with which it is frequently associated.

make hay while the sun shines is a proverb cliché meaning to take advantage of any good opportunity that occurs, as *The skiing season there does not last very long and so the local hoteliers have to make hay while the sun shines*. The saying dates from the early sixteenth century and in origin refers to the necessity for farmers to get as much hay-making as possible done in dry weather. It is often abbreviated into an allusion cliché **make hay**, as *We might as well make hay while there is plenty of work around. It usually tails off towards the end of the year.*

make no bones about it is an idiom cliché meaning to be absolutely open and frank about something, often something that one might expect someone to be reticent about, as *She made no bones about it. She told us she was marrying him for his money*. The expression has been popular since the eighteenth century and is still very commonly used today. The origin is uncertain. The most widely held theory is that it refers to bones in a soup or stew, although it has been suggested that its derivation relates to dice-throwing. The idea is that because dice were originally made of bones **make no bones about it** meant literally to throw the dice without any unnecessary delay or preparation.

make no mistake is a hackneyed phrase used for emphasis, as *Make no mistake, he*

will live to regret this, and *He has a terrible life with her, make no mistake*. It is sometimes extended to **make no mistake about it**. Both expressions are often used by people to whom they have simply become a habit and who are often not aware of it. They are frequently a source of irritation to their listeners. The phrases date from the end of the nineteenth century.

make one's day is a hackneyed phrase meaning to make one very happy, as *Granny's been ill. It will really make her day if you go and see her*. The expression has been popular since around the 1940s and is still common today, being used in informal contexts. Nowadays it is often used ironically, as *The boss has just made my day. He's told me to work late and I have tickets for a show*.

make or break is a hackneyed phrase used to refer to a crucial situation which will end in either complete success or failure, as *He's taking a bit of a gamble. This new job will either make or break his career*, and *This year it'll be make or break for the firm*. The expression has been popular since the middle of the nineteenth century, although it has a very modern ring to it. An earlier form of the expression was **make or mar**.

make short work of is a hackneyed phrase meaning to dispose of something very rapidly, as *The champion made short work of her competitor in the final*. It is often used humorously, as *The children made short work of the jelly and ice cream at the party*. The expression dates back to the sixteenth century and is still popular today, being used in informal contexts.

make the best of a bad job is a hackneyed phrase used to mean to get along as well as one can in unfortunate or adverse circumstances, as *We don't have enough volunteers* to help in the campaign but we'll just have to make the best of a bad job, and *There was too little food for the number of people who turned up but we made the best of a bad job*. As a cliché it dates from the middle of the nineteenth century, although the sentiment goes back to the seventeenth century. It is still popular today. An earlier form of the expression was **make the best of a bad bargain**.

make the supreme sacrifice is a hackneyed phrase originally meaning to give up one's life either for one's country or to save someone else's life, as *Having made the supreme sacrifice for his fellow officer he was buried with full military honours*. In this sense it was common from the late nineteenth century on, being particularly popular during World Wars 1 and 2. The expression is still used today, although it is considerably rarer than it once was, and is frequently used humorously or ironically in a variety of contexts indicating some form of minor sacrifice, as *He stayed a bachelor until he was forty and then he made the supreme sacrifice*, and *I know you want to watch the football but could you make the supreme sacrifice and help me with the supermarket shopping?* An alternative form is **make the ultimate sacrifice**.

make waves is an idiom cliché meaning to cause trouble, as *The committee used to agree on most things until a new member was elected and started making waves*. The expression became a cliché in the second part of the twentieth century and has a nautical origin, referring to a ship causing waves in still water by passing through it.

makes you think, it is a hackneyed phrase that has become a catchphrase cliché. The expression dates from around the late nineteenth century, becoming popular around the 1930s. It is still popular in informal contexts today, as *It makes you think. Unemployment can happen to any of us*. The expression is often extended to **it makes you think, doesn't it?**, as *She was so young to die. It makes you think, doesn't it?* Both phrases are sometimes used simply as filler clichés by people to whom they have become a habit.

making tracks, be is a hackneyed phrase meaning to take one's departure, often rather rapidly, as *Heavens, is that the time? I'd better be making tracks*. The expression **make tracks** is American in origin and dates from the nineteenth century. As a British cliché **be making tracks** is found in informal contexts. In origin it refers to leaving tracks or footsteps in the ground as one leaves.

man and boy is a hackneyed phrase meaning all of someone's life or all of someone's working life, as *He's worked for that firm man and boy and he still earns a pittance*. It is still a popular cliché and it has retained its masculine status, since its female equivalent is not commonly found.

man Friday is a hackneyed phrase meaning assistant, often with the sense of invaluable assistant, as *The manager's always saying he doesn't know what he would do without his man Friday, but he gave his personal assistant a very poor pay rise*. It is still found as a modern cliché although it has declined in popularity, perhaps because it sounds rather patronizing. In the middle of the twentieth century, its female counterpart → **girl Friday** became popular particularly in relation to office jobs. In origin the expression refers to Daniel Defoe's novel *Robinson Crusoe* (1719) in which the hero found a young native man on the desert island on which he was stranded. The young man, called Friday because Crusoe met him on a Friday, became his faithful servant.

man in the street, the is a hackneyed phrase meaning the ordinary person, as *The politicians are always pretending to be interested in the views of the man in the street.* The term dates from the early part of the nineteenth century and became a cliché later in the same century. It is still popular today, frequently being used by journalists or by people in public life whose fate depends on said man in the street. Sometimes it is used in a derogatory way by people who think that they are above the social level of the man in the street, as *The man in the street is only interested in his beer and cigarettes.* 'Man' in this context is usually now used to cover both sexes. It is objected to by some feminists and efforts have been made to popularize **person in the street** but with far from widespread success. An alternative form of the expression is **the man on the Clapham omnibus**, but this is now much rarer.

manna from heaven is an allusion cliché used to refer to sudden and unexpected assistance or advantage, as *The car broke down in the middle of nowhere and it was like manna from heaven when a tractor came along and gave us a tow.* The expression is now often used in humorous contexts, this humorous association dating from the early eighteenth century. The allusion is Biblical, 'manna' being used in *Exodus* (16:15) to refer to the food that God miraculously sent to the Israelites on their journey into the wilderness from Egypt.

man of the house, the is a hackneyed phrase used to refer to the man in charge of a household. The phrase is not confined to the role of husband or father but is extended to the oldest male in a household, as *Now that your father's dead, you'll have to be the man of the house and look after your mother and sisters.* Despite the fact that women now run many households with-

out a man, the phrase is still found. Salesmen have a habit of using it without ascertaining whether or not there is a man of the house, as *Could I come and demonstrate our double-glazing system when the man of the house is at home?* See also **lady of the house**.

man of the world, a is a hackneyed phrase meaning a man with experience of the world, a sophisticated man as, *I'm sure your story won't shock John. He's a man of the world after all.* The expression in this sense probably dates from the nineteenth century but originally it referred to a man who was married. As a cliché it is still common today and has its counterpart in **a woman of the world**, as *I thought that she was far too much of a woman of the world to get pregnant accidentally.*

man's gotta do what a man's gotta do, a is a catchphrase cliché indicating that there are some things which simply have to be done, whatever one feels about doing them, as *I don't really want to get rid of my assistant but I can't afford her. A man's gotta do what a man's gotta do.* It is usually now used in humorous or ironic contexts, as *I'll have to force myself to go on holiday next week. A man's gotta do what a man's gotta do.* The expression, whose popularity dates from the 1940s, is American in origin. Although its ultimate source is uncertain, it is thought to have been popularized by Western films.

man the pumps is an idiom cliché meaning to lend a hand in an emergency of some sort, as *If we are going to get this export order finished on time everyone will have to man the pumps.* Its popularity dates from the twentieth century and as a cliché is still found today, although it is perhaps rather dated. The expression is nautical in origin.

man to man is a hackneyed phrase meaning frankly. The sentiment contained in the expression dates from the days when there were many areas of interest from which women were excluded and when they were considered too delicate or sensitive to cope with forthrightness. Despite the change in the status and perception of women the phrase still persists today, as *She was very embarrassed when her father said that he wanted to talk man to man with her fiancé.* The expression is often used adjectivally, as *'Well, son, now that you are fifteen it's time that you and I had a man-to-man talk.'* As a cliché it dates from the late nineteenth century. Its female counterpart **woman to woman** is occasionally found, although this implies intimacy.

man who has everything, the is a hackneyed phrase used to refer to someone who is so wealthy that he already has all the consumer goods he could possibly want. It is commonly found in the promotion of luxury goods in the context of gift-giving, as *This diamond pen-holder is the perfect gift for the man who has everything.* The expression is American in origin and probably dates from the early part of the twentieth century. As a modern cliché it is often used of people who are not necessarily wealthy but who have everything that they want. Many women would include most older men in this category. *What do you give the man who has everything for Christmas? I always end up giving my father socks.* The phrase is not restricted to the male of the species, **the woman who has everything** also being found, although perhaps more rarely both linguistically and actually.

many are called but few are chosen is a quotation cliché, being a Biblical reference to *Matthew* (22:14) 'For many are called but few are chosen.' As a cliché the expression dates from the middle of the nineteenth century. It

is found today in humorous or ironic contexts, as *I've been turned down for promotion again. Ah well, many are called but few are chosen,* being mostly used by people of rather a literary bent.

many hands make light work is a proverb cliché usually used to encourage those who do not really wish to be involved in a project, as *If you give me a hand with these dishes we'll get them done in no time. Many hands make light work.* A proverb of long standing, it is still a popular cliché today, often being used by parents or grandparents in an attempt to get younger members of the family to help out with chores.

marines, tell that to the see *tell that to the marines*

marking time is a hackneyed phrase meaning allowing time to pass without making any progress or taking any definite action. As a cliché it dates from the late nineteenth century and is still popular nowadays, as *He is in rather a dead-end job but he is just marking time until he goes to university.* In origin it is a military term, referring to soldiers retaining a marching rhythm by moving the feet up and down as if marching but without actually moving from the spot.

mark my words is a hackneyed phrase used either for emphasis or as a filler cliché, as an introduction to a remark, as *Mark my words, that boy will end up in jail,* and *Mark my words, it will rain today.* As a cliché it dates from the middle of the nineteenth century. Nowadays it is often quite meaningless, being used by people to whom it has become a habit. It is often prefaced by 'you'. See also *you mark my words*.

matter of fact, as a see *as a matter of fact*

matter of life and death, a is a hackneyed phrase used to refer to something that is of vital importance, as *Please could you give us a lift to the hospital. It's a matter of life and death.* Frequently the urgency is exaggerated, as *I've got to get this letter in the post tonight. It's a matter of life and death.* As a cliché it dates from the middle of the nineteenth century. It is sometimes used in the form **a matter of life or death** which is more logical but less common.

may all your troubles be little ones is a hackneyed phrase used as a toast to a bride and groom. It is also a euphemism cliché since it is simply a *double entendre* indicating a wish that the couple will have children. It is used only by people who are given to finding this phrase amusing. To others it is at best trite and usually cringe-making, especially to the unfortunate couple on the receiving end of it.

May and December is an idiom cliché used to refer to a relationship or marriage between two people, one of whom is much older than the other, as *It's a real case of May and December. Her husband is old enough to be her father.* The expression is often used adjectivally, as *People say these May and December affairs never last but they've been married for ten years now.* Formally the relationships tended to involve an older man and a younger woman, but it is now quite common for women to be involved with younger men. The idea of comparing relationships is an old one. Chaucer in his *Merchant's Tale* refers to May and January, but May and December has existed since the early seventeenth century.

meaningful relationship, a is a vogue cliché that became popular in the 1970s and reached its peak in the 1980s. Supposedly it refers to a particularly special and deep relationship, as *She thought that she had a really meaningful relationship with Jim but he suddenly went off with someone else.* However, the 'meaningful' part is often practically meaningless, simply being added for the sake of pretentiousness. Its popularity has waned rather in the 1990s but just as one thinks it has gone, it pops up again.

meanwhile back at the ranch is a catchphrase cliché used, usually in the course of rather an involved conversation or story, to indicate that one has returned to the main thrust of the conversation or story or to the main location. In origin it refers to the old silent Western films, where it was a familiar caption indicating that the action had switched to the ranch from the scene of the fight, etc. It probably dates from the early 1920s and is still used today in humorous contexts, as *Mary and Jim were in Greece, Paul and Jane were in Spain, and meanwhile back at the ranch we were looking after all their children.*

meet one's match is a hackneyed phrase meaning to come up against someone who is as good as one is at something, as *She was used to beating the other members of the tennis club easily but she met her match when she played Mary.* The expression was originally to **find one's match** and this dates from the fourteenth century. By the late sixteenth century **meet one's match** was in existence and is a common cliché today.

meet one's Waterloo is an idiom cliché meaning to experience a major defeat or disaster, as *He was boasting that no one could beat him at chess but he met his Waterloo when he played against the defending champion.* In origin it refers to the defeat of the French under Napoleon by the English under Wellington at the Battle of Waterloo in 1815, a defeat that marked the end of Napoleon's power in Europe. The figurative expression probably dates from around the middle of the nineteenth century and is still common today.

message received is a catchphrase cliché indicating that one has understood what has been said or implied, as *Message received. We shall have nothing more to do with him.* In origin the expression dates from radio communications in World War 2, becoming more generally used later in the 1940s and still found as a cliché today. In radio communication the expression was usually **message received loud and clear** and this is also found as a cliché, as is **message received and understood**.

method in one's madness is an allusion cliché referring to the fact that, although someone's action seems strange or foolish there is an underlying purpose to it, as *The teacher lets the children do as they please for a while, but there is method in her madness. They soon tire of it.* The allusion is to Shakespeare's *Hamlet* (2:2) 'Though this be madness, yet there is method in it,' although the idea predates this. It has been a cliché since the early part of the nineteenth century.

Midas touch, the is an allusion cliché meaning the ability to make an undertaking successful or profitable, as *He seems to have the Midas touch. All his companies are doing very well even in the middle of the recession.* The allusion is to a Greek legend in which Midas, a king of Phrygia, asked the gods to turn into gold everything that he touched. The god Dionysus granted his request but Midas regretted it when even the food which he tried to eat turned to gold, and he asked for things to return to normal. By the seventeenth century the idea

was being used figuratively and it is still common today.

mid-life crisis is a vogue cliché used to describe a stage in someone's middle age, often around the age of forty, when he or she assesses his or her life, finds it lacking and often does something out of character, like going off on a completely different course, as *I think he had some kind of mid-life crisis. He suddenly left his wife and children and went to live by himself on a remote island.* The expression became popular in the 1970s and by the early 1980s practically everyone of the appropriate age, particularly if male, was having such a crisis. Its popularity was spread by the many journalists who wrote about it. The cliché is still common today, although probably less so than formerly.

millstone round one's neck, a is an allusion cliché used to refer to a heavy burden or responsibility. The allusion is a Biblical one, referring to *Matthew* (18:6) 'But whosoever shall offend one of these little ones who believe in me, it were better for him that a millstone were hanged about his neck and that he were drowned in the depth of the sea.' A millstone was one of a pair of heavy circular stones used to grind grain. The expression began to be used figuratively around the sixteenth century. As a cliché it is still common today, as *We thought buying this old house was a good idea but it is so expensive to renovate that it's just a millstone round our necks.*

mind boggles, the is a hackneyed phrase used to indicate extreme surprise – to boggle means to baffle – as *The mind boggles at what he might do when he finds out.* The expression has been in existence since the 1950s but became particularly popular from the 1970s. As a cliché it is still common today.

mind how you go! is a hackneyed phrase used as a greeting when parting from someone, as *You'd better get off now if you want to get home tonight. Mind how you go!* It urges people to be careful, meaning the same as → **take care** and has been common since the 1940s. As a modern cliché it is still popular in informal contexts.

mind one's p's and q's is a hackneyed phrase meaning to be very careful about what one does or says, as *You'd better watch your p's and q's when you visit my grandparents. They're very strict and old-fashioned.* The expression dates from the seventeenth century, becoming a cliché in the nineteenth century. It is still used today, being found in informal, and sometimes humorous, contexts. The origin of the expression is obscure. There are various theories. One is that the derivation points to the similarity of the letters p and q to children when they are learning to write. Another is that the two letters are respectively short for pints and quarts as they appeared in the accounts of the owners of taverns.

mind you is a hackneyed phrase either used to emphasize what one is about to say, as *He says that he's telling the truth. Mind you, I don't believe him*, or is used as a filler cliché by people to whom it has become a habit and who are unaware of the fact.

miss the boat is an idiom cliché meaning to be too late to take advantage of an opportunity, as *We were going to put in an offer for the house on the corner but we've missed the boat. It's already been sold*, and *She heard there was a job going in the factory but she applied too late and missed the boat.* The expression dates from around the beginning of the twentieth century and

is a popular cliché today, being used in informal contexts. An expression expressing the same idea is **miss the bus**.

moment of truth, the is a hackneyed phrase meaning a crucial point, the point at which something will be proved to have been successful, etc or otherwise, as *Jim says that he has mended the television set but the moment of truth will be when he switches it on*, and *I followed the instructions for making the cake faithfully but the moment of truth will come when I open the oven door.* In origin the expression is a translation from Spanish of *el momento de la verdad* which refers to the point in a bullfight at which the matador is about to kill the bull. This was described by Ernest Hemingway (1932) in *Death in the Afternoon*. The English expression then transferred to the general language and is a popular cliché today. It is often used of situations that are relatively minor and is frequently found in humorous or ironic contexts.

money is the root of all evil is a quotation cliché, being a misquotation of a Biblical passage. The actual quotation is 'The love of money is the root of all evil' (*1 Timothy* 6:10). The misquotation is commonly used today to indicate that much evil and wrongdoing comes about because of money and materialism, as *There was a big family quarrel over the will when their father died and they have never spoken to each other since. It's true what they say about money being the root of all evil.* Today it is sometimes used in satirical contexts.

month of Sundays, a is a hackneyed phrase meaning a very long time, as *I haven't seen him in a month of Sundays.* The expression dates from the nineteenth century and was probably a cliché by the early part of the twentieth century. The cliché is still popular today, being used in informal contexts. **A month of Sundays** could take some thirty-one weeks.

moot point, a is a hackneyed phrase meaning a debatable or doubtful point, as *It is a moot point whether or not she is a more talented pianist than her sister.* In origin the term meant a case to be discussed by a meeting or 'moot' of law students. It began to be used more generally from the eighteenth century and is a common cliché today, although it is sometimes used wrongly.

more haste, less speed is a proverb cliché used to advocate care and caution against too great a hurry, as *You'll just make mistakes if you rush at that. More haste less speed.* It can be a very annoying cliché to have directed at one, especially if one has no choice but to do something in a hurry. Sometimes the cliché is used to apply to one's own actions, as *Damn! I've laddered my tights. More haste less speed!* The proverb is of long standing and the cliché is still widespread today.

more . . . than you've etc. had hot dinners, I've etc. had is a catchphrase cliché used to emphasize one's wide experience of something, as *I've been involved in more business deals than you've had hot dinners,* and *She's been on more trips abroad than you've had hot dinners.* The expression is used in informal or slang contexts and dates from the twentieth century. Originally the phrase had sexual associations, being used by men to boast of their sexual conquests, as *I've had more women than you've had hot dinners.*

more the merrier, the is a proverb cliché indicating that the more people there are participating in something the more successful it will be, as *Why don't you and your friend come to the cinema with us? The more the merrier,* and *Yes we could do with some more volunteers. The more the merrier.* It has been a cliché since the nineteenth century, although as a proverb it dates from around the sixteenth century. It has been suggested that James 1 of Scotland may have been the first to use the expression (circa 1423).

more to it than meets the eye is a hackneyed phrase indicating that the speaker feels that a situation, problem, etc is more involved, more significant, etc than at first appears to be the case, as *He seemed to be the obvious thief but the police thought that there was more to it than met the eye,* and *It looked as though the child had fallen off the wall but the doctor thought that there was more to his bruises than met the eye.*

morning after, the is a hackneyed phrase traditionally used to describe the hangover that often follows a night of celebration, as *I wouldn't ask Jack to do too much today. He is suffering from the morning after.* The expression dates from the late nineteenth century and both it and the condition it describes are still extremely common today. Occasionally the expression is extended to mean the unpleasant effects of something other than a drinking bout. The phrase is a shortening of **the morning after the night before** and the full expression is still used.

move heaven and earth is an idiom cliché meaning to make every effort, to go to a great deal of trouble, as *They will move heaven and earth to keep their son out of prison,* and *The villagers will have to move heaven and earth to get the council to keep the local school open.* The expression dates from the eighteenth century and became a cliché towards the end of the nineteenth century. As a cliché it is still used today, although the expression is often a gross exaggeration of the effort put into something.

move the goalposts is a vogue cliché which became extremely popular in the 1980s to describe a situation in which the rules or conditions are changed after the action is underway, as *When we agreed to merge our firm with his we were quite pleased with the arrangements but he keeps moving the goalposts*. Its origin lies in ballgames, such as football.

much of a muchness is a hackneyed phrase used to refer to things or situations which are very similar, as *It doesn't really matter which of the candidates we choose for the job. They're all much of a muchness*. The expression dates from the eighteenth century and has been popular since the middle of the nineteenth century. It is still common today.

multitude of sins see *cover a multitude of sins*

mum's the word is a hackneyed phrase used to urge someone to keep quite about something, as *We're organizing a surprise birthday party for Mary, so mum's the word*. The actual expression probably dates from the early eighteenth century but the association of the word 'mum' and silence is much older, perhaps dating from the fourteenth century. Mum is imitative of the sound made when one's lips are closed. The cliché is still used today in informal contexts.

Murphy's law see *anything that can go wrong will go wrong*

mutton dressed as lamb is a hackneyed phrase used to describe in a derogatory way someone, usually a woman, who is dressed in the style of a much younger person, as *Did you see what she was wearing to the wedding? Talk about mutton dressed as lamb!* The expression dates from the late nineteenth century and is still common today. In origin it refers to a butcher trying to make mutton (meet from an older sheep) look like lamb.

my brother's keeper, I am not see *keeper, I am not* . . .

my heart bleeds for you is an idiom cliché used ironically to indicate that one does not feel a bit sympathetic towards someone, as *She says that she can only afford to buy one new dress a month. Poor soul! My heart bleeds for her*. Presumably the expression was once used in a sincere way, but it has been used in its present sense probably since the late eighteenth century and has been a cliché since the 1940s. It is still common today.

my, how you've grown is a hackneyed cliché much used by people to children whom they might not have seen for some time. It is a cliché which most children dread because there is nothing much that can be said in reply and because it embarrasses them. Adults should note that this particular piece of patronization is best avoided.

my lips are sealed see *lips are sealed, my*

my wife doesn't understand me is a catchphrase cliché used by a man to obtain the sympathy of another woman, usually with a view to having an extra-marital sexual relationship with her, as *You mustn't worry about the fact that I am married. My marriage is virtually over. My wife doesn't understand me*. The truth of the matter is that the wife usually understands him all too well and it is the misfortune of the other woman that she might not understand him. Nowadays the cliché is usually used in a consciously humorous way.

N

nail in someone's coffin, a is an idiom cliché meaning something that will harm or destroy someone, as *Having a row with the boss was another nail in his coffin. He's in trouble already for unpunctuality.* The expression dates from the late eighteenth century and is a common cliché today. In origin the phrase refers to the fact that a coffin was nailed down after the corpse was put in it but before it was put in the grave.

nail on the head, hit the see *hit the nail on the head*

name is mud, his/her is a hackneyed phrase meaning that someone has been discredited in some way, as *Her name is mud in the office since she reported her colleague to the boss.* The term dates from the early part of the nineteenth century when it was used in the British Parliament to describe an MP who had brought disgrace on himself in some way. As a modern cliché it is used in informal contexts and is often used humorously, as *My name will be mud if I forget to send my mother a birthday card.* The origin of the expression is uncertain. It may be derived from the fact that 'mud' was an eighteenth century slang term for a fool, or it may simply be that mud is a dirty, slimy substance.

name names, to is a hackneyed phrase meaning to specify the people involved in something, as *The teacher knows who committed the crime but she has not yet named names.* The expression is often used by people who are proud of the fact that they know something that others do not and want to sow seeds of suspicion, as *I won't name names but one of the bosses is having an affair with his secretary.*

name of the game, the is a vogue cliché that became popular in Britain in the 1970s. It is one of those clichés which is used rather vaguely or even meaninglessly but it usually refers to the thing that is important or central in something, as *In business the name of the game is profit.* The cliché is not so popular today as it was in the 1970s and early 1980s, although it is still fairly common, usually in rather informal contexts. The expression originated in America in the early 1960s.

name to conjure with, a is a hackneyed phrase used to refer to someone who is well-known or famous in a particular field, as *That's a name to conjure with. He was one of the best cricketers of his generation.* The expression became popular in the late nineteenth century and as a cliché is still used today, usually by people who have a fairly formal way of speaking and writing. In origin it derives from words used by conjurors or magicians when performing their tricks, the name in question being a name that could work wonders.

napping, caught see *caught napping*

nearest and dearest is a hackneyed phrase used to refer to someone's relatives and sometimes also to close friends. As a modern cliché it is usually used ironically, as *Her nearest and dearest never go to see the old lady*. The expression dates from the sixteenth century and it has been used ironically as well as literally from its inception.

neat as a new pin is a simile cliché used as the stock phrase to describe something that is exceptionally neat and tidy, as *The whole lived family in one room but it was always as neat as a new pin*. The expression dates from the late eighteenth century and is still widespread.

necessity is the mother of invention is a proverb cliché referring to the fact that people who are in dire need or trouble tend to be inventive and resourceful about finding ways to solve their problems. The expression dates from the late seventeenth century when it was used by playwright William Wycherley in *Love in a Wood* (1671), although the sentiment goes back to the ancient Greeks. As a modern cliché it is frequently used by people who like to be platitudinous about other people's misfortunes, as *If you can't afford to have the roof repaired you should have a go at it yourself. Necessity is the mother of invention*.

neck and neck is an idiom cliché used to refer to the closeness of some form of competition, as *The two teams at the top of the league are neck and neck at the moment*, and *Just before the general election the two parties were neck and neck*. In origin the expression refers to horse-racing where two runners who were close together were literally neck to neck. It began to be used more generally in the early nineteenth century. As a cliché it dates from the twentieth century and is widespread today.

neck of the woods is a hackneyed phrase meaning area or neighbourhood, as *He's*

certainly the best doctor in this neck of the woods. The expression is American in origin, originally referring to an area that was a forest settlement, and dates from the middle of the nineteenth century. It later transferred to Britain where it is still a popular cliché in informal or slang contexts.

needle in a haystack, a is an allusion cliché used to describe something that is very difficult to find, as *Empty country cottages are like needles in haystacks round here these days*. The allusion is to the proverb **to look for a needle in a haystack** which derives from medieval Latin and has its equivalent in several other languages. The aptness of the metaphor has meant that it has retained its popularity through the centuries.

needless to say is a filler cliché used by some to indicate that something need not be said since it is so obviously the case, although in fact the thing that need not be said follows the cliché, as *Needless to say, he never returned the money*. It is frequently used meaninglessly by people to whom it has become a habit. The expression dates from the sixteenth century and is still a popular cliché today. See also **goes without saying, it**.

need like a hole in the head is a simile cliché used to indicate how unwanted or undesirable something is, as *I needed another guest like I needed a hole in the head, but I really couldn't refuse to put them up*. The expression is American in origin, dating there from the 1940s. It spread to Britain where it is still a popular cliché in very informal or slang contexts.

needs no introduction is a filler cliché beloved of public speakers and used to indicate that the person in question is so well-known that he or she does not require to be formally introduced to an audience. The expression is completely unnecessary since it is invariably followed by an introduction, often one of some length, as *I am happy to announce the presence with us today of James White who needs no introduction to an audience of booklovers. He is . . .* The cliché dates from the late nineteenth century and is still heard in halls all over the country.

neither here nor there is a hackneyed phrase used to indicate that something is of no consequence or relevance, as *The fact that I didn't vote is neither here nor there. He lost by a huge margin.* The expression dates from the sixteenth century and has been a cliché since the late nineteenth century. It is still widespread today.

never the twain shall meet is an allusion cliché used to indicate the difference or disparity between two people, as *There's no point in trying to get those two together. He is a devout Tory, she is a devout Socialist and never the twain shall meet.* It is an allusion to a quotation from Rudyard Kipling's *The Ballad of East and West* 'East is East and West is West and never the twain shall meet.' The cliché dates from the twentieth century and is still fairly popular today, mostly in humorous contexts

new broom is an allusion cliché used to refer to someone who has just taken up some kind of new post and who is making changes often of a radical nature, as *The whole filing system has been changed. The new office manager is a bit of a new broom.* It is an allusion cliché to the proverb **a new broom sweeps clean**. As a cliché it dates from the middle of the nineteenth century and is still much used today.

new lease of life, a is a hackneyed phrase meaning renewed or refreshed vigour,

enthusiasm, etc, as *Her hip replacement has given her a new lease of life.* As a cliché it dates from the middle of the nineteenth century and owes its origin to the renewing of property leases.

nice work if you can get it is a hackneyed phrase used to congratulate someone on his or her good fortune and usually said in rather envious tones. It does not necessarily relate to a work situation, as *I hear Frank's gone to France for three months. Nice work if you can get it!* The cliché dates from the twentieth century and is still popular today.

nick of time, in the is a hackneyed phrase meaning just in time, as *I found my ticket in the nick of time. The train was about to leave.* As a cliché it dates from the early part of the nineteenth century. The expression was originally in the nick, 'nick' having the obsolete sense of critical point.

nine-days' wonder is a hackneyed phrase for something that gives rise to much interest and gossip but for a short time only, as *The whole village is talking about her son going to prison but it will be a nine-days' wonder.* As a cliché it dates from the nineteenth century and it is still widespread today. The idea goes back to a saying popular in Chaucer's time.

nip in the bud is an idiom cliché meaning to put an end to something potentially harmful or dangerous before it can develop very far, as *The teachers tried to nip the pupils' protest in the bud before it affected the rest of the school.* The expression dates from the sixteenth century and became a cliché about the middle of the eighteenth century. In origin it may refer to a gardener's method of preventing a plant from flowering, or from an early frost that kills off flower buds.

nitty gritty, the is a hackneyed phrase that was a vogue cliché in the late 1960s and 1970s. Although it has declined somewhat in popularity it is still common today in all but the most formal contexts meaning the basic points or issues of a situation, as *We've discussed the theoretical advantages of the project. Now let's get down to the nitty gritty.* It is held to be Black English in origin, perhaps referring to the grit-like nits that are difficult to remove from the scalp.

no accounting for tastes, there's is a hackneyed phrase used to refer to the seeming inexplicability of other people's tastes and preferences, as *I can't believe they actually chose that wallpaper. Still, I suppose there's no accounting for tastes.* An earlier form of the expression was **there is no disputing about tastes** but the present form was in existence by the early nineteenth century. This wonder at the taste of others remains popular today.

no better than she should be is a hackneyed phrase used to refer to a woman who is felt to be lacking in moral standards, as *His parents are concerned about him marrying her because she's had so many other boyfriends. They think she's no better than she she should be.* Since the cliché dates from the times, which may still be with us, when there was one moral standard for men and another for women, there is no male equivalent of this cliché.

no can do is a catchphrase cliche used to indicate that one cannot do something, that something is impossible, as *You want me to paint your house by next week. No can do!* The phrase is pidgin English in origin and became popular in general English around the beginning of the twentieth century. It is still popular today in very informal or slang contexts.

no comment is a hackneyed phrase used to indicate that someone would prefer to say nothing in response to questions. These questions, sometimes of a personal nature, are frequently set by members of the media to someone who for some reason is newsworthy, as *When asked about the possibility of a divorce, the film actor said, 'No comment.'* It is a response that is given not only by individuals but also by the police and other official bodies.

no expense spared is a hackneyed phrase used to indicate that a lavish amount has been spent on something, as *They had a huge society wedding, no expense spared.* It is often now used ironically, as *We thought we had been invited to dinner but all we got was sherry and peanuts. No expense spared!*

no laughing matter is a hackneyed phrase meaning a serious or grave issue. It is often used in situations in which there is no question of humour, as *You should report her disappearance to the police. It is no laughing matter.* The expression dates from the sixteenth century and is a popular cliché today.

no names, no pack drill is a catchphrase cliché meaning that one is unwilling to give a name to anyone, such as someone who is guilty of something, as *It wasn't Jim who stole the money. I know who it was, but no names, no pack drill.* The expression is military in origin, probably dating from the late nineteenth century and was originally used by soldiers who did not wish to mention any colleague's name in relation to any deed or offence in case he was punished. Pack drill was a form of punishment by which soldiers had to march up and down with all their equipment on their backs. It is now rather dated.

no news is good news is a proverb cliché used to indicate that to hear nothing suggests that all is well since if there has been any form of accident or other disaster notification would have been given by the police, etc. The expression dates from the seventeenth century.

no problem is a hackneyed phrase used as a conventional reply meaning literally that there is no difficulty about a situation. It used to mean much the same as **don't mention it** or as a term of general acquiescence, as *Certainly, I will give you a lift. No problem!* The expression originated in America in the middle of the twentieth century, becoming popular in Britain in the 1970s and now sometimes reaching epidemic proportions. **No sweat** is a more informal version of it. An Australian equivalent which is being popularized in Britain by the Australian soaps shown on British television is **no worries**.

no rest (or peace) for the wicked is a catchphrase cliché used in rather resigned tones simply to indicate that one is very busy, as *I've just got home from work and I have to go to the supermarket and cook the evening meal. Ah well, no rest for the wicked!* The reference to wicked is purely facetious. In origin it may be an allusion to a Biblical passage in *Isaiah* (48:22) 'There is no peace, saith the Lord, unto the wicked.' The phrase was being used by the early nineteenth century and was a cliché by the late nineteenth century.

nose out of joint, put someone's see *put someone's nose out of joint*

no show without Punch is a catchphrase cliché used to refer to a person who seems to have the knack of always turning up at events, usually events that are interesting, exciting, controversial, etc in some way, as *I*

might have known it. There's Mary over there with the protest group. No show without Punch! It became popular around the late nineteenth century and is common today in informal contexts. In origin the expression refers to the traditional Punch and Judy Puppet show, in which Punch is a leading character.

no skin off my nose, it's is a catchphrase cliché meaning it does not matter to me or affect me in any way. It has been popular since the early part of the nineteenth century and is common today in very informal or slang contexts, as *You can move out of the flat if you like. It's no skin off my nose!* In origin it probably refers to boxing or to an exchange of blows.

nose to the grindstone see *keep one's nose to the grindstone*

no smoke without fire, there's is a proverb cliché meaning that every rumour has some foundation or some element of truth in it, as *He's promised her faithfully that he's not seeing another woman but she's heard about it from various people and there's no smoke without fire.* It is an extremely popular cliché, especially among people who love to gossip and cause trouble. An alternative form of the saying is **where there's smoke there's fire**. The sentiment appeared in John Heywood's collection of 1546 having the wording **there is no fire without smoke**.

no spring chicken is an idiom cliché used in a derogatory way to indicate that a woman is no longer young. It often carries the connotations that said woman tries to appear or act younger than she actually is, as *She goes to discos every night but she's no spring chicken. She was at school with my mother's elder brother.* An alternative form is **no chicken**. The expression became a cliché in the nineteenth century, although **no chicken** was used in the early part of the eighteenth century. It is still common today in an informal context but has not yet been affected by unisex considerations in that men seem immune from the term.

not fit to hold a candle to see *fit to hold a candle to, not*

not for all the tea in China is a hackneyed phrase indicating that nothing would induce someone to do something, as *I wouldn't live in that part of town for all the tea in China*. The expression originated in the late nineteenth century and spread to Britain. It is still a popular cliché today in informal contexts.

nothing to write home about is a catchphrase cliché used to indicate that something is very ordinary or mediocre, as *We went to see the new play that got rave reviews but it was nothing to write home about*. The expression dates from the late nineteenth century and in origin may refer to soldiers writing letters when stationed away from home. It is still popular today in informal contexts.

nothing ventured, nothing gained is a proverb cliché meaning that nothing is achieved unless one is prepared to take risks, as *I hesitated about putting money into his new business but then I thought, 'nothing ventured, nothing gained'*. An alternative form of the proverb is **nothing venture, nothing gain**. An older form was **nothing venture, nothing have** which was in use in the time of Chaucer.

not in my back yard is a hackneyed phrase which was something of a vogue cliché in the 1980s. It is frequently abbreviated to **nimby** and sums up the attitude of one who has no objection to something being

built as long as it is not built anywhere near where one lives and so long as it does not inconvenience one. The attitude can be applied to things that are obviously objectionable, such as nuclear waste dumps, but can also be applied to things that are necessary and worthy, such as hostels for the homeless.

not just a pretty face is a catchphrase cliché used to highlight one's skill or intelligence, as *I told you I could fix the TV set. I'm not just a pretty face!* Originally it was used by a woman to a man to remind him that women have intelligence as well as good looks. It became popular around the middle of the twentieth century and is still popular today, although it is now often used ironically or humorously and sometimes by men. A standard facetious response is **you're not even a pretty face**.

not know from Adam is a hackneyed phrase meaning not to know someone at all, to be totally unacquainted with someone so that one would not recognize him or her, as *This man at the party greeted me like a long lost friend but I didn't know him from Adam*. The expression dates from the middle of the nineteenth century and the cliché is still common today, being used of women as well as men. The Adam in question is presumably Adam referred to in the Bible but the origin is otherwise unclear.

not out of the woods is an idiom cliché meaning that someone or something is not out of danger or trouble, as *The patient is very much better but she is not out of the woods yet*, and *The firm has improved a bit financially but it's not out of the woods yet*. An alternative form is **not out of the wood**. In origin it may refer to an old proverb **do not shout until you are out of the wood**. The idea of woods and forests being associated with danger goes back to Roman times. As a cliché it is still popular today being often used as an informal medical cliché.

not to be sneezed at is a hackneyed phrase used to indicate that something, such as an offer or opportunity, should not be dismissed lightly but should be taken seriously, as *Their offer for your house may not be as high as you wanted but it's not to be sneezed at.* The expression was in use by the early nineteenth century and is still popular today in informal contexts.

not to have a leg to stand on is an idiom cliché meaning to have no plausible defence or excuse to offer for one's behaviour, etc., as *He's bound to be found guilty of murder. The defence does not have a leg to stand on.* The expression dates from the sixteenth century and is still common today. Its origin is the obvious one of having no means of support.

not to know whether to laugh or cry is a hackneyed phrase indicating conflicting emotions, as *She didn't know whether to laugh or cry when the last of her children left home. She was glad to have more time to herself but she knew that she would miss them.*

The expression has been a cliché since the nineteenth century although the idea is much older. It is still in common use today.

not to let the grass grow under one's feet is an idiom cliché which is also a proverb cliché meaning not to delay or be inactive, as *If you see a suitable job advertised you should apply for it right away. Do not let the grass grow under your feet.* The expression dates from the sixteenth century and is still popular today in various forms, but always with negative connotations, as *If you want to change jobs you might as well do it now. There is no point in letting the grass grow under your feet.* In origin the expression refers to the supposed fact that if you stand in one place long enough the grass will start growing under your feet.

nudge, nudge is a hackneyed phrase used to indicate some sexual reference, often one that is illicit, as *He says that he needs to take his secretary to the conference. Nudge, nudge!* It is a shortened version of **nudge, nudge, wink, wink** which has the same connotations. The latter originated in the early 1970s in the TV series *Monty Python's Flying Circus* and was probably a cliché by the late 1970s. It is still popular today.

O

odds and ends is a hackneyed phrase used to refer to a miscellaneous collection of articles, as *The drawer of the kitchen table is full of odds and ends*. The expression dates from the eighteenth century and has been a cliché from around the middle of the nineteenth century. It is still widespread today. The original of the term may have been 'odd ends' meaning leftovers from rolls of cloth.

off the beaten track is a hackneyed phrase meaning in rather a remote place, as *The holiday cottage is a bit off the beaten track*. It is also used figuratively meaning unusual or original, as *His ideas on child-rearing are rather off the beaten track*. The cliché dates from the late nineteenth century and is still common today.

off the cuff is an idiom cliché meaning extemporaneously, without preparation, as *The speaker hadn't turned up. We'll have to get someone to speak off the cuff*. The expression originated in America in the early part of the nineteenth century and spread to Britain. In origin the phrase is said to refer to the fact that some speakers, such as after-dinner speakers, write some informal notes on their shirt cuffs as a memory aid rather than prepare a speech completely beforehand. It is still common today in informal contexts and is also used adjectivally, as *He made a few off-the-cuff remarks when introducing the speaker*.

of the first magnitude is a hackneyed phrase derived from the grading of the brightness of a star, the brightest being the first. When used figuratively the phrase originally meant of the highest quality, as *The college produces students of the highest magnitude*. It is also used ironically meaning greatest, as *He is a fool of the first magnitude*. The expression dates from around the seventeenth century and has been a cliché since the middle of the nineteenth century.

of which more anon is a hackneyed phrase used to indicate that one is going to say more about the subject later, as *There was the most terrible disaster at the wedding, of which more anon. I must rush now*. The cliché dates from the nineteenth century. Although it sounds archaic ('anon' meant soon) it is still used now, although usually humorously.

oil and water is an idiom cliché used to refer people or things which are completely incompatible, as *I'm not surprised they've separated. I'm surprised they ever got together in the first place. They're oil and water*. The expression has been a cliché since the nineteenth century. In origin it refers to the fact that oil and water do not mix.

old as the hills, as is a simile cliché meaning extremely old. The expression dates from around the beginning of the nineteenth century and is still common today, as *Some of the local traditions are as old as the hills*. It is also used facetiously of people, as *Children often think that their* *parents are as old as the hills*. It has its origin in geology.

old boy network is a hackneyed phrase used to describe a group of people, usually upper-class people, who have social connections with each other and who help each other in careers, etc, as *James was one of the few students who got a job and that was due to the old-boy network. His father was at school with the chairman of the firm*. The cliché dates from around the middle of the twentieth century and, in common with the phenomenon which it describes, it is still common today. It is mostly used of men, although women are also now beginning to network.

old enough to be her father is a hackneyed phrase used of someone who is in a relationship or marriage with someone much older than herself. The expression is used in a derogatory and disapproving way, as *She must be marrying him for his money. He is old enough to be her father*. Previously a relationship with a marked disparity in ages usually applied to an older man and a younger woman, but now older women often enter relationships or marriage with younger men. Disapproval is shown to them with **old enough to be his mother**.

old enough to know better is a hackneyed phrase meaning that someone is old enough to show maturity and good judgement, as *You children are old enough to know better than to play in the street*. The expression dates from the nineteenth century and is still common today. It is very often directed at children.

old hat is an idiom cliché meaning old-fashioned, unoriginal and uninteresting, as *I'm not going to hear his lecture on psychology. His ideas are old hat*. In origin it

probably refers to the fact that hats go out of fashion before they actually wear out. The expression dates from the late nineteenth century and is a widespread cliché today in all but the most formal contexts.

once and for all is a hackneyed phrase meaning finally. As a cliché the expression dates from the twentieth century and is still common today, as *She was told once and for all that she must get to work on time or she would be sacked*. It is often used by people who are delivering ultimatums. The previous form of the expression was 'once for all' which dates from around the middle of the fifteenth century.

once bitten, twice shy is a proverb cliché indicating that if one has been harmed, exploited, etc once by someone or in a particular situation, one will be extremely cautious in future dealings so as to avoid being harmed, exploited, etc again, as *He was very unhappily married once and I don't think he'll marry again. I think it is a case of once bitten, twice shy*. The saying dates from the middle of the nineteenth century.

once in a blue moon is an idiom cliché meaning extremely rarely, as *She goes to see her parents once in a blue moon, although they're now very old*. It is often used as a gross exaggeration. The expression dates from the nineteenth century, although references to a blue moon go back to the early sixteenth century. It is still very common today in informal contexts.

one foot in the grave is an idiom cliché indicating that someone is either very ill or very old. The idea goes back to the sixteenth century. As a modern cliché it is often used in humorous contexts, as *Their teacher is only about 35 but the children think she's got one foot in the grave*.

one for the road is a hackneyed phrase used to describe one last drink before people set off, as *It's nearly closing time. Let's have one for the road.* It probably applies to drivers who were having one last drink before driving home, the expression and the idea both predating modern drink-driving laws. As a cliché it dates from the twentieth century.

one good turn deserves another is a proverb cliché indicating that if one person does another a favour the other person should return it. It is usually said by someone who is in the act of returning a favour, as *You lent me your lawn-mower and so please feel free to borrow my electric hedge-clipper. One good turn deserves another.* The proverb appears in John Heywood's collection of 1546 but it goes back to the fourteenth century. It is still a common cliché today.

one in a million is a hackneyed phrase used to praise someone's good qualities, as *Her father was one in a million. He would have helped anyone.* In origin it refers to statistics and points to the rarity of such a good person. It dates from the twentieth century and is a common cliché today, being used in informal contexts.

one of those days is a hackneyed phrase used to indicate that the user has had a dreadful day when everything has gone wrong, as *Oh, I'm glad to be home. It's been one of those days!* The expression became popular in the 1920s and, like the experience which it describes, it is still widespread today.

one of those things, just see *just one of those things, it's*

one over the eight is a hackneyed phrase meaning one alcoholic drink too many, that is a drink that makes one drunk, as *He always gets aggressive when he's had one over the eight.* As a cliché it dates from the twentieth century. It is still used today in informal contexts, although it is rather dated.

one that got away, the is a hackneyed phrase originally used by anglers to describe a fish of exceptional size which was nearly caught but got away at the last minute, as *Keep away from old Fred at the bar. He's been fishing and he's just dying to tell someone about the one that got away.* In this sense it dates from the early part of the twentieth century but around the middle of the 1940s it came to be applied to a person who escaped from danger. It is often used facetiously in this sense, as *That's the one she married and that's the one that got away.* As a cliché today the first sense is still common but the second is rather dated.

only time will tell is a hackneyed phrase used to indicate that the outcome of something is not likely to be known for some time, as *They think they have caught her illness but only time will tell.* It is a cliché used by people who can think of no other ending to what they have said or written, whether or not there is any suggestion that the long-term outcome is uncertain.

only too pleased is a hackneyed phrase used to indicate that someone is very pleased to do something, such as help in some way, as *I'll be only too pleased to lend you the book after I've finished it.* It is often used simply for the sake of politeness, the user of the phrase being anything but pleased, but being too polite to say so, as *Why of course, I'll be only too pleased to look after all the animals while you're on holiday.* The cliché dates from the early 1920s and is still common as a polite convention today.

on the ball is an idiom cliché meaning quick and alert. It carries connotations of being extremely well-informed and up-to-date, as *If you're going to take up a job in the money market you'll really have to be on the ball.* In origin it refers to someone taking part in a ballgame who watches the ball closely so as to be ready if it comes to him/her. The cliché is American in origin and dates from the twentieth century. It is still popular today, being used in informal or slang contexts.

on the dot is a hackneyed phrase used in relation to time and meaning exactly, as *The bus will leave at 6 o'clock on the dot.* The expression is used for emphasis. It dates from around the beginning of the twentieth century and is still widespread in informal contexts today.

on the side of the angels is a hackneyed phrase indicating what is perceived to be the right or moral side of a situation, according to the circumstances, as *She thought for one minute that he was one of the planners but then she realized that he was on the side of the angels and was one of the protesters against building on the green belt.* Exactly who the angels are depends on your point of view. It sounds rather formal although it is in fact quite a common cliché today. The cliché dates from the late nineteenth century. In origin it refers to a speech given by Disraeli at the Oxford Diocesan Conference in 1864. 'The question is this; Is man an ape or an angel? I, my lord, am on the side of the angels.' The original meaning of the expression was to be on the side of those taking a spiritual view.

on the spur of the moment is a hackneyed phrase meaning suddenly, impetuously, as *He was passing the travel agents when on the spur of the moment he went in and booked a holiday to Greece.* As a cliché it dates from the late nineteenth century, although the expression has been in existence since the late eighteenth century. It is still widespread today. The 'spur' in the phrase refers to something that goads a horse to action.

on the tip of one's tongue is an idiom cliché indicating that someone was just about to say something, as *His name is on the tip of my tongue but I just can't think of it.* The expression has been a cliché since the middle of the nineteenth century and it is still widespread today.

on the wagon is an idiom cliché meaning abstaining from taking alcoholic drink, as *He used to drink like a fish but he has been on the wagon since he was up on a drink-driving charge.* The expression is American in origin and dates from the early part of the twentieth century. It then crossed the Atlantic and became a cliché in Britain and it is still popular today in informal and slang contexts. The expression was originally **on the water wagon** and in origin refers to the horse-drawn water wagon which was used to spray dirt roads to keep the dust down.

on the warpath is an idiom cliché meaning in a very angry mood, often seeking revenge, as *I should keep out of your mother's way. She's on the warpath since she discovered you'd damaged the car.* In origin it means engaged in battle and refers to American Indians. The figurative expression originated in America in the late nineteenth century and then spread to Britain. It is still a common cliché in informal contexts.

on this auspicious occasion is a filler cliché used by public speakers on supposedly important occasions, as *We are* *delighted to welcome the mayor to the school on this most auspicious occasion.* Since 'auspicious' means fortunate or favourable, the occasion in question is usually a celebratory or social one, such as the opening of a new building. The cliché dates from the late nineteenth century. Nowadays it is frequently used satirically or by people who are consciously sending the phrase up. As a straight cliché it is rather dated.

on with the motley is a catchphrase cliché meaning it is time to get on with things, whatever has happened. It is usually used in rather a humorous or ironic way, as *I got in very late last night and I don't really feel like going to work. Still, I suppose it's on with the motley.* The cliché dates from the twentieth century and was originally used to indicate that it was time for a show or some form of entertainment to begin, whatever had happened. It carries much the same sentiment as **the show must go on**. In origin it derives from the cry of the clown, *'vesti la giubba'*, in Leoncavallo's opera *I Pagliacci* (1892) which is the traditional story of the clown who has to make others laugh when his heart is breaking. 'Motley' is an obsolete term for jester and also refers to his costume.

on your bike! is a hackneyed phrase used informally and rudely to tell someone to go away, as *No I don't want to buy any double-glazing. On your bike!* The expression has bee popular since the 1960s. Interest in it was revived by advice given to the unemployed by **Margaret Thatcher's** government in the early 1980s that they should get on their bikes and go out of their own area to find work. Norman Tebbit in his address as Employment Secretary to the Conservative Park Conference in 1981 spoke of how his father had 'got on his bike' to look for work in the depression of the 1930s.

open a can of worms see *can of worms, a*

opening gambit is a hackneyed phrase used to refer to someone's opening point in a discussion or to someone's initial course of action or stratagem, often a cunning one, as *Her opening gambit was that her child was not to blame,* and *I think that their opening gambit will be to try to discredit the opposition.* The phrase is tautological, the word 'opening' being unnecessary, since 'gambit' on its own suggests openings. Gambit is an opening move in chess, being the sacrifice, or the offer of such a sacrifice, of a piece in order to acquire some advantage. **Opening gambit** is still widely used today.

open secret is a hackneyed phrase which seems like a contradiction in terms. It is used to refer to something which is supposed to be highly secret or confidential but in fact is extremely well-known, because it has been leaked to so many people, as *It is an open secret that they are planning to marry,* and *They are trying to suppress rumours about the merger but it is already an open secret.* It became popular in the nineteenth century and, since gossip is always a favourite pursuit of us all, it is still common today. In origin it is thought to refer to the title of a play, *Il Pubblico Secreto* translated in 1769 by Carlo Gozzi from *El Secreto a Voces* (The Noisy Secret), a Spanish play by Calderon.

open sesame is a hackneyed phrase used to refer to an event, situation, etc that leads to success of some kind, as *That first audition in the town hall was the open sesame for a glittering career in the threatre.* In origin the expression refers to the story of *Ali Baba and the Forty Thieves,* one of the stories in *The Arabian Nights' Entertainments* (circa 1375). In the story 'open sesame' is the secret password that opens the door to the robbers' treasure cave. By the nineteenth century **open sesame** was becoming a synonym for a password, particularly a password to success. It is a common cliché today.

open the floodgates is a hackneyed phrase meaning to remove some form of restriction or control and so release a great, often overwhelming, amount or number of something, as *When the restraints on wage increases were lifted it opened the floodgates to claims from all the other Unions*. In origin it refers to the opening of gates at a lock or reservoir that hold back a great volume of water. As a cliché it dates from the twentieth century and is common today. As is the case with such clichés it is often used as a gross exaggeration. It is also often used as an excuse for not going ahead with the removal of some form of restriction, as *If we give permission for one of the pupils to go on holiday during term time it will open the floodgates and we'll get a rush of demands from other parents*.

or words to that effect is a hackneyed phrase sometimes used as a filler cliché indicating that something is more or less what was said, as *Her employer said that he was sorry to lose her but that he had no choice, or words to that effect*. It is used to indicate that what one has said is a reasonably close approximation, but it is also used meaninglessly by people to whom the cliché has become simply a habit. The cliché dates from the twentieth century and is still in common use.

OTT is an abbreviation of → **over the top** which itself is used as a cliché in informal or slang contexts, as *He deserved to be punished but it was a bit OTT to expel him*.

out of the blue is an idiom cliché meaning suddenly and unexpectedly, as *I wasn't thinking of changing jobs but this offer came out of the blue*. In origin the phrase refers to

something dropping unexpectedly from the sky. As a cliché the expression dates from the twentieth century and is still widespread today.

out of the mouths of babes and sucklings is an allusion cliché indicating that young and inexperienced people often show unexpected cleverness or judgement, as *Our young daughter asked us why they were digging up nice trees to build a new road. Out of the mouths of babes and sucklings*. Sometimes the expression is shortened to **out of the mouths of babes**. A cliché since the nineteenth century it is now used mostly by people of a literary bent. It is an allusion to the Bible, to *Matthew* (21:16). 'Out of the mouths of babes and sucklings thou hast perfected praise,' and to *Psalms* (8:2) 'Out of the mouths of babes and sucklings hast thou ordained strength.'

out on a limb is an idiom cliché meaning to have opinions that are completely different from the rest of a group, etc, as *She's out on a limb by wanting to diversify their range. The rest of the company want to stick to what they know*. An alternative meaning is in a dangerous or disadvantageous position. In origin the expression refers to an animal being at the end of a branch of a tree and so far from the main tree and safety.

over a barrel, have someone see *barrel, have someone over a*

over and done with is a doublet cliché used to emphasize the fact that something has come to an end, as *There was a feud between the families for many years but that is over and done with now*. The cliché dates from the twentieth century and is still common today.

over my dead body is a hackneyed phrase indicating one's strong opposition to something, as *They'll pull down that tree over my dead body*, and *She'll be invited to the party over my dead body*. The expression is American in origin and dates from the early nineteenth century. As a cliché it is still much used today in all but the most formal contexts by people wishing to emphasize the extent of their opposition.

over the hill is an idiom cliche meaning past one's prime or too old for something, as *He was a magnificent singer in his youth but he is a bit over the hill now*. In origin the phrase refers to a climber who has reached the top of a hill or mountain and is descending the other side. The cliché dates from the second part of the twentieth century and is still common in informal, derogatory contexts today. As the age at which people are supposed to be effective and employable diminishes, so the number of people liable to have the cliché applied to them is increasing.

over the moon is an idiom cliché meaning extremely happy or pleased, as *She was over the moon when she discovered she was pregnant*. As a cliché the phrase dates from the twentieth century and around the 1970s became particularly associated with the reactions of the manager or players of a winning football team when being interviewed after a match. In origin it may be connected with the old nursery rhyme in which 'the cat jumped over the moon.'

over the top is a hackneyed phrase meaning indicating that something is too much, too great, exaggerated, over-dramatic, etc, as *The leading man was good in the play but the leading lady was over the top*, and *It was a bit over the top to sack him just for saying what he thought*. As a cliché the expression dates from the 1980s and is extremely common today. In World War 1 **go over the top** meant to leave the comparative safety of the trench and go over the top or parapet to launch an attack on the enemy.

own goal, an is an idiom cliché used to refer to some misfortune that is the result of some action of one's own, as *The politician tried to start a smear campaign against one of the other election candidates but it turned out to be an own goal when she got a huge sympathy vote*. The popularity of the cliché dates from the second part of the twentieth century and has its origin in football where to score an own goal means to put the ball into one's own net and so give a point to the other side.

own worst enemy, to be one's is a hackneyed phrase meaning to cause oneself more harm or misfortune than anyone else does, as *He's his own worst enemy. Every time he gets a job he loses his temper and walks out*. As a cliché the expression dates from the twentieth century and is still widespread. The idea goes back to Greek and Roman times.

✤ P ✤

paddle one's own canoe is an idiom cliché meaning to be independent, to be self-reliant, as *Now that both her parents are dead she has no choice but to paddle her own canoe.* The expression is American in origin and dates from around the beginning of the nineteenth century. It then crossed the Atlantic and became popular in Britain. As a cliché it is still common today in informal contexts.

paint the town red is an idiom cliché meaning to go out celebrating, especially by going to bars, clubs, etc as *As soon as we heard that we had all passed the exams we started painting the town red.* The expression originated in America in the late nineteenth century, becoming popular in Britain in the twentieth century. It is still common today in informal contexts. Apart from the fact that its origins are American the derivation of the phrase is uncertain. It may simply refer to the fact that red is a cheerful, gaudy, passionate colour.

pale into insignificance is a hackneyed phrase used to mean that in comparison with something else something seems minor or trivial, as *She was feeling very sorry for herself at being on her own with a child, but her troubles paled into insignificance when she met a woman who was a widow with four children under five.* As a cliché the expression dates from the late nineteenth century. Despite the fact that it has rather a formal ring, it is still quite common today.

panic stations! is a catchphrase cliché used to indicate some form of emergency. As a modern cliché it is used humorously, as *Panic stations! My mother's coming round. We'd better do some clearing up fast.* In origin the phrase refers to a naval expression **be at panic station** meaning to be prepared for the worst. **Panic stations** in a humorous context dates from around the 1940s and as such is still common today.

paper over the cracks is an idiom cliché meaning to pretend that everything is fine and try to cover up any mistakes, disagreements, etc, as *Although they quarrelled all the time, they decided to try to paper over the cracks in their marriage for the sake of the children,* and *I know that you have major disagreements on the board but you will have to paper over the cracks if you want to sell the company.* In origin it refers to the practice of putting wallpaper on walls to hide the cracks. The expression was said to have been used by Otto von Bismarck in 1865 to describe the outcome of the Convention of Gastein by which it was agreed that Austria would administer the Danish province of Holstein and Prussia would govern Denmark. Its translation into English in 1910 is thought to have popularized the phrase in English. As a cliché and as a concept it is still popular today.

par for the course is an idiom cliché meaning what might be expected, usually something bad, as *I don't know why you were surprised that he let you down. It's par for the course as far as he's concerned.* The expression originates on the golf course where 'par' is used to describe the number of strokes regarded as standard for a particular hole. The expression began to be used figuratively in the general language from the early 1920s and as a cliché is common today, in informal, often derogatory contexts.

part and parcel is a doublet cliché used to refer to something that is an essential part of something, as *Taking the children to school is part and parcel of her job*. The expression was originally a legal term dating from the sixteenth century. It began to be used more generally from the early nineteenth century and is a common cliché today.

parting shot, a is a hackneyed phrase used to refer to an apt or effective remark that one makes as one is leaving, as *As he packed his clothes to leave her, her parting shot was that she had never loved him anyway*. As a cliché the expression dates from the late nineteenth century and is still common. In origin it is a variation of 'Parthian shot' which refers to the habit of the Parthians, famous archers and horsemen of the first century BC, of discharging arrows at their enemy as they rode away.

party line, the is a hackneyed phrase used to refer to the official policy of a political party, government, organization, etc, as *If he follows his conscience he will have to go against the party line and vote against the proposal*. The expression with regard to political parties originated in America in the nineteenth century but it came to be applied more generally in the middle of the twentieth century. It is still a common cliché today, often being found in the phrase **toe the party line**. See also *toe the line*.

party's over, the is an idiom cliché indicating that something, usually something pleasant, successful, etc, has come to an end, as *We're used to long summer holidays from school. Now we're starting work and the party's over. From now on we'll get only two weeks*. The expression has been popular since around the middle of the twentieth century and is still a common cliché today in informal contexts.

pass muster is an idiom cliché meaning to meet a required standard, as *This essay would just about pass muster in the exam but it is not up to your usual standard*. The expression is military in origin and means to pass a review without fault being found. As a cliché it probably dates from around the nineteenth century and is still popular today in rather informal contexts.

pass the buck is an idiom cliché meaning to try to avoid responsibility for something by passing it to someone else, as *It was the school bully who broke the school window but he tried to pass the buck by blaming the younger boys*. The expression originated in America in the nineteenth century, and was originally a term used in poker to refer to a piece of buckshot or other object that was passed to a player to remind him that he was the next dealer. In its figurative version the expression spread to Britain where it became a cliché in the twentieth century. It is still common today in informal or slang contexts. **The buck stops here** is a development of the expression. It means that the ultimate responsibility lies with the person referred to, as *The teacher in charge at the time will not be asked to take responsibility for the behaviour of the pupils. I am the headmaster and the buck stops here*. It was used by Harry S Truman, President of the United States, around 1949 and later became a cliché in both America and Britain, being used in informal and slang contexts.

pass one's sell-by date is an idiom cliché indicating that someone or something is no longer considered useful or effective, as *They're declaring people of my age redundant in the firm and taking on younger people. They think we're past our sell-by date.* As a cliché it dates from the later part of the twentieth century, being used in informal and often humorous or ironic contexts. In origin it refers to the date stamped on perishable goods, such as foodstuffs.

patience of Job is an idiom cliché meaning extraordinary patience or forbearing, as *She must have the patience of Job to look after all those young children and never lose her temper.* As a cliché it dates from the nineteenth century although Job's patience was recognized in print long before that. Job was a character in the Old Testament who bore all his trials with extreme patience although the actual expression, **patience of Job**, does not appear in the *Book of Job* in the Bible.

patter of tiny feet is a hackneyed phrase meaning children, being particularly applied to someone who is expecting, or is likely to be expecting, a baby, as *Jim and Mary have just got married and I wouldn't be surprised if we hear the patter of tiny feet before long.* The expression dates from the late nineteenth century. As a cliché today it is often used humorously or satirically. When used straight it sounds rather coy or twee.

pave the way is an idiom cliché meaning to prepare the way for something or to lead up to something, as *His early research paved the way for the discovery of the new drug*, and *It is hoped the informal discussions will pave the way for formal peace talks.* The expression dates from the sixteenth century and became popular in the nineteenth century. As a cliché it is much used today in a variety of

contexts. In origin it refers to the paving of a road which will make progress along it easier.

pay through the nose is an idiom cliché meaning to pay a great deal of money for something, as *They really paid through the nose for that house and now property prices have slumped and they can't sell it.* The expression dates from around the seventeenth century. Although the origin of the phrase is uncertain, it has been suggested that it is a reference to the 'nose tax' imposed in Ireland in the ninth century, by the Danes, those who did not pay it having to face the punishment of having their noses slit. As a cliché it is widespread today in informal contexts.

pays your money and you takes your choice, you is a hackneyed phrase used to mean that the choices before one are very similar in some way and so one might as well trust to luck when deciding, as *All of the essay questions seem equally difficult. It is a case of you pays your money and you takes your choice*, and *I haven't heard of any of these films that are on at the cinema. It will be a case of you pays your money and you takes your choice.* The expression dates from the nineteenth century and appeared in a nineteenth-century rhyme 'Whatever you please my little dears, You pays your money and you takes your choice.' As a cliché it probably dates from the late nineteenth century. It is still used today in informal and humorous contexts.

pearls before swine is an allusion cliché used to refer to something that someone is not capable of appreciating, as *You should never have suggested taking her to the opera. That's a case of pearls before swine if ever I heard one.* The expression refers to a Biblical passage, to *Matthew* (7:6) 'Neither cast ye pearls before swine.' As a cliché it dates from the nineteenth century. It is often used by rather snobbish people who look down on those who do not share their acquired tastes.

pecking order is an idiom cliché referring to the order of importance or rank in a group of people, as *We can't just sit at any table at the dinner. There is a very strict pecking order. All the senior executives sit at the tables near the top.* The popularity of the expression dates from the twentieth century. The phrase is based on the fact that scientists observed a social system in domestic hens by which each hen in a group is allowed to peck the hen below except for the hen at the end of the row who has to submit to being pecked but cannot do any pecking. This system mirrors similar strict chains of rank.

penny dropped, the is an idiom cliché used to indicate that one has just, and usually somewhat belatedly, understood the significance of a remark, act or situation, as *I couldn't understand why Mary kept shaking her head at me while I was telling Frank about Jim's affair with Jenny. The penny dropped when I realized that Frank is now going out with Jenny, and I didn't get the point of John's joke until I was going home in the bus and then the penny suddenly dropped.* In origin it refers to the dropping of a coin in a slot machine which works a piece of machinery. The expression dates from the early twentieth century and is still a popular cliché today.

penny for them, a is a hackneyed phrase used to ask someone what he or she is thinking about, as *You haven't heard a word I've said. A penny for them.* The expression is a shortened version of **a penny for your thoughts,** a saying which goes back to the sixteenth century, having appeared in John Heywood's proverb collection of 1546.

Both expressions are clichés today but the shorter form is the more common.

pick up the threads is an idiom cliché meaning to resume something from where one left off some time before, as *She took time off from her career to look after her children and she's now trying to pick up the threads again,* and *He lost touch with his old school friends when he went away to university but he picked up the threads during the summer holidays.* In origin it refers to beginning to use thread again in sewing. The expression became popular in the twentieth century and is still common today.

picture of health, the is an idiom cliché indicating that someone is looking extremely well. The expression dates from the late eighteenth century and has been a cliché since the late nineteenth century. It is still popular today being used as a compliment to someone's air of well-being, as *She has been ill but she's just returned from holiday and she is looking the picture of health.*

pièce de résistance is a foreign cliché, used to refer to the best example of something or the best part of something, as *He has painted many fine portraits but the one of his sister is the pièce de résistance.* It was originally used in France around the late eighteenth century to refer to the main or finest course of a meal. The expression was adopted into English and was applied in more general contexts. It is still popular today, there being no phrase in English which is quite so apt.

piece of cake is an idiom cliché used to refer to something that is extremely easy or simple, as *He said he thought the exam was a piece of cake but he failed it.* The expression was used by the armed forces in World

War 2 to describe an easy mission. Its ultimate origin is uncertain but it may be connected with 'cakewalk', originally a contest, popular among black Americans in the middle of the nineteenth century, in which couples had to devise innovative and intricate steps while promenading, the winners receiving a cake as a prize. As a cliché it dates from the twentieth century and is still popular today in informal contexts.

pie in the sky is an allusion cliché used to refer to the promise of some form of success or advantage that will never materialize, as *He says that he is planning to get a job abroad but it's all pie in the sky.* The expression is an allusion to a song sung by the International Workers of the World in the early part of the twentieth century. 'You will eat, bye and bye, in the glorious land above the sky! Work and pray, live on hay, you'll get pie in the sky when you die.' It became a cliché in America later in the century and crossed the Atlantic to Britain where it is still popular today in informal or slang contexts.

pig in a poke, buy see *buy a pig in a poke*

pin one's hopes on is a hackneyed phrase meaning to rely on something or someone to bring about the realization of one's hopes or dreams, as *They can't afford the price of the house but they're pinning their hopes on his aunt lending them some money* and *Their team are lying second at the moment and they're pinning all their hopes on their relay team winning the competition for them.* The expression dates from the nineteenth century, an earlier form having been **pin one's faith on**. It may have its origin in the badges which were once worn by troops to show who their leader was.

plain sailing is an idiom cliché used to refer to trouble-free progress, as *We had expected to have trouble getting planning permission for our new house but in fact it was all plain sailing.* The expression which dates from the nineteenth century is derived from the nautical phrase 'plane sailing' in which navigational calculations were made by plotting them on a flat plane rather than on the surface of a globe. As a cliché it is in widespread use today.

platform on which to build is a hackneyed phrase used to indicate a basis from which other things can be developed, as *These are not our final plans for nursery education but they are a platform on which to build.* As a cliché the expression dates from the second part of the twentieth century, being much used today by politicians and people in public life.

play ball is an idiom cliché meaning to cooperate, as *I thought we could form a car pool to take the kids to school but the other parents wouldn't play ball.* As a cliché the expression dates from the twentieth century and is common today in informal or slang contexts. In origin it refers to the cooperation required in order for two or more people to play a game with a ball.

play one's cards right is an idiom cliché meaning to use one's opportunities cleverly so as to gain maximum advantage, as *They are obviously interested in the project. If you play your cards right I think they might invest some money in it.* When used literally the expression obviously refers to card games. As a figurative expression the phrase dates from the eighteenth century, probably becoming a cliché in the nineteenth century. An earlier form of the cliché was **play one's cards well**.

play with fire is an idiom cliché meaning to do something very risky or dangerous, as *He knew that he was playing with fire having* an affair with his best friend's wife, and Someone should warn Jim that he's playing with fire by teasing Jack. The figurative use of playing with fire is a very old one. It became popular in the late nineteenth century and is a common cliché today.

pleased as Punch is a simile cliché meaning delighted, as She is as pleased as Punch at winning the competition, although the prize is a small one. The phrase refers to Punch of the traditional Punch and Judy Puppet show, in which Punch is portrayed as being very pleased with himself. The expression became popular in the middle of the nineteenth century and is a common cliché today.

plot thickens, the is a catchphrase cliché used to indicate that the situation is getting involved and dramatic. It originally referred to the plot of a play getting very involved. The expression was used by playwright George Villiers in his comedy The Rehearsal (1672) 'Ay, now the plot thickens very much upon us.' The phrase was used seriously in some Victorian and Edwardian melodramas and mystery stories. As a modern cliché it is usually used humorously or satirically, often being applied to situations that are not at all involved and certainly not dramatic, as Mary received some flowers at work and we all thought Jim had sent them, but Jim said he hadn't. The plot thickens.

pocket, in one's is an idiom cliché meaning influenced or controlled by someone, as Many people think that some of the council members are in the pocket of the local builder. The influence or control is often based on dishonesty and often involves bribes. As a cliché it dates from the twentieth century and in origin the phrase refers to the fact that people keep money in their pockets.

point of no return is a hackneyed phrase indicating a critical point in a project or situation which marks the stage after which there is no possibility of turning round or stopping, as Setting up the new business was so expensive that we thought of giving up but we had reached the point of no return. If we had given up we would have lost all our money. The term originated in aviation where it referred to the stage in a flight beyond which there would not be enough fuel to return to one's destination. It was used by airmen during World War 2, becoming a cliché in the second part of the twentieth century.

poor are always with us, the is a quotation cliché which is a slight misquotation from Biblical passages, such as Matthew (26:11) 'For ye have the poor always with you but me ye have not always', a statement made by Jesus to his disciples. As a cliché the expression dates from the twentieth century. It is used today mostly in humorous or ironical contexts, as She says her parents-in-law are like the poor, always with them. They are constantly popping in uninvited.

poor thing but mine own, a is a quotation cliché being a misquotation from Shakespeare's As You Like It (5:4) in which Touchstone says of Audrey 'an ill-favoured thing, sir, but mine own.' It is used as a deprecatory way of referring to a possession, although often one is quite proud of the possession so referred to, as Do you like my new car? It's a poor thing but mine own. As a cliché it dates from the middle of the nineteenth century. It is still used today but often by people of a literary bent.

pop the question is a hackneyed phrase meaning to propose marriage, as Did he go down on bended knee when he popped the question? The expression dates from the eighteenth century and is commonly used today in informal, and often humorous or satirical contexts, although some people would regard it as rather coy. In origin it refers to the person who is proposing marriage being so nervous or embarrassed that he blurts out the proposal as though it were exploding from him. In these enlightened times, of course, the popper of the question can be female.

pound of flesh is an allusion cliché meaning what is due or owed to one, as *I'm sure that our landlord will charge us for the broken chair. He is always one to exact his pound of flesh.* In origin it refers to Shakespeare's *The Merchant of Venice* (4:1) in which the moneylender, Shylock, demands the pound of flesh that was promised him when he lent Antonio money. As a cliché the expression dates from around the later part of the nineteenth century. It is still a widespread cliché today.

pour oil on troubled waters is an idiom cliché meaning to bring calm to an angry or troubled situation, as *Her brother and sister are always quarrelling and it is left to her to pour oil on troubled waters and restore family peace.* As a cliché the expression dates from the middle of the nineteenth century and is still common today. In origin it refers to an ancient practice of pouring oil on rough seas to try and create a calm surface.

powder one's nose is a euphemism cliché sometimes used by women to indicate that they are going to the toilet, as *I must just powder my nose before dinner.* Despite the fact that we live in a society where things are now discussed or mentioned that would once have been considered taboo or not polite, this cliché is still used today, although sometimes in humorous contexts. In origin the expression refers to the fact that women often freshen up their

make-up in a toilet or bathroom as well as attending to more basic bodily functions.

powers that be, the is an allusion cliché being a reference to a Biblical passage, to *Romans* (13:1) 'The powers that be are ordained of God.' It refers to those in authority. As a cliché the expression dates from the late nineteenth century. It is still used today, sometimes in humorous or satirical contexts, as *The powers that be have decided that our school summer holiday will be shorter this year*, and *The powers that be have sent a memo round saying we can work flexitime from now on.*

practice makes perfect is a proverb cliché indicating that the more one does something the better one gets at it. The proverb dates from the fifteenth century and has an equivalent in several other languages. As a cliché it is still popular today, often being used by parents to encourage their children in a pursuit that the parents favour but on which the children may resent spending time, as *You should spend more time at the piano. Practice makes perfect and you might get to play at the school concert.* It is sometimes used humorously or ironically, as *Why don't you try getting to work on time? You may find that practice makes perfect.*

prey on one's mind is an idiom cliché meaning to cause distress or anxiety to, as *Memories of the accident preyed on her mind for years*, and *It preyed on his mind that he might have been able to save the child's life if he had acted more promptly.* In origin it refers to an animal preying on another for food. As a cliché it dates from the later part of the nineteenth century but the expression is older than that.

prick up one's ears is an idiom cliché meaning to start listening attentively, as *The child pricked up his ears when he heard* his mother mention the word picnic. As a cliché it dates from the nineteenth century and is still popular today, mostly in informal contexts. The expression itself dates from the sixteenth century and in origin refers to a horse or other animal pricking up its ears at a sudden noise.

pride and joy is a hackneyed phrase used to refer to someone or something of which one is very proud, as *Their grandson is their pride and joy*, and *Those roses were your father's pride and joy and the dog has just dug them up*. The expression comes from a poem, *Rokeby* (1813) written by Walter Scott in which it was used to describe children. As a cliché it is still common today.

pride of place is a hackneyed phrase used to describe the prominent position given to something, as *Pride of place on their mantelpiece goes to the graduation photograph of their grandson*. As a cliché the expression dates from the middle of the nineteenth century and is still common today.

prime mover is a hackneyed phrase used to indicate the person or thing that has been the cause of something or that has been most effective in getting something started, as *The local headmistress was the prime mover in the campaign to keep the school open*, and *The murder of the child was the prime mover in the reform of the law*. As a cliché it dates from the twentieth century and is still popular today in a wide of contexts.

prime of life is a hackneyed phrase used to refer to the most vigorous period of one's life or to the time at which one's talents are at their peak, as *Her father died recently although he was in the prime of life*, and *Many people thought that the actress was in*

the prime of life when she decided to retire. As a cliché the expression dates from the middle of the nineteenth century although the idea of a period of life that is particularly vigorous goes back to ancient times and was defined by Plato in *The Republic* as a period of about thirty years in a man's life. Women came off a good deal worse with a period of only twenty years. A related expression is **in one's prime**, popularized by the character of Jean Brodie in Muriel Spark's novel *The Prime of Miss Jean Brodie* which was made into a film (1969). Both expressions are still common today, sometimes being used in humorous or ironic contexts.

proof of the pudding is an allusion cliché referring to a proverb **the proof of the pudding is in the eating**. Both the shorter version and the full proverb are still in common use today. The proverb indicates that it is possible to judge whether something is successful or not only when it has been put to the test and when one has found out whether it does what it was intended to do, etc, as *John is confident that he can mend the car himself but the proof of the pudding will be in the eating*, and *The education authorities think that the new exam system will be more effective but some of the teachers have doubts. The proof of the pudding will be in the eating*. The proverb dates from around the early part of the seventeenth century and in origin refers to the fact that one does not know whether a pudding mixture has been successful until it has been cooked and eaten.

proud parents is a hackneyed phrase often used by journalists, for examples as a caption to a picture, as *The proud parents congratulate the champion*, and *The proud parents leave the hospital with their baby son*. As a cliché the expression dates from the nineteenth century and is still popular today.

public enemy number one is a catchphrase cliché used to describe a person who is undesirable in some way to a particular group or person. The expression was originally applied to a notorious American Midwest outlaw, John Dillinger, by the then Attorney General, Homer Cummings, in the early 1930s. The expression spread to Britain and became popular after World War 2. It is a common cliché today, often being used in humorous or ironic contexts, as *He has been public enemy number one with Mary since he bought the car that she had her eye on*, and *I'm public enemy number one since I told the children they would have to finish their homework instead of going to the cinema*. In America the FBI keeps a list of the ten most wanted criminals but they are not individually ranked.

pull one's finger out is a hackneyed phrase often used as a vulgar instruction to someone to start working faster or more effectively, as *For goodness' sake pull your finger out or we won't get these orders out today*. It is not always used in the form of an actual instruction, as *If you don't pull your finger out we'll all have to work overtime tonight*. As a cliché it dates from the twentieth century, having its origins in RAF slang of the 1930s and is common today in less polite circles of society. An alternative form of the expression is **get one's finger out**.

pull one's socks up is an idiom cliché used to mean to make an effort to do better. It is often children who are at the receiving end of this cliché, as *If you don't pull your socks up you will find yourself repeating the year*, although its use is not confined to them. In origin it refers to smartening oneself up by pulling socks up that have slipped round one's ankles, a common problem for schoolboys wearing short trousers. As a cliché it dates from the twentieth century

and is a common exhortation today, much loved by people in authority.

pull out all the stops is an idiom cliché meaning to do one's utmost, as *If we pull out all the stops we may just get this work finished tonight* and *They pulled out all the stops to find a hospital bed for the sick child*. In origin the expression refers to organ playing. An organ's stops are used to change its sounds and by pulling them all out and bringing into play all the ranks of pipes, an organist can achieve the loudest possible sound. The term began to be used figuratively in the second part of the nineteenth century and is a widespread cliché today in all but the most formal contexts.

pull someone's leg is an idiom cliché meaning to tease or fool someone, as *I don't believe we're getting another week's holiday. You're pulling my leg!* The expression dates from the nineteenth century and was probably a cliché by the end of the twentieth century. It is still common today as an expression of incredulity in informal contexts. In origin it refers to tripping someone up by catching one of his or her legs on something such as a stick.

pull strings is an idiom cliché meaning to use one's influence or power to help bring something about, often secretly, as *At first he was turned down for the job but his father's an executive with the firm and he pulled a few strings*. As a cliché it dates from the twentieth century and is still common today in informal contexts. It is related to **pull the strings** which means to be the person who really, though not apparently, controls affairs or controls the actions of others, as *Mr Brown is the managing director but it's his deputy who pulls the strings*. The expression dates from around the late nineteenth century, being originally used in political contexts and then becoming more general. Both **pull strings** and **pull the strings** refer to puppetry where the puppet master operates the puppets by pulling strings. —

pull the other one is a catchphrase cliché used to express one's disbelief at something someone has said, as *You say the car is worth £12,000. Pull the other one!* The expression is a shorter version of **pull the other one, it's got bells on**. The latter may be a reference to the bells that were associated with the traditional court jester or fool. The expression is thought to date from the early 1920s and is a popular cliché today in very informal or slang contexts, the shorter version being the more common. See also **pull someone's leg**.

pull the wool over someone's eyes is an idiom cliché meaning to deceive or hoodwink someone, as *She was out with her boyfriend but she tried to pull the wool over her parents' eyes by saying she was at the library studying.* In origin it refers to someone pulling a wig, once generally worn, over someone's eyes so as to prevent him or her seeing clearly. The expression dates from the early nineteenth century. Like the practice it defines, the expression is still common today.

pull yourself together is a hackneyed phrase used to someone who is very upset about something and is showing emotion in some way. It is a typically British piece of advice given by people who believe one should **keep a stiff upper lip** and is often wrong advice since it is sometimes important to give rein to one's emotions, as in the case of grieving for a loved one. The expression dates from the twentieth century and is still commonly used today. In origin it refers to someone having fallen apart.

put in the picture is an idiom cliché meaning to give someone up-to-date information about something, as *Could you put me in the picture about what's been going on while I've been away?* The cliché dates from the twentieth century and is still common today in informal or slang contexts.

put one's best foot forward is an idiom cliché meaning to make the best attempt possible to succeed, as *The first year of the business is going to be difficult but we'll just have to put our best foot forward.* The expression dates from the sixteenth century and became a cliché around the middle of the nineteenth century. It is still popular today. The origin of the expression is obscure.

put one's foot in it is an idiom cliché meaning to do or say something tactless or clumsy, as *You certainly put your foot in it when you criticized Jane in front of John. She is his fiancée.* The expression has been in use since the eighteenth century and is still commonly used today in all but the most formal contexts.

put one's shoulder to the wheel see *shoulder to the wheel, put one's*

put on one's thinking cap is an idiom cliché meaning to devote some time to thinking or reflection, as *We have to find ways of raising money for the youth club. We'd better all put on our thinking caps.* The expression dates from the late nineteenth century, becoming a cliché in the twentieth century. The origin is uncertain. It has been suggested that it was a cap worn by judges when considering the appropriate sentence for a wrongdoer. An earlier form of the expression was **put on one's considering cap** but this is now obsolete.

put someone's nose out of joint is an idiom cliché meaning to hurt someone or make someone jealous by making him or her feel supplanted or displaced, as *His nose has been put out of joint since his parents brought home the new baby, although everyone is treating him very affectionately.* The expression dates from the sixteenth century and is still very common today. In origin it probably refers to someone getting a blow in the face which breaks his nose, although the nose does not actually have a joint.

put the cart before the horse see *cart before the horse, put the*

put two and two together is an idiom cliché meaning to work out or realize something on the basis of the information that one has, as *I don't know why she didn't put two and two together when he said he was working late at the office so much. Everyone else knew he was having an affair.* The implication is often that there is something suspicious about the situation that the information relates to. The expression dates from the nineteenth century and is a common cliché today. In origin it refers to simple arithmetic. An extension of the expression, and with the same meaning, is **put two and two together and make four**. A related expression is **put two and two together and make five** which means wrongly to deduce something from the facts.

Q

quality of life is a vogue cliché used to describe the non-materialistic side of life, as *If we move right into the country we shall take a huge cut in income and facilities but the quality of life for the children will be greatly enhanced. They will have lots of fresh air and plenty of room to play.* As a cliche it began to become popular in the 1970s and has stayed popular, with the increase in awareness of the importance of leisure and the environment.

quality time is a vogue cliché used to describe the time that a person devotes solely to a child, partner, etc, being too busy at work to spend any more time, as *We pick our daughter up from nursery at 6 o'clock and then we have an hour's quality time before she goes to bed.* The expression originated in America and has been a cliché in Britain since the mid 1980s. It is often the outward expression of an inward guilt complex about not spending more time with one's family.

quantum leap is a vogue cliché meaning a significant advance, a sudden breakthrough, as *The patient's recovery took a quantum leap when they treated her with the new drug.* The term comes from nuclear physics, a quantum leap being a sudden transition from one energy state to another within the submicroscopic atom. In physics the term dates from around 1950 and it began to be used figuratively a few years later, becoming a vogue cliché in Britain in the 1970s. It is one of several clichés that have scientific or specialist origins.

queer the pitch is an idiom cliché meaning to spoil things for someone, to make it impossible for someone to do something effectively, as *He had just persuaded her to go out with him when his sister told her that he was married and queered the pitch.* In origin a pitch was the place where a stall was set up and so if someone queered it, he or she prevented the trader from being able to sell things from it. The expression has been a common cliché since the late nineteenth century

quick as a flash is a simile cliché used to emphasize the speed of someone or something, as *The police were just about to arrest the burglar when, quick as a flash, he leaped over a fence and disappeared*, and *I told her to keep my news a secret but, quick as a flash, it was all round the village.* In origin the phrase refers to a flash of lightning, the expression **quick as lightning** also being common but not as common. The expression probably dates from the eighteenth century.

quick one, a twentieth century hackneyed phrase for a quick alcoholic drink. It is usually used in an informal context, as *Have you time for a quick one after work?*

quid pro quo (Latin for 'this for that') is a foreign cliché meaning tit for tat, the same in return. The expression has been in existence in English since the time of Shakespeare who used it in *Henry VI, Part 1* (5:3) 'I cry you mercy, 'tis but quid pro quo.' As a cliché it is still used today, as *It was a case of quid pro* quo; *they withdrew their ambassador and we withdrew ours,* but not in informal contexts. It tends to be used by people of a literary or academic bent but it is also used somewhat pompously by others who are trying to impress and who might well not know exactly what the expression means. The phrase is used in legal circles.

quiet as a mouse is a simile cliché used to emphasize the silence of someone or something, as *The child was told to be quiet as a mouse while she watched the robin feeding her young,* and *The whole house was quiet as a mouse when the burglar crept in.* The expression has been in existence since the sixteenth century and is an extremely widespread cliché. In origin it refers to the necessity of a mouse to keep absolutely silent in the presence of an enemy, such as a cat, although mice can be extremely noisy if they are scampering around behind woodwork.

quite frankly is a filler cliché usually used virtually meaninglessly, as *Quite frankly, I am strongly opposed to the scheme.* Some people use it extremely frequently without being aware of their somewhat annoying habit.

quite the reverse is a hackneyed phrase meaning the opposite of what has just been stated, as *She is not as naive as she appears; quite the reverse.* As a cliché it dates from the twentieth century. It is still quite common but it tends to be used by people who use rather a formal style of *speech.*

QT, on the is an abbreviation cliché meaning secretly or clandestinely, as *He has just got engaged to Mary but he is still going out with another girl on the QT.* The expression, which is short for **on the quiet**, is still used as a cliché by some people but it is rather dated nowadays.

R

race against time, a is a hackneyed phrase used to refer to an extremely urgent situation, as *I wish the ambulance would come. It's going to be a race against time to get her to hospital on time before the baby is born.* The cliché dates from the twentieth century and is still the standard phrase used today to express urgency. In common with many such phrases the level of urgency is frequently exaggerated. In origin the expression refers to the fact that time is often represented as being swift-moving, as in phrases such as **how time flies**.

rags to riches is a hackneyed phrase meaning from extreme poverty to wealth, usually as a result of one's own efforts, as *His story is one of rags to riches. He was a labourer's son who became a wealthy factory-owner.* It is often used in a business context. The expression became popular in the second half of the twentieth century and is still popular today. Stories of people who go from poverty to riches are the stuff of which dreams and fiction are made. The fairy tale *Cinderella* is a well-known example. A development of the theme is **rags to rags** which is used satirically to describe a person, family or firm who has gone from poverty to wealth and back to poverty again. It is used, for example, of a family firm which was started by someone very go-ahead and talented and then run down by successive family members of a singularly less talented nature.

rain cats and dogs is a hackneyed phrase meaning to rain very heavily, as *We had to cancel the picnic because it was raining cats and dogs*, and *It looks as though it's going to rain cats and dogs.* The expression probably dates from the eighteenth century and has been a cliché since the middle of the nineteenth century. It is still widespread today, in informal contexts, as befits a climate where the phenomenon is extremely common. The origin of the expression is uncertain. One suggestion is that in the days before there was efficient street drainage, cats and dogs could drown in the gutters during a heavy downpour.

rain or shine is a hackneyed phrase meaning come what may, as *Don't worry I'll be there, rain or shine.* As a cliché it dates from the twentieth century and is still popular today. In origin it refers to uncertain weather conditions which can often affect the holding of events or people's attendance at them.

rainy day, a is an idiom cliché used to refer to a time when one might be in financial difficulties. It is mostly used in the phrase **keep** or **save something for a rainy day** meaning to save some money while one has it against the day when one might not, as *He's getting a lot of overtime just now but he's spending the money as he earns it. He should be saving some of it for a rainy day.* The concept dates from the sixteenth century. As a cliché the expression dates from the late nineteenth century. In origin it refers to wet days when agricultural workers could not work and so would not earn any money.

rarin' to go is a hackneyed phrase meaning eager to get started on something, as *The child didn't want to start school at first but now she's rarin to go*. In origin it refers to a horse 'rearing' because it is anxious to be off. As a cliché it dates from the twentieth century and is still popular today in informal contexts. It is sometimes used ironically, as *Monday morning and everybody's rarin' to go to work*.

rat race, the is an idiom cliché used to refer to the relentless competitive struggle to stay ahead of one's competitors at work, in commerce, etc. It is often used just to describe the average work situation or modern life generally, as *He was a senior executive in the company but he got tired of the rat race and went to run a croft on a remote island*. The expression originated in America and became a cliché in Britain around the second half of the 1970s. As the struggle to get ahead gets ever fiercer the expression has got ever more popular.

rats deserting a sinking ship see *desert a sinking ship*

read my lips is a hackneyed phrase used to emphasize the truth of what one has just said. The phrase was popularized by US President George Bush in his speech accepting the Republican nomination for president in 1988 when he made a promise not to raise taxes, no matter how much Congress tried to persuade him 'I'll say no, and they'll push, and I'll say no, and they'll push again, and I'll say to them "Read my lips, no new taxes".' The phrase in fact predates this and is thought to have its roots in 1970s rock music. As a cliché today it is often found to emphasize a negative statement, as *Read my lips! I will not give you money to go to the cinema*.

ready for the fray see *eager for the fray*

red-carpet treatment is a hackneyed phrase used to indicate special treatment, usually when applied to that given to important guests, as *Of course the mayor didn't realize how bad the hospital food is. She got the red-carpet treatment and had a gourmet menu*. In origin it refers to a strip of red carpet traditionally laid out for a royal person or other VIP to walk on when making an official visit. The expression dates from the early twentieth century. It is still common today although it is often found in contexts that are critical of the practice.

red-letter day is an idiom cliché used to indicate a special or memorable day of some kind, as *Tuesday is a red-letter day for the children because they are appearing in the school play*. It is often a day which gives rise to a celebration but this is not always the case, as *It was a red-letter day for the whole family when the youngest daughter left home*. As a cliché it dates from the nineteenth century, although it goes back at least until the eighteenth century, and is widespread. In origin it refers to the practice, common from the fifteenth century on, of printing saints' days and feast days on calendars and almanacs in red.

red rag to a bull, like a is a simile cliché used to indicate that someone or something is a source of anger or fury to someone else, as *Don't mention his name to my mother. It's like a red rag to a bull. He once did her out of a lot of money*. As a cliché it dates from the late nineteenth century and is still widespread today. In origin it refers to the erroneous idea that bulls are infuriated by the sight of a piece of red cloth being waved in front of them, hence the red lining of the matador's cape in bull-fighting. In fact, bulls are colour blind and it is the movement, not the colour of the cape, that infuriates them.

red tape is an idiom cliché used to refer to unnecessary bureaucracy and the delays that this often leads to, as *She thought she would get permission to do her research work here fairly rapidly but she had reckoned without the red tape.* The expression is thought to have become popular in the nineteenth century and, in keeping with the fact that the phenomenon plays such a major role in our lives, it is still widespread today, always being used in a derogatory way. In origin it refers to the reddish ribbons that lawyers and bureaucrats use to tie their documents.

reinvent the wheel is an idiom cliché meaning to start from the beginning when there is no need to do so, to fail to take advantage of previous developments or experience in a situation, as *The new managing director has no knowledge of the business and refuses to ask other people for advice. He keeps trying to reinvent the wheel.* The expression dates from the second part of the twentieth century and is still popular today, especially in business contexts.

reliable source, a is a hackneyed phrase used to testify to the authoritative and dependable nature of one's sources for a story or for a piece of gossip, as *I have it from a most reliable source that he is planning to leave her.* It is frequently used by journalists who do not wish to reveal the identity of the source of a story. Frequently the sources are far from reliable, particularly when a piece of gossip is being handed on, it usually being the bush telegraph, rather than a reliable source, that has given rise to the information. As a cliché it dates from the twentieth century and it is as common today as the sources are unreliable.

rest is history, the is a hackneyed phrase used to indicate that no more need be said because it is already well-known, as *She married him when she was very young, She went off with someone else, He killed her lover and the rest is history*, and *He was born of very poor parents, got a scholarship to university, graduated in science and the rest is history*, As a cliché it dates from the twentieth century and may be based on the rather dated cliché **the rest is silence** from Shakespeare's *Hamlet* (5:2).

ride off into the sunset is a hackneyed phrase used to indicate the departure of someone or the ending of something in more or less happy circumstances, as *I didn't think those two would ever get together but they did and they've ridden off into the sunset.* The origin of the expression is not linguistic but visual since it refers to the classic ending of a Western film, popular from the 1930s on, in which the victorious hero literally rides off into the sunset having accomplished what he set out to do.

right as rain is a simile cliché meaning fine, all right, as *She's been ill but she's as right as rain now.* The expression dates from the late nineteenth century and is widespread today. The origin is uncertain but it may refer to the original meaning of 'right' as straight.

ring a bell is an idiom cliché meaning to call something to mind, to remind someone of someone or something, as *His name rings a bell but I cannot quite place him.* The expression dates from the early twentieth century and is still popular today, being used in all but the most formal contexts. In origin it refers either to the memory being alerted in the way that a doorbell or telephone bell alerts a person to make a response, or to the bell that rings on a machine that acts as a trial of strength in a fairground and rings a bell if the competitor is successful.

ring the changes is an idiom cliché meaning to vary one's choice of things, actions, etc, within a possible, and often limited, range, as *She doesn't have many clothes but she manages to ring the changes by wearing different skirts with different sweaters each day*. In origin the expression refers to the ancient art of bell-ringing in churches in which a series of church bells are rung in as many different sequences as possible. The expression took on a figurative meaning around the early seventeenth century. As a cliché it is still popular today, often being used with reference to clothes.

ring true is an idiom cliché meaning to seem likely to be true, as *Everyone else seemed to find her story convincing but it didn't ring true to me*. The expression dates from around the early twentieth century and is still a popular cliché today, having the alternative form **have the ring of truth**. In origin it refers to the practice of judging the genuineness of coins, in the days when they were made of precious metals, by striking them against a counter or something similar to see if they produced the right sound. If made of counterfeit metal they did not.

rising tide is an idiom cliché meaning an increasing amount or trend, as *There has been a rising tide of opposition to the scheme*. The expression began to be popular in the nineteenth century and is still common today, particularly among journalists. It has the obvious origin of the incoming sea tide.

risk life and limb is a hackneyed phrase, meaning to risk death or serious injury, whose alliteration has probably done much

to popularize it. The idea has been current since the seventeenth century and the expression has been a cliché since the middle of the nineteenth century, as *Volunteers risk life and limb to rescue climbers who get into difficulties on the mountain*. As a modern cliché it is used either in rather formal contexts or in humorous contexts where the degree of danger is deliberately exaggerated, as *Do you expect me to risk life and limb to get your kite down from that tree?* It is also use by journalists to heighten the danger in their accounts of rescues.

rock the boat is an idiom cliché meaning to disturb the stability of a situation, to cause trouble, as *The firm is just about financially stable again so don't rock the boat by asking for a huge salary increase*, and *We had all just agreed to forget about our difference of opinion when along came Jack who started rocking the boat*. The expression dates from the 1920s and was popularized by the title of a song 'Sit Down, You're Rockin' The Boat' in the musical *Guys and Dolls* (1950). It is still a common cliché today and has its origin in someone risking a small boat capsizing by moving around carelessly in it.

Roger is a catchphrase cliché which was originally used as a codeword of acknowledgement in the RAF and then in the general armed forces in World War 2. The letter R became Roger in the phonetic alphabet introduced in 1941. It had originally been Robert and stood for received (and understood). After the war the catchphrase spread to civilian life. It is still used today to indicate that something has been understood and agreed, but it tends to be used by older people with a military background or by people who are using it in a consciously humorous or ironic way.

rolling stone is an allusion cliché meaning someone who keeps moving around and never acquires much in the way of money or possessions, as *She hopes that he's going to get a job in the local factory and marry her but he's always been a rolling stone and doesn't want to settle down.* The phrase alludes to the proverb

a rolling stone gathers no moss which simply emphasizes the meaning of the shortened version. The proverb dates from the sixteenth century and is still popular today, despite the fact that in modern times moving on from job to job is often thought to be a good thing from the point of view of promotion.

roll on! is a hackneyed phrase used to indicate that one is awaiting the arrival of something with impatience, as *Roll on pay day! I'm absolutely broke!* and *Roll on summer! This weather is getting me down!* The cliché dates from the twentieth century and derives from military catchphrases of World War 1. These were **roll on the big ship** which expressed the wish that the war would end and a ship would come to take the troops home, and **roll on duration** which also expressed the wish that the war would come to an end, duration being a reference to the fact that volunteers in 1914 had joined up for the duration of the war. The cliché is still commonly used today in a variety of contexts.

Rome was not built in a day is a proverb cliché used to encourage someone to have patience by reminding him or her that aims can take a long time to achieve, as *I know your leg seems to be taking a long time to heal, but try to be patient. Rome wasn't built in a day, you know.* As a proverb it dates from the twelfth century and appeared in John Heywood's proverb collection of 1546. As a cliché it is still popular today. It is beloved of people who like to

make platitudinous remarks about other people's lives and it is resented by enthusiastic people who do not regard patience as a virtue.

rose between two thorns, a is an idiom cliché used of someone or something very attractive and placed between two people or things that are not attractive, as *It's a beautiful house but you should see the buildings on either side of it. Talk about a rose between two thorns!.* It has been a cliché since the nineteenth century and is now mostly used facetiously and ironically, as *Old Fred insisted on sitting between the twins at their eighteenth birthday party. He called himself the rose between two thorns.*

rose by any other name, a is an allusion cliché indicating that it is the basic qualities of people or things that count, not what they are called. As a cliché it probably dates from the nineteenth century. It is still popular today, especially with people of rather a literary bent and it is often used ironically, as *I used to be called his secretary. I'm now his personal assistant but I don't get any more money. A rose by any other name,* and *The ad is for cleansing operatives but they're looking for street cleaners. A rose by any other name.* The allusion is to a quotation from Shakespeare's *Romeo and Juliet* (2:2) and the quotation itself a **rose by any other name will smell as sweet** is also found as a cliché.

roses, roses all the way is an allusion cliché used to refer to a life of ease and comfort. As a modern cliché it is usually used in negative, often ironic contexts, as *He's been in and out of prison all his life. If she marries him it's not exactly going to be roses, roses all the way.* As a cliché the expression is often shortened to **roses all the way**, as *We now have a successful business but I can tell you that it has been far* *from roses all the way.* The phrase is an allusion to *The Patriot* by Robert Browning (1812–89). The cliché dates from the twentieth century and it is still common today, mostly being use by people of rather a literary bent.

rough diamond, a is an idiom cliché used to describe someone who is unsophisticated and rather uncouth in his or her manners and appearance, but who is usually an extremely worthwhile or kind person, as *He's a bit of a rough diamond but he's a very good worker,* and *She's a rough diamond but she was the only neighbour who offered to look after the children when their mother was in hospital.* In origin it refers to the fact that an uncut, unpolished diamond does not look attractive or valuable but may be extremely attractive and valuable after it is cut and polished.

rule the roost is an idiom cliché meaning to be in charge, to be dominant, as *There's no question of any discussions about anything in their house. Their father rules the roost and what he says goes,* and *The deputy manager loves ruling the roost when the boss is away.* As a cliché it dates from the twentieth century and is still popular today. It is found in all but the most formal contexts and is usually used in a derogatory way. In origin it may refer to a cockerel being in charge of hens and choosing which hen should roost near him but an alternative suggestion is that it is a variation of **rule the roast**, a term that originated in the fifteenth century with the same meaning as the present **rule the roost**. It probably referred to the fact that the person who was in charge of the roast (meat) was in charge of the household.

rule with a rod of iron is an idiom cliché used of someone in charge and meaning to be very strict or tyrannical, as *No one misbehaves in that class. The teacher rules them with a rod of iron.* In origin it may be a Biblical reference to

Revelations (2:27) 'Thou shalt break them with a rod of iron.' As a cliché it probably dates from the late nineteenth century and is still widespread today.

rumour hath it is a hackneyed phrase indicating that there is a rumour circulating about something, as *Rumour hath it that there is a new woman in his life.* As a cliché it dates from the late nineteenth century. Although it sounds rather archaic it is still used today, often by people of a literary bent and frequently in a humorous way.

run around like headless chickens is a simile cliché meaning to act in a totally disorganized, often panic-stricken, way, as *The managing director knew everything about the firm. Since he's resigned, the board are running around like headless chickens trying to find a suitable replacement,* and *The opposition accused the government of running around like headless chickens in the face of their economic difficulties.* In origin it refers to the fact that chickens continue to move convulsively for a time after having their heads removed. As a cliché it dates from the late part of the twentieth century.

run it up the flagpole is an idiom cliché, often used as a business cliché, meaning to give something a trial in order to gauge reactions to it, as *We can't decide on a cover for this book. Let's get a trial one done and give it to the salesmen to run it up the flagpole,* and *They have some doubts about the new product. They're going to run it up the flagpole and do a limited production run.* It is American in origin and dates from around the middle of the twentieth century, being a shortened form of **run it up the flagpole and see who salutes**. The longer expression points to the origin. As a cliché in Britain it is more recent, having become popular from the late 1970s. It is still common today, particularly in business circles.

run rings round is an idiom cliché meaning to defeat or surpass someone utterly, as *When it comes to marketing our firm can run rings round theirs*, and *You shouldn't worry about the tennis final. You will run rings round your opponent*. The term dates from the late nineteenth century and is still popular today in informal contexts. It is, for example, favoured by journalists when referring to a sporting rout. In origin it refers to the fact that a runner is so much better than the other competitors that he or she can move along the course while running in circles, rather than in a straight line, and still win.

run round in circles see *go round in circles*

Russian roulette, play is an idiom cliché used to mean to take part in a very risky undertaking the outcome of which is potentially ruinous or fatal, as *Jim's playing Russian roulette going out with Frank's wife while he's abroad. He'll kill him if he finds out*, and *Despite all the warnings about unsafe sex she still goes in for one-night stands. She certainly believes in playing Russian roulette*. In origin it refers to a game played by Russian officers at the court of the Czar in which each player, using a revolver that contained one bullet, spun the cylinder of the gun and aimed it at his head. Since the cylinder contained six chambers there was one chance in six that he would kill himself. As a cliché it dates from the first part of the twentieth century and is still widespread today.

S

safe and sound is a doublet cliché used to emphasize that someone is free from danger and unharmed. The expression, probably because of its alliteration, is a very old one, dating from around the beginning of the fourteenth century and remaining in use through the centuries. It is a popular cliché today, being much used by journalists among others, as *The missing child has been found safe and sound.*

sail close to the wind is an idiom cliché meaning to come very close to breaking the law or rules, as *The police have their eye on the market trader. He has never been prosecuted for receiving stolen goods but he sails very close to the wind.* In origin the expression refers to a ship or boat sailing so close to the wind that it is dangerous. The figurative expression dates from the nineteenth century and became a cliché towards the end of the century. Like the practice which it describes, the cliché is still common today, being found in all but the most formal contexts. An older form of the expression is **sail near to the wind**.

salt of the earth, the is an allusion cliché, to a Biblical passage (*Matthew*, 5:13) in which Jesus told those who were persecuted for him and his beliefs 'Ye are the salt of the earth.' The metaphor refers to the fact that salt was a very valuable commodity since it was used not only to give flavour to food but also to preserve it. As a cliché it dates from the middle of the nineteenth century and refers to people who are really worthwhile, having all the sterling qualities, such as kindness, loyalty, etc, as *We really miss our next door neighbour. She was the salt of the earth.*

sauce for the goose is sauce for the gander, what is is a proverb cliché basically indicating that people should be treated equally whatever their gender. The proverb appeared in John Ray's collection of 1678. It could be said to be the forerunner of equality for women although it took a long time for actuality to catch up with the proverb. As a cliché it is still popular today, as *Why shouldn't she have an affair? Her husband's had a mistress for years. What is sauce for the goose is sauce for the gander.* It is often now shortened to **what is sauce for the goose**, the rest of the proverb being understood, as *If he thinks that he can go out on Saturday afternoons without the children, why shouldn't she? After all, what's sauce for the goose.*

saved by the bell is an idiom cliché used to indicate that because of the chance intervention of someone or something, one has been saved from some form of difficult or dangerous situation, as *My mother has just asked me how I had done in my college exams when the first of her guests arrived for the party. Saved by the bell!* In origin it refers to the bell rung at the end of a round of boxing. As a cliché it dates from the second part of the twentieth century and is still popular today.

save for a rainy day see *rainy day, a*

163

saving grace, one's is a hackneyed phrase used to refer to someone's redeeming feature which compensates for his or her negative qualities, as *She was an absolutely dreadful boss. Her saving grace was her sense of humour*. As a cliché it dates from the late nineteenth century and is common today. In origin it refers to the theological concept of grace which delivers people from eternal damnation.

say the least, to is a hackneyed phrase used to indicate that one is stating the case as mildly as possible, as *It will be, to say the least, a difficult journey*, and *The repairs, to say the least, will be rather expensive*. It is sometimes used more or less meaninglessly by people to whom it has simply become a habit. As a cliché it dates from the middle of the nineteenth century and is still in current use.

school of hard knocks, the is a hackneyed phrase used to refer to experience of life. It is often used to contrast that with further education, often in rather a rancorous way, as *They've started employing young graduates at management level. That doesn't give much of a chance to those of us who were educated at the school of hard knocks*. The expression dates from the nineteenth century and is still common in some contexts today. It is particularly favoured by those who have made a lot of money without benefit of formal education.

sea change, suffer a see *suffer a sea change*

seamy side of life, the is an idiom cliché used to describe the unpleasant, dirty, etc side of life, perhaps the realistic aspect, as *She wants to be a social worker but she'll never cope with the seamy side of life. She has very wealthy parents and has led a very sheltered life*. In origin it refers to the side of a garment which has the seams of the cloth on it. Shakespeare used the idea in *Othello* (4:2) 'He turned your wit the seamy side without', and it has been a popular concept ever since. As a cliché it dates from the later part of the nineteenth century.

second to none is a hackneyed phrase used to indicate that someone or something is outstanding, as *He is second to none in English cricket at the present time*. It is often used as a gross exaggeration, as *I am not surprised the village fête was a success. As an organizer she is second to none*. The idea probably goes back to Chaucer's day but the expression itself first appeared in Shakespeare's *The Comedy of Errors* (5:1) 'Of credit infinite, highly beloved, Second to none that lives here.' It became a cliché around the middle of the nineteenth century and is still common today.

search me is a catchphrase cliché used to indicate that one has no knowledge or information on the subject at issue, as *Search me! I've no idea where he gets his money from*. The expression is American in origin and dates from the early part of the twentieth century. It is a common cliché today being used as an exclamation in informal contexts. In origin it refers to someone being searched to see if he or she had any information.

see a man about a dog is a catchphrase cliché used in humorous contexts to indicate that one does not wish to reveal one's destination when one leaves a room, as *Well it's time I went. I have to see a man about a dog*. It is sometimes a euphemism cliché for going to the toilet (see also powder one's nose) and is mostly used by men. The expression has been popular since the late nineteenth century and is still current.

see eye to eye is an allusion cliché meaning to agree but usually used negatively, as *I wouldn't ask them both to be on the committee. They do not see eye to eye on anything. There is no point in continuing the discussion. We will never see eye to eye.* The cliché is a reference to a Biblical passage in *Isaiah* (52:8) 'Thy watchmen shall lift up the voice; with the voice together shall they sing; for they shall see eye to eye, when the Lord shall bring again Zion.' As a cliché it dates from the later part of the nineteenth century and is still common today.

see how the land lies is an idiom cliché meaning to check out and consider the circumstances of a situation before taking action, as *I am not sure how long we will stay with our friends. It depends how many of their family are at home. We shall just have to see how the land lies.* As a cliché it dates from the middle of the nineteenth century and is still popular. It is originally a nautical idiom meaning to get one's bearings.

see the wood for the trees, cannot is an idiom cliché used to indicate that someone is unable to obtain a general or comprehensive view of a situation because of paying too much attention to detail, as *There is no point in asking Mary to review our staffing levels. We'll get such a detailed report that we won't have time to read it. She just can't see the wood for the trees.* The expression is always used in the negative although the negative takes various forms, as *Peter is taking weeks to work out population trends in the area. He never could see the wood for the trees.* The expression dates from the sixteenth century, probably becoming a cliché around the beginning of the twentieth century. It is a common way today of describing someone who is over-meticulous. In origin it suggests that someone is so intent on looking at the individual trees that he or she misses the general view of the wood.

see with one's own eyes is a hackneyed phrase meaning to witness something for oneself or have personal proof of something, as *I would not have believed that she would hit a child if I had not seen her do it with my own eyes.* The expression dates from around the beginning of the eighteenth century, becoming a cliché later in the century and being still current today.

see you later! is a hackneyed phrase used as a greeting to someone on parting from him or her, as a substitute for goodbye or cheerio. The expression is used whether or not the two people concerned are likely to meet again. For example a hairdresser might use it to a chance customer. The expression became popular in the 1980s and is still extremely popular today.

sell down the river is an idiom cliché meaning to act treacherously towards someone, as *They thought he was a trusted employee but he sold the company down the river by telling their competitors their trade secrets.* In origin the expression refers to the practice in America of slave-owners in the upper Mississippi selling slaves down river to the much harsher life on the cotton and sugar plantations of Louisiana. The expression began to be used figuratively in the late nineteenth century and is still common today.

sell like hot cakes is a simile cliché meaning to be sold very quickly, to be a great commercial success, as *His new novel is selling like hot cakes.* The expression is American in origin and refers to the rapid sale of hot cakes, such as pancakes, at fairs, etc. As a general expression in America it dates from the middle of the nineteenth century. It became a cliché in Britain in the twentieth century and is still common today in all but the most formal contexts.

separate the sheep from the goats is an allusion cliché which refers to a Biblical passage *Matthew* (25:32) 'And before him shall be gathered all the nations; and he shall separate them one from the other, as a shepherd divideth his sheep from the goats. And he shall set the sheep on his right hand but the goats on the left.' The expression means to separate the good from the bad, the clever from the stupid, the competent from the incompetent, etc, as *I think this exam will separate the sheep from the goats.* As a cliché the expression probably dates from the nineteenth century and is still common. There are two other clichés which also refer to the good and bad, the superior and the inferior, etc being divided into their categories by some form of test. They are **separate the grain from the chaff** which as a cliché dates from the nineteenth century and **separate the men from the boys** which dates from the twentieth century.

serious money is a vogue cliché of the 1980s, a decade in which money was considered even more important than it usually is. It has survived into the present decade and means money in considerable quantities, as *You would get a stake in that company only if you had serious money to invest,* and *there is serious money to be made in the antiques trade.*

set the Thames on fire is an idiom cliché meaning to be very successful or famous. It is always used in negative, or implied negative, contexts, as *He was a hard-working pupil but we knew he would never set the Thames on fire,* and *Mark will make her a good enough husband but he's not the kind you can imagine setting the Thames on fire, is he?* The expression dates from the eighteenth century and has been a cliché since the middle of the nineteenth century. The expression has been used of other rivers in other languages.

seventh heaven, in is an idiom cliché meaning to be extremely happy, as *She was in seventh heaven when she discovered that she was going to have a baby.* In origin it refers to the fact that both Moslems and the ancient Jews recognized seven heavens in their faiths, the seven heavens corresponding to the seven planets. The seventh and highest of these was the abode of God and the angels. The expression began to be used without any religious significance in the nineteenth century and as a cliché dates from the middle of the nineteenth century. It is still a standard expression of happiness today.

sex rears its ugly head is a catchphrase cliché used to indicate that sex has become involved in a situation, as *We thought that Frank and Jenny were just friends but sex seems to have reared* its ugly head, and *You never get very far in a modern novel before sex rears its ugly head.* The expression became popular in the 1930s. It is still current today in humorous or satirical contexts. The origin is uncertain. It may refer to the rising of a penis or it may refer to the rearing of a serpent's head, perhaps an allusion to the serpent in the Garden of Eden. Other things can be substituted for 'sex' in the expression as **money rears its ugly head**.

shadow of one's former self a is an idiom cliché used to indicate that someone has become much thinner and weaker than before, as *This was the first time I had seen him since he had been ill. I was shocked to see that he is a shadow of his former self.* The expression is also used to indicate a diminution in power or fame, as *It is amazing to think he was one of the world's major political leaders. He is now a shadow of his former self and living in obscurity.* As a metaphor for emaciation the phrase has been in use since the sixteenth century. As a cliché the expression dates from the middle of the nineteenth century and is still common.

shape of things to come, the is a quotation cliché, the expression having been popularized by the title of H G Wells' novel, *The Shape of Things to Come* (1933), although the idea was referred to by Shakespeare in *Troilus and Cressida* (1:3) 'giant mass of things to come.' The phrase became a cliché not long after its use by Wells and is still common, as *We should have known when the first few people lost their jobs because of computerization that this was the shape of things to come.*

shape or form, in any is a doublet cliché meaning of any kind whatsoever. As a cliché it dates from the later part of the nineteenth century and is still a common form of emphasis, as *She will not eat meat in any shape or form.*

share and share alike is a hackneyed phrase meaning to divide something equally. The expression dates from the sixteenth century and has been a cliché since the later part of the nineteenth century. As a modern cliché it is frequently used to children in an effort to get them to share with their friends or siblings, as *It is selfish to keep all your chocolate to yourself. You should offer some to your friends. Share and share alike.*

shed light on is an idiom cliché meaning to explain or clarify something, as *No one can shed any light on the mystery of how the burglar got into the house.* The expression was used literally from the fourteenth century. The figurative expression became a cliché in the later part of the nineteenth century and is still common.

shipshape and Bristol fashion is an idiom cliché meaning tidy and orderly, as *We'd better leave the place shipshape and Bristol fashion for the next tenant coming in.* The expression is nautical – Bristol was a famous English port – in origin and has been a general cliché since the middle of the nineteenth century. It is still found today but it is rather dated and is mostly used by older people.

ships that pass in the night is an allusion cliché used to describe people who meet briefly and then go their separate ways, as *People who meet at conferences are often ships that pass in the night. Very few of them keep in touch with each other.* It is a reference to a passage in a poem by Henry Wadsworth Longfellow. The poem was published in 1873 in *Tales of a Wayside Inn* as 'The Theologian's Second Tale'. The reference is 'Ships that pass in the night and speak to each other in passing.' As a cliché it dates from the later part of the nineteenth century. It is often used today with reference to brief relationships, sometimes of a sexual nature, as *He didn't know that she had had a child by him. He thought he and she were just ships that passed in the night.*

shoot oneself in the foot is an idiom cliché meaning to harm oneself or do oneself a disservice, often while trying to cause harm to someone else, as *The politician was trying to cause embarrassment to the government but he ended up by shooting himself in the foot.* The expression originated in America, the derivation being the obvious one of having an accident with a gun while getting ready to shoot someone, although it sometimes implied that the 'accident' was deliberate to escape military service. As a cliché in Britain it dates from the later part of the twentieth century. Like the practice it describes, it is common today, being used in informal or slang contexts.

short and sweet is a hackneyed phrase used to indicate that something, although brief, is pleasant, lively, satisfactory, etc, as *If you are asked to write a report on a meeting it is best to keep it short and sweet*. The saying dates from the the sixteenth century and has been a cliché since the late nineteenth century. It is often now used ironically, as *He didn't spend much time telling us we were redundant. It was short and sweet*.

shot one's bolt is an idiom cliché meaning to have done all that one is able to do, to have exhausted one's resources, as *They came up with a series of threats to try to make us do as they asked, but we went on refusing and it became obvious that they had shot their bolt*, and *The champion started the marathon race at a very fast pace but halfway through it was obvious that he had shot his bolt and had to retire from the race*. The expression comes from an old proverb **a fool's bolt is soon shot** which probably dates from the thirteenth century. In origin it refers to medieval archery in which the bolt was a short, heavy, blunt-headed arrow fired from a crossbow. An archer who had shot all his bolts was in a perilous position. The expression to **have shot one's bolt** has been a cliché since the middle of the nineteenth century and is still common.

shoulder to the wheel, put one's is an idiom cliché meaning to begin to make a vigorous effort or to work hard, as *The workforce is really going to have to put its shoulder to the wheel if this order is going to be ready in time*. The expression has been popular since the eighteenth century and is still a common cliché today, usually being used to exhort people to maximum effort. It is often used in humorous contexts, as *As usual the headmaster will be telling us to put our shoulders to the wheel and our noses to the grindstone if we want to get through the exams*. In origin it refers to someone pushing a cart that had got stuck in mud.

show must go on, the is a catchphrase cliché meaning that everything must go on as normal, no matter what happens, as *Half the sales assistants are off with flu but the show must go on. The customers are queueing to get in*. The expression was originally a theatrical one, literally meaning that the show had to go, irrespective of what had happened, and in this context dates from the nineteenth century. It became a more general cliché in the twentieth century and is still common today.

sick and tired is a hackneyed phrase meaning completely tired, bored or annoyed at something, as *I am sick and tired of listening to her complaining*, and *We are sick and tired of having to ask our neighbour's son to turn his CD player down*. As a cliché it dates from the twentieth century and is still common today.

sick as a dog is a simile cliché meaning to be very sick, to vomit violently, as *We were both sick as a dog after we ate the mussels. They must have been off*. The expression dates from the sixteenth century and is still common today in informal contexts. There is no obvious reason for believing that dogs are more likely to be sick than any other animals.

sick as a parrot is a simile cliché meaning very unhappy or depressed, often at one's own failure and another's success. As a cliché it dates from the second part of the twentieth century, as *She was sick as a parrot when her friend bought the house that she had wanted*, and is still common today in informal contexts. In the late 1970s it became associated with the reaction of those connected with a losing football team, as *When asked by the commentator how he felt at the end of the match, the manager said that he was sick as a parrot*. The origin of the phrase is unclear. It may be connected with psittacosis, a disease of parrots and other birds that can spread to humans. It may also be connected with an older expression **melancholy as a parrot**.

sight for sore eyes, a is an idiom cliché used to refer to someone or something that is a pleasure to see, as *How nice to see you! You're a sight for sore eyes*, and *The little country cottage was a sight for sore eyes. It was so pretty.* As a cliché it dates from the late nineteenth century and is still common, being used in informal contexts. The implication of the phrase is that the person, etc is such a welcome sight that he or she will bring pleasure to, and so cure, sore eyes.

signed, sealed and delivered is a hackneyed phrase used to indicate that something has been brought to a satisfactory conclusion. Originally it referred to legal documents, such as property deeds, but it came to be used in more general contexts, becoming a cliché in the twentieth century, as *Here are our holiday tickets. Signed, sealed and delivered.*

sign of the times, a is an allusion cliché used to indicate that something is typical of the times we live in, as *It's terrible seeing all these people sleeping rough. Still, I suppose it's a sign of the times. There is so much poverty around.* The expression is a reference to a Biblical passage. According to *Matthew* (16:3), Jesus, when asked by the Pharisees to show them a sign from heaven said, 'O ye hypocrites, ye can discern the face of the sky; but can ye not discern the signs of the times?' As a cliché it dates from the twentieth century and is still common.

silent majority, the is a hackneyed phrase used to describe the bulk of the population who attract less attention than their more vocal counterparts, it being the assumption that they are quite happy with their lot and with how things are going, as *The politician says that the silent majority are in favour of more roads, and that there are just a few protesters who go from site to site.* It is often used in political contexts, being much favoured by politicians and others in public life and by journalists. The expression probably dates from the 1920s and was popularized by Richard Nixon, President of the United States, in a speech on the Vietnam War made in 1969.

sixes and sevens, at is a hackneyed phrase meaning in a state of confusion or disorder, as *There are so many people sick that we have been at sixes and sevens all morning.* The expression has its origin in a game of dice, although which game is not clear. As a cliché the expression probably dates from the twentieth century and is common today in informal contexts.

six of one and half-a-dozen of the other is a hackneyed phrase indicating that there is little or no difference between two things or people, as *It doesn't matter which of the trains you take. It's six of one and half-a-dozen of the other. They go by different routes but get in at about the same time*, and *Either of the candidates would be suitable for the job. It's six of one and half-a-dozen of the other.* As a cliché it dates from the later part of the nineteenth century and is common today in informal contexts.

sixty four thousand dollar question, the is a hackneyed phrase used to describe a question which is very difficult or impossible to answer, as *When do we expect to finish painting the house? That's the sixty four thousand dollar question.* American in origin, the expression dates from the 1950s before becoming a cliché in Britain in the late 1960s. In origin it refers to the title of an American television quiz show on which

$64,000 was the top prize. An earlier expression was **the sixty-four dollar question** which was derived from a CBS radio quiz show 'Take it or Leave It', in which the top prize was $64 dollars and which was broadcast in the 1940s.

skeleton in the cupboard, a is an idiom cliché used to refer to a shameful secret, as *Every family has the odd skeleton in the cupboard*, and *The press are snooping around to see what skeletons in the cupboard they can find in the politician's family*. In origin it refers to a murder victim being hidden away in a cupboard until he or she became a skeleton. As a cliché it dates from around the middle of the nineteenth century. The cliché is still popular today and the skeletons still common.

slave over a hot stove is a hackneyed phrase used to refer to cooking or loosely to refer to housework generally. As a cliche it dates from the twentieth century and is still common today, often being used in humorous or satirical contexts, as *I've been slaving away all day over a hot stove and now they've phoned to say they can't come to dinner*, and *She says that she rushes home from work to slave over a hot stove but in fact she has a housekeeper*.

slight technical hitch, a is a hackneyed phrase used as an excuse for the breakdown of a machine or the delay or non-running of a service. It was common with regard to transport until very recently, as *We apologize for the delay to the 15.30 Edinburgh train. This is due to a slight technical hitch*, and *We apologize to passengers travelling on the 16.00 flight to Milan. The plane has been delayed owing to a slight technical hitch*. Recently those not providing the promised transport service have tended to offer seemingly more specific, but no more enlightening,

reasons, as *We apologize to the delay to the 17.00 service to Aberdeen. This is due to trouble with the overhead lines at Berwick*. This supposed increase in information may well have occurred as passengers grew suspicious and intolerant of 'slight technical hitches'.

slip on a banana skin see *banana skin, a*

slowly but surely is a hackneyed phrase meaning steadily, as *At first the favourite was away out in front. Then slowly but surely the other horse gained on him*. As a cliché the expression dates from the middle of the nineteenth century. In origin it refers to Aesop's fable about the hare and the tortoise in which the steady progress of the tortoise made him a victor in his race against the apparently faster hare.

smell a rat is an idiom cliché meaning to suspect that something is not quite right, as *We smelled a rat when the supposed council workman couldn't find his identification card*, and *The neighbours smelled a rat when they saw the open window. They phoned the police who caught the burglar*. The expression has been in use since the sixteenth century and has been a cliché since the middle of the eighteenth century. In origin it refers to a dog or cat sniffing out a rat.

social whirl, the is a hackneyed phrase used to describe a full social life or social life generally. As a cliché it dates from the late nineteenth century. It is still used today but often in humorous or ironic contexts, as *I left work, picked up the children, went to the supermarket then cooked the evening meal. Just the usual social whirl*.

Sod's law see *anything that can go wrong will go wrong*

so far so good is a hackneyed phrase indicating that progress up till now has been good, with the implication that one cannot rely on this favourable state of affairs continuing, as *It's very tricky driving along this narrow track but so far so good*. As a cliché the expression dates from the middle of the nineteenth century and it is still popular today.

some of my best friends are . . . is a catchphrase cliché which is often used as an excuse for prejudice or bigotry, as *I have absolutely nothing against homosexuals. Some of my best friends are gay*. The expression dates from the 1940s or earlier and was originally used of people of Jewish descent, as *I am not anti-semitic. Why some of my best friends are Jewish*. It is still common today but often in humorous or satirical contexts, as *I don't think we should get rid of the male sex. Some of my best friends are men*, and *I support animal rights but I care about human rights too. After all, some of my best friends are humans*.

some other time is a hackneyed phrase often used as a delaying technique or as an attempt to postpone something indefinitely, as *I would love to have lunch with you some time, but I am very busy just now. Some other time, perhaps*. Frequently it is effectively a euphemism cliché for never. It is an expression with which children become familiar at an early age, as *No, I'm sorry we can't go to the beach today, but some other time when mummy and daddy are not so busy*. As a cliché it dates from the twentieth century.

son and heir is a hackneyed phrase used to refer to the eldest son of a family and frequently to the first, and possibly only, son born to a family, irrespective of whether or not there is anything much to be heir to. It reflects an inheritance law which favours the first born male child. As a cliché the expression probably dates from the late nineteenth century, but it goes back to Shakesperian times. Nowadays it is frequently used by journalists, as *Pictured right are Mr and Mrs Brown with their son and heir leaving his christening ceremony*, or in humorous contexts.

so near and yet so far is a hackneyed phrase used to indicate that something is close but still not attainable, sometimes with the implication that it will never be attainable, as *He very nearly broke the record for the course, but he fell just before the finishing line. So near and yet so far*. As a cliché the expression dates from the later part of the nineteenth century, although the idea goes back to Roman times. Nowadays it is frequently used in humorous contexts, as *Although he had drunk so much, he almost made it home before he was sick. So near and yet so far!*

sour grapes is an idiom cliché used to describe the attitude of someone who disparages something which he or she would like to have but, for some reason, cannot have, as *Don't worry about what Mary says about your new car. It's just sour grapes. She can't afford one*. In origin the expression refers to Aesop's fable about the fox and the grapes in which the fox says that the grapes are sour when he cannot reach them. As a cliché the expression dates from the nineteenth century

speak the same language is an idiom cliché used of people who understand each other very well, often sharing the same attitudes, views, etc, as *They don't mix socially but when it comes to business they speak the same language*. As a figurative expression it dates from the nineteenth century, becoming a cliché in the twentieth century and being still popular today.

spend a penny is a euphemism cliché for going to the toilet. Even in these enlightened days, euphemisms for attending to basic human functions are thought to be necessary and there is the problem of the half-remembered conventions about whether toilet is acceptable, whether one should call it lavatory, or whether one should play safe but informal and just go to the loo. In origin the expression refers to the penny that one had to put in the slot of a cubicle in a public toilet before gaining admittance. See also *powder one's nose* and *see a man about a dog*.

spend more time with one's family is a euphemism cliché used instead of admitting that one has had to leave one's job for some reason, either because one has been sacked or because one has resigned for some rather personal or complex reason. The expression became popular in the 1980s being an excuse given by some politicians in ministerial positions for resigning. It is now frequently used in humorous or satirical contexts.

spick and span is a hackneyed phrase meaning neat and clean, as *My mother says we can do some baking as long as we leave the kitchen spick and span*. The expression is made up of two obsolete words. 'Spick' means a spike or nail and 'span' means a wood chip. The expression refers to the time of sailing ships when a ship that was spick and span was one in which all the spicks and spans were new. As a figurative expression, it has been popular since the the later part of the nineteenth century and is still common.

spill the beans is an idiom cliché meaning to reveal something that was meant to be kept secret, as *We wanted to know what had happened at the confidential meeting, so we persuaded Jim who was taking the notes to*

spill the beans. The expression is American in origin and has been a cliché since the first part of the twentieth century.

spilled milk see *cry over spilled milk*

spirit is willing, the is an allusion cliché to a Biblical passage. It is a reference to *Matthew* (26:41) where Jesus gives advice to his disciples at the last supper 'Watch and pray, that ye enter not into temptation; the spirit indeed is willing, but the flesh is weak.' As a cliché it dates from the late nineteenth century. As a modern cliché it often means simply that, though one would very much like to do something, one simply does not feel up to it, as *I'd love to come to the cinema but I've just got home from working late and I'm exhausted. The spirit is willing but the flesh is weak*. It is often used in humorous contexts.

square peg in a round hole, a is an idiom cliché used to describe someone who is not at all suited to his or her current position, or who is not at all comfortable with it, as *His father was a doctor and persuaded him to study medicine, but he is a square peg in a round hole and hates it*. As a cliché it dates from the later part of the nineteenth century and is still widespread today.

stalking horse is an idiom cliché used to describe some form of pretext, or someone who takes part in some form of pretext. In origin it refers to the practice of some hunters, when stalking deer or other game, of dismounting and hiding behind their horses until they are within shooting range of their prey. In the 1980s and 1990s it has become particularly associated with political candidacy where someone who is not a serious contender for a position, such as the leadership of a party, pretends to be so in order to make it easier for someone else to put himself or herself forward. The figurative use of the expression has been in use since the sixteenth century, Shakespeare having used it in *As You Like It* (5:4) 'He uses his folly like a stalking-horse and under the presentation of that he shoots his wit.'

stand up and be counted is an idiom cliché meaning to show publicly or otherwise obviously one's opinion, attitude, loyalty, etc, especially if this is held only by a minority of people or if it is unpopular, as *We feel that there is a great deal of opposition to the new motorway but sometimes those who are opposed to it are reluctant to stand up and be counted.* The expression is American in origin and refers to standing up so that one's vote can be counted in some form of poll. As a cliché it dates from the twentieth century and is still popular today.

stem the tide is an idiom cliché meaning to halt the course of something, as *The government is trying to stem the tide of opposition to their economic policies.* As a cliché the expression dates from the late nineteenth century and is still popular today. In origin it refers to the holding back of the ocean tides.

storm in a teacup, a is an idiom cliché meaning a fuss over nothing, as *The two families won't speak to each other but it was all a storm in a teacup over two children fighting.* As a cliché it dates from the later part of the nineteenth century and is still popular today as indeed are fusses over nothing.

straight and narrow, the is a hackneyed phrase which is probably an allusion cliché to a Biblical passage 'Strait is the gate, and narrow is the way, which leadeth unto life.' (*Matthew* 7:14). The expression, which

means virtue or a virtuous way of life, became popular in the nineteenth century, becoming a cliché in the middle of the century. It is often used today in humorous or ironic contexts, as *I'll have to stick to the straight and narrow for a few weeks. I'm studying for my final exams.*

straight from the shoulder is an idiom cliché meaning in a frank or outspoken manner, as *I hate it when doctors try to hide things. I wish they would just give it to me straight from the shoulder.* The expression has its origin in boxing where someone is given a full-force blow. As a figurative expression it dates from the late nineteenth century, becoming a cliché in the twentieth century. It is often used by people who pride themselves on their bluntness, which is often in fact rudeness.

straw in the wind, a is an idiom cliché used to refer to something that is an indication of how things might develop, as *The reaction of the health unions to their small pay increase is a straw in the wind. There will be general industrial unrest.* As a cliché the expression dates from the twentieth century, although the idea is much older, and is still common today. In origin it refers to using a straw to indicate which way the wind is blowing.

strike while the iron is hot is a proverb cliché meaning to take advantage of an opportunity or favourable circumstances when they present themselves, as *If you want to borrow some money from your father now would be a good time to ask. He has just won some money on the lottery, so you can strike while the iron is hot.* The proverbial saying dates from the fourteenth century and has been a cliché since the nineteenth century, being still common today. In origin it refers to the work of a blacksmith in his forge – iron has to be very hot before it can be hammered into shape.

suffer a sea change is an allusion cliché meaning to undergo a marked change, often for the good, as *This area's certainly suffered a sea change since I last visited it. It used to be a derelict site.* The expression refers to a passage in Shakespeare's *The Tempest* (1:2) 'Nothing of him that doth fade, but doth suffer a sea change into something rich and strange.' As a cliché it dates from the middle of the nineteenth century. It is still used today, particularly by people of a literary bent, and frequently in humorous or ironic contexts. The expression is sometimes shortened simply to **sea change**.

suffer fools gladly, not to is an allusion cliché, being a reference to a Biblical passage 'For ye suffer fools gladly, seeing ye yourselves are wise.' (2 *Corinthians* 11:19) In the passage Paul is pointing out to the Corinthians that those who tolerate fools are themselves fools. As a cliché it dates from the nineteenth century and is still common today, often being used of someone who is intolerant of people generally.

survival of the fittest, the is a hackneyed phrase used to indicate that in the long run it is the strongest who will succeed, as *There is no point in going in for the marathon race if you are unfit. It'll certainly be a case of the survival of the fittest,* and *This firm is so full of office politics that people come and go very quickly. It's a case of the survival of the fittest.* The expression was originated by Herbert Spence in *Principles of Biology* (1864) when describing Charles Darwin's theory of natural selection. As a cliché it dates from the twentieth century and is still common, sometimes being used in humorous or ironic contexts.

sweetness and light is an allusion cliché being a reference to a passage in Jonathan Swift's *The Battle of the Books* (1697). The expression was popularized by Matthew Arnold in *Culture and Anarchy* (1869). It became a cliché in the late nineteenth century and is common today but mostly in ironic contexts, as *He treats his wife and children appallingly badly, but to the rest of the world he is all sweetness and light,* and *Mary has a hangover this morning and so she is not exactly sweetness and light.*

swings and roundabouts is a proverb cliché being a shortened version of the saying **what you win/gain on the swings you lose on the roundabouts**. Both expressions indicate that the advantages that one achieves in some things are often offset by disadvantages suffered in other things, as *His venture into the stock market was a case of swings and roundabouts,* and *I just got a salary increase when I had to pay a huge car repair bill. What you win on the swings you lose on the roundabouts.* A more optimistic version of the longer expression is **what you lose on the swings you win/gain on the roundabouts**. As clichés the expressions date from the twentieth century and are still used to demonstrate a philosophical acceptance of fate.

take a leaf out of someone's book is an idiom cliché meaning to follow someone's example. This mostly refers to a good example, as *I wish you would take a leaf out of your sister's book and keep your room tidy*, but not always, as *I think I'll take a leaf out of Fred's book and start doing as little as possible*. As a cliché the expression dates from the late nineteenth century and it is still popular today. In origin it refers to taking a page out of one's exercise book to copy.

take care is a hackneyed phrase used when taking one's leave of someone. It is used in informal contexts to someone whom one knows fairly well. Literally it urges the other person to take good care of himself/herself but it is frequently used meaninglessly in the way that → **see you later** is used. As a cliché it dates from the later part of the twentieth century.

take it from me is a hackneyed phrase used as a filler cliché. It is either used to emphasize the truth of what is about to be said, as *Take it from me. He is up to no good* or is simply used meaninglessly by someone to whom it has become a habit. The expression has a modern colloquial ring, but it was in use in the seventeenth century. As a cliché it is still popular today, sometimes taking the form **you can take it from me**.

take one's life in one's hands is a hackneyed phrase meaning to do something very risky, as *You take your life in your hands when you cross this road. The traffic*

goes very fast. It originally referred to physical risk but it now refers to other forms of risk and is often use in humorous or ironic contexts, as *You'll be taking your life in your hands if you disagree with our next-door neighbour about animal rights.* As a cliché it dates from the middle of the nineteenth century and is still popular today.

take pot luck is a hackneyed phrase meaning to accept an invitation to a meal which is made up of just what the host or hostess was going to have anyway, rather than one which has been specially prepared for a guest, as *You are welcome to have dinner with us as long as you don't mind taking pot luck.* The expression has been popular since the late eighteenth century. It is still a common cliché today, being found in all but the most formal contexts. It refers literally to whatever happens to be in the cooking pot.

take the bull by the horns is an idiom cliché meaning to meet any danger or difficulty with boldness or courage, as *I don't like upsetting her but I'm going to have to take the bull by the horns and ask her to leave. There's just not enough room here.* The expression has been popular since the late nineteenth century and is a common cliché today.

take the law into one's own hands is a hackneyed phrase meaning to take it upon oneself to see that what one perceives as justice is done, as *When the man who attacked his daughter got off with just a fine, he took the law into his own hands* *and went out and beat him up*. The expression was in existence by the early seventeenth century and is still common today.

take the rough with the smooth is an idiom cliché meaning to be prepared to accept the bad or disadvantageous side of something as well as the good or advantageous side, as *If you go and live in the country you'll have to take the rough with the smooth. It's lovely in the summer but the roads are often blocked in the winter and supplies can't get through.* As a saying the expression dates from the fifteenth century and as a cliché from the twentieth century, being still generally popular today.

take the words out of someone's mouth is an idiom cliché indicating that someone has just said something that one was about to say oneself, as *I was just about to suggest going to the cinema. You took the words out of my mouth.* The expression goes back to the sixteenth century and has been a cliché since the nineteenth century. It is still common today in fairly informal contexts.

take to the cleaners is an idiom cliché meaning to take a great deal of money from someone. It is frequently used in relation to divorce settlements, as *He says that his ex-wife took him to the cleaners but in fact she got very little.* The expression is American in origin and dates from the second part of the twentieth century. As a cliché it is common today in informal or slang contexts. It is related to the idea of being cleaned out, in the sense of having no money left.

talk of the devil is a hackneyed phrase used as a comment on the fact that the person about whom one has just been talking has appeared on the scene, as *Well, talk of the devil! Here's Frank and we were just saying that we hadn't seen him*

for ages. In origin the cliché refers to the saying **speak of the devil and he's sure to appear**. The cliché probably dates from the nineteenth century and is still common today in informal contexts.

tall, dark and handsome is a hackneyed phrase used to refer to the appearance of a supposedly ideal man. The expression is American in origin and dates from the early 1920s. It was probably popularized by being the title of a film (1941) in which Cesar Romero played the lead. Although tastes as to what constitutes an ideal man come and go as frequently as they do in relation to an ideal woman, the expression is still a popular cliché today, often being used in humorous or satirical contexts, as *I wouldn't exactly call him tall, dark and handsome, more small, fat and balding.*

tarred with the same brush is an idiom cliché indicating that someone has the same faults or bad qualities as someone else, as *He is tarred with the same brush as his cousin. They are both conmen.* The expression became popular in the middle of the nineteenth century and is still common in fairly informal contexts today. In origin the phrase probably refers to the former practice of shepherds of applying tar to a sheep's sores with a brush.

teach one's grandmother to suck eggs is a proverb cliché meaning to try to show someone, usually someone more experienced than oneself, how to do something that he or she can do perfectly well, usually better than one can oneself, as *I know perfectly well how to operate the stove. Don't teach your grandmother to suck eggs.* As a cliché the expression dates from the middle of the twentieth century and, although it sounds rather archaic, it is popular today, often among older people who feel that they are being patronized by younger people.

teething troubles is a hackneyed phrase used to refer to the difficult early stages of something, as *We've had a few teething troubles with our new catering business but everything's going smoothly now*. As a cliché it dates from the twentieth century and is still common today in all but the most formal contexts. In origin it refers to the pain that babies experience when their teeth are coming through.

tell me about it is a hackneyed phrase used to emphasize one's agreement with what has just been said, as *'What a pity you didn't get the job,' said Mike. 'Tell me about it!' said Jane*. As a cliché it dates from the later part of the twentieth century. A slightly older phrase which expresses the same sentiment is **you're telling me**.

tell that to the marines is a catchphrase cliché used to indicate that one does not believe something and that only a fool would do so, as *You expect me to believe that he would take a cut in salary. Tell that to the marines!* The expression dates from the early nineteenth century and in origin it refers to the fact that sailors thought marines inferior to them, a marine being a soldier who serves at sea. As a cliché it is rather dated today.

tender loving care is a hackneyed phrase whose meaning is self-evident, as *The child comes from a very unhappy home and is desperately in need of some tender loving care*, and *After her operation she'll need lots of tender loving care*. The expression became popular in the second part of the twentieth century, although Shakespeare makes an early reference to it in *Henry VI* (3:2) 'Go, Salisbury, and tell them from me, I thank them for their tender loving care.' It

was well established as a cliché by the 1980s and is still popular today, often being abbreviated to **TLC** (or **tlc**) which is used mostly in informal contexts.

tender mercies, leave to someone's is a hackneyed phrase meaning to leave someone or something in the care of someone who is inefficient, imcompetent, unsympathetic, etc, as *I'm a bit worried. I've had to leave the dog to Jane's tender mercies. She's so vague she'll probably lose him*, and *We're going on holiday and leaving the house to the tender mercies of our son. Do you think you could keep an eye on things?* As a cliché used ironically the expression dates from the twentieth century. It is still popular today, always being used ironically.

terra firma (Latin for 'firm ground') is a foreign cliché meaning dry land, as opposed to the sea. As an English cliché it dates from the middle of the nineteenth century. It is still used today, as *The sea was so rough that I was glad to get off the ferry and back onto terra firma*. It is rather dated.

thankful for small mercies is a hackneyed phrase indicating that one should appreciate benefits or advantages, however small, as *We've waited ages for a bus and it's so cold. Still, we should be thankful for small mercies. At least it isn't raining*. As a cliché it dates from the late nineteenth century and it is still common today, sometimes being used in humorous or ironic contexts.

thanks but no thanks is a hackneyed phrase which is used to convey an emphatic rejection, *'We're reducing the budget and we've had to make you redundant but we can re-employ you on a short-term contract'. 'Thanks but no thanks'*. It is often rather an impolite rejection, a fact which is made clear only by the tone when spoken. The popularity of the expression dates from the later part of the twentieth century.

that'll be the day is a catchphrase cliché used to indicate the unlikelihood of something, as *You seriously think he would lend us some money? That'll be the day!* The catchphrase dates from the early part of the twentieth century and is still a common cliché today.

that's a good question is a catchphrase cliché which is often used as a filler cliché while someone thinks how best to answer a question, as *How would we solve the present economic problems? That's a good question.* The catchphrase dates from around the middle of the twentieth century and is a popular time-wasting cliché today.

that's all I need is hackneyed phrase indicating much the same idea as the last straw, as *That's all I need. My husband has asked his boss to dinner and I've already got a mountain of things to do.* The expression dates from around the middle of the twentieth century and, as befits an expression of exasperation, it is a common cliché today. An alternative form is **that's all I needed**.

that's for me to know and for you to find out is a catchphrase cliché used as an evasive way of dealing with a question. The cliché dates from the twentieth century and was originally used to answer children in the rather high-handed attitude that adults adopt to children, as *What age am I? That's for me to know and for you to find out.* As a cliché it is now rather dated and is mostly used in humorous contexts.

that's life is a hackneyed phrase used to indicate a resigned attitude towards the misfortunes of life, as *Our team were*

beaten in the closing minutes of the game. Still, I suppose that's life! As a cliché it dates from the second part of the twentieth century and is still common today among those who are less than optimistic.

that's the way the cookie crumbles is a hackneyed phrase indicating a resigned attitude to fate meaning that is how things are and there is nothing we can do about it, as *I wish that I hadn't lost my job just before my holiday but I suppose that's the way the cookie crumbles.* The expression is American in origin, as is 'cookie' meaning biscuit, and has been current since the middle of the twentieth century. Although it is American English in form, the phrase is still a common cliché in Britain today.

that would be telling is a hackneyed phrase used to indicate that one knows the answer to a question but that one has no intention of revealing what one knows, as *What did we do last night? That would be telling.* The expression in its present form probably became popular in the twentieth century, although **that's telling** is an earlier form, dating from the early part of the eighteenth century

there are thousands worse off than you is a hackneyed phrase used to console people who have suffered some form of misfortune and are inclined to grieve or complain about it. It is a bracing phrase meant to make people aware of the triviality of their misfortune in a world context. In fact it usually simply makes matters worse, as the person suffering from the misfortune is not in the mood for worrying about the rest of the world, and the person making the comment usually sounds rather smug since he or she has not suffered misfortune. The cliché dates from the twentieth century and is still common.

there are ways and means is a hackneyed phrase used to indicate the fact that if something absolutely has to be done, a way can be found to do it. The suggestion conveyed by the cliché is that this way is not always honest or even legal, as *The bank has refused to lend him money for his new business but I'm sure he will get it from somewhere. There are ways and means.* As a cliché the expression dates from the twentieth century.

there but for the grace of God go I is a catchphrase cliché used to indicate that one might well have been in the same unfortunate position that someone else now is, as *Jim was booked for speeding on the road into town last night. There but for the grace of God go I – and most of the other drivers on that road!* It is frequently used in humorous or satirical contexts, as *I hear Jane is getting married to Frank today. There but for the grace of God go I! I went out with her for a while until I realized what she was like.* As a cliché the expression dates from the nineteenth century and it is still common today. In origin the phrase is said to quote John Bradford who made the remark on seeing some criminals being taken to their execution around 1553. In fact his words, if he uttered them, proved prophetic for he himself was burned at the stake in 1555 for his religious beliefs. The words have also been ascribed to John Wesley and John Bunyan.

thereby hangs a tale is a hackneyed phrase indicating that there is a story, or a bit of juicy gossip, attached to something that has just been said or written, as *I hear that he has decided to take early retirement and thereby hangs a tale*, the implication being that the user of the phrase is about to tell the story. The expression has probably been a cliché since the nineteenth century. It was used by Shakespeare in several of his plays, including *As You Like It* (2:7) although he did not originate it. In origin it is a pun on a tail hanging from an animal.

there'll be dancing in the streets tonight is a catchphrase cliché indicating that an event has taken place that will give rise to general celebration. It is frequently used as a cliché by sports commentators to refer to the celebration that will greet a team's victory in their home town, as *There'll be dancing in the streets of Glasgow tonight.* Sometimes it indicates that the victory was unexpected. The cliché dates from the twentieth century and has the alternative form **they'll be dancing in the streets tonight**.

there's a lot of it about is a hackneyed phrase often used as a medical cliché, as *If you have a sore throat you should go home and take an aspirin and go to bed. There's a lot of it about.* It is often used humorously or satirically in non-medical context, as *Mark's wife has just gone off with Jane's husband. There's a lot of it about.* The cliché dates from the twentieth century.

there's many a slip is an allusion cliché reminding one of the fact that many things can go wrong between a plan or project being conceived and it actually being carried out or achieved, as *I know you're excited that the bank are going to discuss your business plan with you, but don't forget there's many a slip.* As a cliché it dates from the twentieth century and is an allusion to the proverb **there's many a slip between cup and lip**, which is itself sometimes used as a cliché. In origin the proverb refers to the fact that accidents can happen between one first raising a cup and it actually coming into contact with one's lips.

there's no fool like an old fool is a proverb cliché meaning that people who are old enough and experienced enough to know better are just as liable, or even more liable, to behave or speak foolishly as young people are, as *He's nearly sixty and he seriously believes that his eighteen-year old girlfriend loves him for himself alone and not for his money. There's no fool like an old fool.* The saying is an old one and appeared in John Heywood's collection of proverbs of 1546. As a cliché it is still common today, sometimes being shortened to **there's no fool**, the rest of the expression being understood.

there's no such thing as a free lunch is a catchphrase cliché used to indicate that one rarely gets anything for nothing. As a cliché it dates from the later part of the twentieth century and has its origins in the world of PR and business. It refers to the fact that anyone, whom one does not know well, is unlikely to invite one to a business lunch unless he or she is planning to get something out of it, such as promotion for a product.

there's one born every minute is a catchphrase cliché used when someone has been duped or conned, as *Jane lent her camera to a child on the beach and he ran off with it. There's one born every minute.* and *They gave the workman the money in advance to pay for materials and they never saw him again. There's one born every minute.* This comment on the universality of folly dates from the twentieth century and is a common cliché today in informal contexts.

these things happen is a hackneyed phrase usually directed at someone who has suffered some form of misfortune in a supposed attempt to get him or her to see the misfortune in a world context and understand that their misfortune is not unique. It is a meaningless phrase, and in common with other phrases used in such a context, is rather fatuous, its only

advantage being that it sometimes so irritates the unfortunate person that he or she forgets temporarily the cause of the misfortune. As a cliché it dates from the twentieth century.

thorn in one's side, a is an allusion cliché being a reference to several Biblical passages, one of which is in *Judges* (2:3) 'They shall be as thorns in your sides.' The cliché means a source of constant irritation, as *That customer is a real thorn in the manager's side. She is always complaining about the service*, and has the alternative form **a thorn in one's flesh**. As a cliché it dates from the middle of the nineteenth century and is still current.

through thick and thin is an idiom cliché meaning whatever the difficulties or dangers, as *The politician has received a great deal of adverse publicity but his constituency party members have stood by him through thick and thin.* As a cliché it dates from the nineteenth century and is still common today. In origin it refers to terrain with both thick and sparse vegetation or woods. The analogy goes back to the days of Chaucer.

throw in the towel is an idiom cliché meaning to give up or to acknowledge defeat, as *The protesters have spent months trying to prevent the authorities closing the village school but they've decided to throw in the towel.* As a cliché the expression dates from the later part of the nineteenth century and is still popular today in informal or slang contexts. An alternative form of the expression is **throw in the sponge**. Both expressions derive from boxing, from the fact that the sponge (later a towel) used by a boxer was thrown into the ring as a sign that he was conceding defeat.

throw the baby out with the bathwater is an idiom cliché to get rid of something useful while disposing of something useless or unwanted, as *The committee threw out the whole proposal for change although there were some good points in it. They simply threw the baby out with the bathwater.* In origin it may be a translation of the German proverb 'Das Kind mit dem Bade ausschütten', to pour the baby out with the bath. The idea has been common in English since the second part of the nineteenth century, sometimes in the earlier form **empty the baby out with the bath**, which was used by George Bernard Shaw in 'Parents and Children' (1914). **Throw the baby out with the bathwater** is still common today in all but the most formal contexts.

throw the book at is an idiom cliché meaning to rebuke or punish someone very severely, as *The headmaster will throw the book at you if you're caught playing truant again.* The metaphor was originally used in a legal context, meaning to sentence someone to the maximum penalty allowed for the crime. It later became more generally used by journalists, among others. In its general use it sometimes applies to situations involving the law, as *If the police stop you in that car they'll throw the book at you. It's got no brake lights, the front number plate is missing and the tyres are bald.*

tickled pink is a hackneyed phrase meaning extremely delighted, as *She was tickled pink by the birthday card which her grandchildren made for her.* In origin it refers to the fact that someone who is being tickled is laughing so much that he or she turns pink. An alternative, and slightly older, form is **tickled to death** which is still current. As a cliché **tickled pink** probably dates from the twentieth century and is still common today, being used in informal contexts.

tie the knot is an idiom cliché meaning to get married, as *I hear that Frank and Jill have at last decided to tie the knot.* The expression may be a reference to a saying that dates from the sixteenth century. 'To tie a knot with one's tongue that one cannot untie with one's teeth.' As a cliché **tie the knot** dates from around the late nineteenth century and is still current today, being used in informal, and often humorous, contexts.

tighten one's belt is an idiom cliché meaning to reduce one's expenditure, to be more frugal. As a cliché the expression dates from the twentieth century, becoming particularly popular during the recessions in the 1980s and 1990s, it is particularly popular among journalists and other commentators on the financial situation, as *Small firms stand a good chance of surviving the recession if they are willing to tighten their belts.* In origin the phrase refers to a person tightening a belt round his waist having lost weight from eating less, having spent less money on food.

till death do us part see *until death do us part*

till the fat lady sings, it's not over is an idiom cliché which is a vogue cliché of the 1990s. It is used to indicate that one should wait until the end of something before expressing one's reaction, making a decision, etc. The expression is used by sports commentators to urge people to wait until the final whistle before commenting, since last-minute goals have been known to happen. In origin it refers to an operatic production, female opera stars traditionally being somewhat large.

time flies see *how time flies*

time heals everything is a hackneyed phrase used by well-meaning people to try to console someone who has just experienced grief or great misfortune. In fact it is of little value because, although time does diminish most emotional pain, the person being so consoled is not in a condition to appreciate the fact. As a cliché the expression dates from the twentieth century.

tip of the iceberg, the is an idiom cliché used to indicate that some misfortune or bad situation is only a minor manifestation of a much worse situation, as *The school admits that about ten percent of pupils regularly play truant but we think that's just the tip of the iceberg*. As a cliché the expression dates from the second part of the twentieth century. In origin it refers to the fact that the bulk of the mass of an iceberg is below the surface of the water and so not visible.

tired and emotional is a euphemism cliché meaning tipsy or drunk, as *I think you should call a taxi for your sister. She's been at the party for hours and has got a bit tired and emotional*. As a cliché it dates from the later part of the twentieth century and is usually used in humorous contexts. In origin it refers to the fact that alcohol can make people tired and maudlin.

to all intents and purposes see *all intents and purposes, to*

to coin a phrase is a hackneyed phrase used by some people not to introduce a phrase which they have just invented but to introduce a well-worn cliché, as *To coin a phrase, the police will throw the book at him*. The expression is American in origin and became popular in Britain in the middle of the twentieth century. It is still widespread today, sometimes, but by no means always, being used humorously or ironically.

toe the line is an idiom cliché meaning to behave strictly according to the rules or standards set down, as *He'll hate staying with his grandmother. He always complains about having to help with the chores but she'll make him toe the line*, and *Their previous teacher was a bit lax about homework being handed in on time, but this one will make them toe the line*. As a cliché the expression dates from the later part of the nineteenth century and is still commonly used today, particularly by people who like the idea of other people being subjected to discipline. An earlier form of the expression was **toe the mark**. In origin the phrase refers to runners lining up at the start of a race.

tomorrow is another day is a hackneyed phrase used to indicate that anything that has not been done or finished today can be done tomorrow, as *It's well after midnight. Could you not finish that essay another time? Tomorrow is another day*. It is a particularly annoying expression if the person to whom it is directed knows perfectly well that tomorrow is another day but knows equally well that the work being done must be done today, or preferably yesterday. The expression is also used as a term of consolation to someone who has just failed at something, as *I know you failed your driving test but you'll get it next time. Tomorrow is another day*. As a cliché the expression probably dates from the beginning of the twentieth century and it is still commonly used today, particularly by the optimists among us. The popularity of the phrase may have been enhanced by its use as the closing line of the film *Gone with the Wind*.

too good to be true is a hackneyed phrase referring to the fact that something seems so wonderful that there must be a snag attached to it, as *I can't believe that holiday is so cheap. It seems too good to be true*. The expression dates from the sixteenth century and was already a cliché when George Bernard Shaw used it as the title of one of his plays in 1932.

too little too late is a hackneyed phrase used to indicate that action taken to rectify a problem or alleviate a situation is inadequate and too late to be any use, as *The refugees are dying in their thousands. Foreign governments are now sending aid but it is too little too late.* The expression was used by American historian Allan Nevins in an article in *Current History* (May 1935) 'The former allies have blundered in the past by offering Germany too little, and offering even that too late, until finally Nazi Germany has become a menace to all mankind.' The expression became a cliché in the later part of the twentieth century and is extremely common today, being a particular favourite of journalists. It is frequently used in the field of politics or international relations.

too many cooks spoil the broth is a proverb cliché meaning that if there are too many people involved in a project, the quality of the project is likely to suffer, as *I think the organizing committee for the charity ball is too large. Too many cooks spoil the broth.* The proverb has been in existence since the sixteenth century and has been a cliché probably since the nineteenth century. The expression is still popular today.

too numerous to mention is a hackneyed phrase supposedly used to indicate that there are too many people or things involved in something to mention them by name. It is, however, frequently, used as a filler cliché to introduce a list of the very names that are too numerous to mention, as *The volunteers who helped with the fête are too numerous to mention. They include . . .* As a cliché it dates from the late nineteenth

century and is still in evidence today in the remarks of public speakers.

touch and go is a hackneyed phrase used to refer to a situation which is extremely precarious or uncertain, as *It'll be touch and go whether the plane lands in time for us to catch our connecting flight*, and *He's had the operation but it'll be touch and go whether he recovers.* As a cliché the expression dates from the middle of the nineteenth century and is still common today. In origin it refers to a vehicle that barely escapes colliding with something.

tough act to follow, a see *hard act to follow, a*

tower of strength is an idiom cliché used to refer to someone who is reliable, supportive and resourceful and so the perfect person to have by one's side in an emergency, as *Their neighbour was a tower of strength to the children when both their parents had to go hospital.* The expression was popularized in 1852 by Tennyson in his poem *Ode to the Duke of Wellington* 'O fall'n at length that tower of strength.' It became a cliché shortly after that and is still popular today.

trials and tribulations is a doublet cliché, trials and tribulations in this context being virtually synonymous, meaning troubles and difficulties, as *The trials and tribulations of being a widow with young children had prematurely aged her.* As a cliché it dates from the late nineteenth century. It is still common today, being often found in humorous or ironic contexts, as *He's just gone out to another business lunch. Oh, the trials and tribulations of being a top executive.*

tried and true is a hackneyed phrase used to refer to something that has been tested in some way and found to be effective or sound, as *She dislike doctors and prefers some of the old tried and true herbal remedies*, and *It was suggested that we overhaul our book-keeping procedures but we decided to stick to our old method that was tried and true*. As a cliché it dates from the twentieth century and is still popular today.

trip the light fantastic see *light fantastic*

true blue is a hackneyed phrase meaning extremely loyal, unwavering. In origin the expression refers to an old proverb, **true blue will never stain**, which dates from the sixteenth century and is now obsolete. The proverb referred to a blue dye that was fast and never ran. The expression **true blue** dates from the eighteenth century and in the late nineteenth century became associated with politics. Nowadays it is very frequently associated with members of the British Conservative party, the colour blue being identified with the party, as *His wife votes Labour but he is a true blue Tory*.

truth will out is a hackneyed phrase used to indicate that sooner or later the true facts will emerge, as *Mary has just found out that Harry's married and she's been going out with him for a year. Truth will out*. The expression dates from the eighteenth century. It is still common today, being often used of some form of scandal.

tug-of-love is a hackneyed phrase much used by journalists, particularly in headlines, to describe a situation in which two divorced or separated parents are fighting over custody of a child, as *Tug-of-love child abducted to Spain*, and *The child at the heart of the tug-of-love row is currently staying with her grandparents*. As a cliché it dates from the second part of the twentieth century. In origin it is an analogy with a tug-of-war, the child acting as the rope.

turn a blind eye to is an idiom cliché meaning deliberately to overlook or ignore something, often something that is either against the rules or something that would not normally be condoned, as *Some of the teachers knew that the senior pupils smoked in the playground but they turned a blind eye to it*. The expression became popular in the nineteenth century. In origin it is said to refer to the behaviour of Lord Nelson at the Battle of Copenhagen (1801). He was second-in-command and he ignored the signals given for the fleet to withdraw by putting his telescope to his blind eye. He then proceeded to attack and the French were defeated and forced to surrender. As a cliché the expression dates from the nineteenth century and is popular today in all but the most formal contexts.

turn a deaf ear is an idiom cliché meaning deliberately to ignore or take no notice of something, as *The children pleaded for mercy for their father but the tyrant turned a deaf ear to their pleas*. The idea goes back to the fifteenth century and a version appeared in John Heywood's proverb collection of 1546. As a cliché the expression dates from the nineteenth century and is still popular in all but the most formal contexts.

turn over a new leaf is an idiom cliché meaning to begin a new and better way of behaving, working, thinking, etc, as *He has been in and out of prison but when his son was born he said that he was going to turn over a new leaf*. The expression dates from the sixteenth century and is a common cliché today, being frequently given as piece of gratuitous advice, as *If you want to pass your exams you'll have to turn over a new leaf and start studying*. In origin it refers to turning the page of a book.

turn the clock back is an idiom cliché meaning to return to the conditions or way of life of an earlier time, as *We are afraid that the present prison legislation will turn the clock back fifty years*. It is often associated with nostalgia or regret for the past, as *She wished she could turn the clock back to the happier times of her youth*, and *Old people often wish they could turn the clock back but they forget how bad social conditions were in the past*. The expression dates from the nineteenth century and is current today. In origin it refers to turning the hands of a clock back.

turn the corner is an idiom cliché meaning to begin to recover. It is frequently used of financial or economic situations, as *The government is trying to convince the electorate that the economy has turned the corner.*, having been used in this sense by Charles Dickens. In this context it is frequently used by journalists. The expression is also used as an informal medical cliché, as *The patient is not completely out of danger yet but I think she has turned the corner*. As a cliché the expression dates from the nineteenth century and is widely used today. In origin it refers to turning a corner and going in a new direction.

turn the other cheek is an allusion cliché being a reference to a Biblical passage where Jesus tells his followers that if someone hit them on one cheek they should offer their attacker the other cheek also 'Unto him that smiteth thee on the one cheek offer also the other.' (*Luke* 6:29). The expression **turn the other cheek** means to accept meekly insults, acts of provocation, attacks, etc, as *It is difficult to ignore their taunts but if you turn the other cheek they'll tire of it and start on somebody else*. As a cliché the phrase dates from the nineteenth century. It is more popular today in these aggressive times than the actual practice it describes.

'twas ever thus is a hackneyed phrase used to reflect on the fact that things do not change, as *The men earn more than the women in the office. 'Twas ever thus!* and *The last bus goes before the end of the concert. 'Twas ever thus*. It is usually said in resigned tones in acceptance of something inconvenient, annoying, etc. As a cliché the expression probably dates from the early twentieth century.

twist my arm! is a catchphrase cliché used in response to a suggested offer, as *I shouldn't really stay and have another drink but twist my arm*, and *Twist my arm! I'd love to stop studying for a while and go to the cinema*. The phrase is from the idiom **twist someone's arm** which means to force someone to do something. The cliché indicates that someone does not really need to be forced but is only too willing to accept the offer. As a cliché the expression dates from the twentieth century and is common today in informal contexts.

two a penny is a hackneyed phrase used to indicate that something is very common, as *Employment conditions are very bad because prospective workers are two a penny*, and *Houses in that area used to be impossible to come by but since the collapse of the property boom they're two a penny*. In origin it refers to things being extremely cheap. As a cliché the expression dates from the twentieth century and is common today, often being used in a derogatory way.

two heads are better than one is a proverb cliché indicating that a problem is likely to be solved more effectively if more than one mind is applied to it, as *Would you like to help me map out our route for tomorrow? Two heads are better than one*, and *I've asked Frank to help me draw up a business plan for the new business. Two heads are better than one and he has a lot of experience of that* *kind of thing*. The proverb is an old one, appearing in John Heywood's collection of proverbs of 1546. As a cliché the expression dates from the twentieth century. It is still widespread today, although not everyone agrees with the sentiment, believing that → **too many cooks spoil the broth**. **two of a kind** is a hackneyed phrase used to indicate in a derogatory way that two people are very alike, as *I wouldn't waste sympathy on Jenny for marrying Jim. I know he's violent but in fact they're two of a kind.* As a cliché the expression dates from the nineteenth century. A previous form of the expression was **two of a trade** but this is now obsolete.

two's company, three's a crowd is a proverb cliché indicating that lovers like to be alone, as *I wouldn't accept their invitation to the cinema. They're just being polite. Two's company, three's a crowd.* The saying is an old one and appeared in John Heywood's proverb collection of 1546. Like love itself, the cliché is common today.

❧ U ❧

ugly duckling, an is an idiom cliché used to describe an unattractive or untalented child who grows into an attractive or talented adult, as *Their youngest daughter is now a famous model but she was a real ugly duckling as a teenager.* In origin the expression refers to a story by Hans Christian Andersen in which a cygnet is adopted by a mother duck and is scorned by her and her ducklings because it is so ugly and clumsy until it grows into a beautiful, graceful swan.

unacceptable face of, is a hackneyed phrase used to indicate the less advantageous, popular, pleasant, etc. aspect of something which is otherwise acceptable as *Bomb attacks involving innocent people were the unacceptable face of the protest movement.* The expression is derived originally from **the unacceptable face of capitalism**, a quotation cliché alluding to a statement made to the House of Commons in 1973 by Edward Heath, the Prime Minister of Britain in reference to a financial scandal in which a former Tory Cabinet minister, Duncan Sandys, accepted a large sum of money from the Lonrho Company in return for giving up his consultancy with the firm, the money to be paid, quite legally, into a tax-free account in the Cayman Islands and the situation taking place when the government was promoting a counter-inflation policy.

unaccustomed as I am to public speaking is a hackneyed phrase used by public speakers, such as after-dinner speakers, irrespective of how experienced they are in the art. Since the middle of the twentieth century the expression has mostly been used in a humorous, ironic or quasi-apologetic way, as *This is, the third fête that I have opened this week and so, unaccustomed as I am to public speaking, I shall tell you the advantages of this one.* By the time Winston Churchill used the expression in 1897 in his first political speech in Bath the non-humorous version was already obviously considered to be a cliché. Nowadays the cliché is sometimes shortened to **unaccustomed as I am** . . . since everyone will know what comes next.

unavoidable delays is a hackneyed phrase usually used in a business or transport context as a non-specific excuse for something not being on time or up to schedule, as *We are sorry that you have not yet received the goods which you ordered but owing to unavoidable delays in production we have been unable to process the orders,* or *Owing to unavoidable delays the train is running half an hour late.* The expression has been popular since the late nineteenth century and is often replaced by seemingly more specific but still vague excuses, as *The plane has been delayed owing to a* **slight technical hitch**.

uncrowned king of, the is a hackneyed phrase originally from around the beginning of the twentieth century, indicating that someone is the virtual ruler of somewhere, although not the official ruler. The expression then came to be used figuratively to refer to people who are generally acknowledged to be exceptionally talented and the best in their fields, although they may not be officially recognized as such, as *At that time he was the uncrowned king of rock 'n' roll.*

under a cloud is an idiom cliché meaning in disgrace or under suspicion of some kind, the image being that the rest of the sky is blue but that there is a cloud over one individual. The figurative expression has been in use since the fifteenth century and has been established as a cliché since the middle of the eighteenth century. It is still widely used nowadays, as *The teacher had had a fine academic career but left the school under a cloud after a relationship with a pupil,* and *Money has gone missing from the classroom and the whole of the class feel that they are all under a cloud until the culprit owns up to the theft.*

under that rough exterior is a hackneyed phrase popular since the late nineteenth century and usually accompanied by the ending **there beats a heart of gold**. The expression is still current but is usually used in a humorous or ironic context. Frequently an ironic ending is added instead of the original, as *Under that rough exterior of his there beats a heart of stone.*

under the sun is a hackneyed phrase usually used for example in some phrases relating to space, as *There is nowhere under the sun that one can be absolutely safe from terrorism,* and *The island has the most pleasant climate under the sun.* The expression has been in use since the fourteenth century and has been common enough to be regarded as a cliché since the seventeenth century. It is still in widespread use today.

under the weather is a hackneyed phrase meaning not very well, slightly ill, as *She*

left work early as she was feeling a bit under the weather. The origin of the expression is uncertain but it may refer to the feeling of tiredness and lethargy that some types of weather, such as hot, humid weather, induce.

university of life, the is a hackneyed phrase used to contrast experience with academic instruction. It is most commonly used by people, especially older people, who did not themselves attend university, to young people who are currently in further education and perceived to be having an easy time, as *It was different in my day. I couldn't afford to spend time reading books. I was educated in the university of life.* An expression which conveys the same sentiment is → **the school of hard knocks**. Both expressions became common in the early part of the twentieth century.

unkindest cut of all, the is a quotation cliché meaning the most unkind or treacherous thing that someone could do. It is in fact a slight misquotation of a passage in Shakespeare's *Julius Caesar* (3:2), the full quotation being 'This was the most unkindest cut of all.' The adjustment was presumably made because the original seems ungrammatical in modern English. The quotation is uttered as Caesar is stabbed by his friends, particularly Brutus. The expression has been common enough to be regarded as a cliché since the latter part of the nineteenth century and is still used, particularly by people of a literary bent.

unsung heroes is a hackneyed phrase which refers to people who have done something extremely brave or noteworthy but who have not received official recognition or acknowledgement. These were heroes whose feats were not sung or written about in the long classical epics by people such as Homer. In his *The Lay of the Last Minstrel* (1805) Sir Walter Scott wrote 'unwept, unhonour'd and unsung.' The expression is still commonly used today, as *They were the unsung heroes of the war effort.*

until death do us part is a quotation cliché used to emphasize the extent of the commitment to a relationship of some kind. In origin it is a quotation from the *Book of Common Prayer* and has been commonly enough used to be considered a cliché since the late nineteenth century. *The Book of Common Prayer* refers to marriage but as a cliché the expression can be used of other associations, as *As schoolgirls we promised to be friends until death did us part.* The expression also exists in the form **till death do us part.**

until one is blue in the face is a hackneyed phrase used to indicate supreme but vain effort, as *You can tell him until you are blue in the face that the system does not work but he will not listen.* In origin the expression refers to the fact that one sometimes goes blue in the face if one makes some kind of hard physical effort.

untimely end, an is a hackneyed phrase indicating a premature death or end, as *She worried in case her sons came to an untimely end when climbing in bad weather conditions,* and *They had high hopes of making a success of the new business venture but it came to an untimely end at the start of the recession.* The phrase has been common enough to be considered a cliché since the middle of the nineteenth century. It is still used today although usually in rather a formal context or by people of a literary bent

untold wealth is a hackneyed phrase meaning vast wealth, as *Some merchants amassed untold wealth by importing goods from the East.* It has been common as a cliché since the late nineteenth century.

up and doing is a hackneyed phrase meaning actively busy, especially after a period of illness or inactivity, as *She has been confined to bed since she was injured in the accident and she can't wait to be up and doing.* The expression is used in informal contexts and has been common as a cliché since the late nineteenth century and is still widespread.

up for grabs is a hackneyed phrase used to indicate that something is available to be taken, bought, etc, as *I've heard that there's a job up for grabs in the local computing firm,* and *She is selling the contents of the house and there might be one or two nice antique pieces up for grabs.* The expression is found only in informal or slang contexts. It is American in origin and has been common in Britain since the early 1970s.

up in arms is an idiom cliché meaning very angry at, or opposed to, something, as *The villagers were up in arms when the local school was threatened with closure.* The expression has been in use since the eighteenth century and has been common as a cliché since the nineteenth century. In origin it refers to people literally taking up arms or weapons against an enemy.

up one's sleeve, have something is an idiom meaning to keep something secret for possible use at a later time, as *I thought that management agreed to our request for money too easily. I think that they have something up their sleeve.* In origin the expression refers to the practice among card-sharps in the nineteenth century of keeping a card, often an ace, up their sleeves, for use at an appropriate moment in the game.

upset the applecart is an idiom cliché meaning to spoil a plan or arrangement, as *We spent ages planning the family holiday and then our daughter upset the applecart by getting mumps.* In origin the expression refers to turning over a cart that is selling fruit in a market, although Grose's *Dictionary of the Vulgar Tongue* (1796) suggests that 'applecart' means the human body. It has been in existence in its present form since the late eighteenth century and has been common as a cliché since the middle of the nineteenth century. An earlier form of the expression was **upset the cart.**

up the creek is an idiom cliché meaning in serious trouble or difficulties, as *If he insists on taking his money out of the firm we'll really be up the creek.* The expression is used in informal or slang contexts, the phrase being sometimes extended to **up the creek without a paddle.** American in origin, it began to become common about the time of World War 2. The ultimate origin of the phrase is uncertain.

up to one's ears is an idiom cliché meaning very busy, as though one were almost completely immersed in something as *I would love to come and have lunch but I am up to my ears in work.* It has been common as a cliché since the late nineteenth century although the expression is much older. The same concept is demonstrated by the expressions **up to one's eyes** and **up to one's eyebrows**.

up to scratch is an idiom cliché meaning having met the required standard, as *If your work does not come up to scratch soon we cannot enter you for the exam.* It has been

common as a cliché since the middle of the nineteenth century and is still widespread today. In origin the expression refers to a line once drawn on the floor in the middle of a boxing ring to which boxers had to go after being knocked down to demonstrate that they were fit to go on fighting.

up to the hilt is an idiom cliché meaning to the utmost, completely. In origin it refers to the hilt or handle of a sword or dagger. If the weapon is pushed very hard into someone or something only the hilt shows. It has been common as a cliché since the middle of the nineteenth century and is still much used today, often with reference to debt or guilt, as *He has a title but no money. His estate is mortgaged up to the hilt,* and *I am sure that he was involved in the robbery up to the hilt.*

up with the lark is a hackneyed phrase meaning rising very early in the morning, as *I don't know how she does it. She never goes to bed before midnight but she is always up with the lark.* The expression has been a cliché since the nineteenth century and is still common today. In origin it refers to the fact that the lark, in common with other birds, starts singing very early in the morning.

U-turn, do a is an idiom meaning to reverse one's actions, opinions, etc totally, as *He used to be in favour of closer ties with Europe but he has now done a U-turn and keeps talking of the importance of sovereignty.* As a cliché the expression became common in the 1980s and has its origin in motoring, where to do a U-turn is to turn round and go back the way one has just come.

V

vanish into thin air is a hackneyed phrase meaning to disappear completely and often suddenly, as *One minute the child was playing in the garden; the next minute she had disappeared into thin air*. Air gets thinner the higher one goes because of a reduction in oxygen, but the origin of the expression probably lies in the supposed sudden disappearance of ghosts. It has been in popular use since the middle of the nineteenth century and is still widespread. Indeed hardly anyone or anything ever vanishes without doing so into thin air.

variety is the spice of life is a quotation cliché meaning that life is much more interesting if there is diversity in it, as *I did not really want to have to change jobs just yet, but I suppose variety is the spice of life*. It is a quotation from a poem, *The Talk* by William Cowper (1785), 'Variety is the very spice of life, That gives it all its flavour', the implication being that diversity adds interest to life as spice does to food. It is still in popular general use today.

ve haf vays of making you talk is a catch-phrase cliché popular from the middle of the twentieth century indicating in a humorous way that the speaker can easily get the information which he or she requires from the person asked. It is said in a mock sinister German accent, being a send-up of members of the Gestapo as portrayed in British war films. It is still used today but mainly by people of an older generation who remember the war films.

vested interest is a hackneyed phrase of legal origin indicating that someone has a personal interest in something, as *I am not surprised that she is organizing a petition against the new supermarket. She has a vested interest in getting planning permission for it turned down. She owns several of the small shops in the area.* John Stuart Mill wrote in *On Liberty* (1859) 'The doctrine ascribes to all mankind a vested interest in each other's moral, intellectual, and even physical perfection,' and the expression is still much used today. Sometimes the interest is financial, sometimes not.

vexed question, a is a hackneyed phrase indicating a difficult problem that is often discussed without being solved, as *The whole community is in favour of a new sports centre but how we are going to fund it is a vexed question*. In origin the expression is a translation of the Latin *quaestio vexata*. As a cliché it dates from the middle of the nineteenth century and it is still widespread today.

vicious circle, a is a hackneyed phrase indicating a chain of events in which the solution of one problem creates another problem, or else exacerbates the original problem, as *Employment among the young seems to be a vicious circle. They cannot find a job unless they have the relevant experience and they cannot get the relevant experience unless they are already in a job.* The expression has been popular since the middle of the nineteenth century and is still widespread today. In origin it derives from logic, and refers to proving one statement by another that itself rests on the first for proof.

vino veritas, in (Latin for 'truth in wine') is a foreign cliché indicating that when people have drunk too much they frequently become loose-tongued and divulge information that they would otherwise keep secret, as *Well, we were all surprised when he said that he was having an affair with his secretary but you know what they say – in vino veritas..* As a modern cliché it is usually restricted to people who have a background in classical languages or a literary background. To those not having experience of these it can appear pompous.

❧ W ❧

wages of sin, the is a quotation cliché, being a Biblical reference to *Romans* (6:23). It occurs in a letter from Paul to the Romans 'The wages of sin is death' and means the consequences of wickedness. The expression has been considered a cliché since the nineteenth century but is nowadays usually used by older people of a literary bent and even then it is more usually used ironically, as *You should think twice about pretending to be ill when you take a day off to go to the football match. The boss might find out and the wages of sin is death.*

wait and see is a hackneyed phrase which was much used by Henry Asquith when he was Prime Minister of Britain at the beginning of the twentieth century. It is a very widespread cliché used to try and suppress impatience in the person with whom one is dealing, or more especially to postpone having to discuss a matter or make a decision. It is particularly commonly used by parents to children, as *I don't know whether we'll be going on holiday this year. We'll just have to wait and see*, in order to postpone having to say no. Children find it a very tiresome stock response and usually recognize its negative implications immediately.

wait hand and foot on is a hackneyed phrase meaning to attend to the every need of, to look after very assiduously, as *Her husband expects her to wait upon him hand and foot.* The expression is usually used in a derogatory way, suggesting that the person doing the waiting is a self-

inflicted martyr in the opinion of the speaker. The expression is very old and has been very common since the late nineteenth century.

walk on air is an idiom cliché meaning to be extremely happy or elated. It has been common since the late nineteenth century and is still widespread, as *She has been walking on air since she discovered that she is pregnant.* The association of supreme happiness and air is also found in *on cloud nine* and → **in seventh heaven**.

walls have ears is an idiom cliché used to caution that someone may be eavesdropping on a conversation, although no one is doing so in an obvious way. The expression is reputedly derived from a story about Dionysius, a tyrant of Syracuse (430–367BC), in which he was so anxious to overhear what his prisoners were saying that he cut an ear-shaped cave into a rock which connected palace rooms and enabled him to eavesdrop. It is a long-standing cliché and is still popular and widespread, as *Watch what you're saying until we're out of the restaurant. I know it's not busy but walls have ears.*

want to know the reason why is a hackneyed phrase used as a kind of threat, usually by people in authority, such as parents and teachers. The expression is rather dictatorial in tone being used as an ultimatum, as *You will clean your room this morning or I shall want to know the* *reason why.* As a cliché it dates from the twentieth century.

warts and all is an allusion cliché to the instructions given by Oliver Cromwell to Sir Peter Lely when he was painting his portrait that the artist should make him appear as he really was, including any imperfections, such as warts 'I desire you would use all your skill to paint my picture truly like me and not flatter me at all; but remark all these roughnesses, pimples, warts, and everything as you see me, otherwise I will not pay a farthing for it.' The expression, which is widespread in modern times, means despite any shortcomings or drawbacks, as *I hope she is going to marry him warts and all and not try to change him.*

wash one's dirty linen in public is an idiom cliché which has its origin in a French proverb. The expression means to make public one's private affairs, particularly when these are of a scandalous or unsavoury nature, as *We all know that she was involved in a messy divorce case but we wish she'd stop washing her dirty linen in public.* It has been common since the middle of the nineteenth century.

wash one's hands of is an idiom cliché meaning to refuse to have anything more do with or to take any responsibility for, as *A local businessman was going to contribute some of the funding for the new club but there has been so much quarrelling among the organizers that he has decided to wash his hands of the whole project.* The expression has been common since the middle of the nineteenth century and is Biblical in origin. It is an allusion to the behaviour of Pontius Pilate, the Roman governor at the time of the trial of Jesus Christ. In *Matthew (27:24)* he is said to have *'washed his hands before the multitude, saying I am innocent of the blood of this just person.'*

was it something I said? is a modern catchphrase cliché used when someone seems to be avoiding one or not behaving in a friendly or usual way towards one, as *Everyone seemed to leave as I arrived at the party. Was it something I said?* The expression is usually used humorously. As a cliché it dates from the later part of the twentieth century.

waste not, want not is a proverb cliché used to warn someone of the dangers of thriftlessness. It became common in the nineteenth century and is still used nowadays, particularly by older people who were made extremely aware of the virtues of making maximum use of something during World War 2, as *Don't throw out those leftovers – you can make a pie with them. Waste not, want not.* The expression is becoming less common in modern society with its love of the disposable.

watched pot never boils, the is a proverb cliché used to caution someone against being impatient or over-anxious, as this in no way speeds matters up. The implication of the saying is that if you go away and forget about a saucepan of water that you have put on to boil, it seems to boil more quickly than it does if you stand and watch it. The expression dates from the middle of the nineteenth century and is still widespread today, as *The jelly won't set any faster if you keep looking at it. The watched pot never boils.*

water under the bridge is an idiom cliché used to refer to something that is over and gone and so not worth thinking any more about. It dates from the twentieth century and is still widespread, as *She used to go out with the boy next door but that's all water under the bridge. She married someone else long ago.*

water, water everywhere is a quotation cliché usually used when there has been a flood or when it is raining very hard, as *When we were on holiday it was a case of water, water everywhere although the local people said it was usually very dry there at that time of year.* The quotation is from *The Rime of the Ancient Mariner* (1798) by Samuel Coleridge. The cliché is sometimes extended to **water, water, everywhere, and not a drop to drink**, which is a misquotation from the same source of 'water, water, everywhere, nor any drop to drink.'

ways and means, there are see *there are ways and means*

we are not amused is a quotation cliché, being an allusion to a remark attributed to Queen Victoria, as *He is bound to come up with an inventive excuse for being late but we shall make it clear that we are not amused.* Nowadays it is usually used in a humorous or light-hearted context.

wear the trousers is an idiom cliché used to refer to a situation in which the female partner in a marriage or relationship is the more dominant person, as *He owns his own business and makes all the decisions at work but at home his wife wears the trousers.* The expression has been common since the eighteenth century and is still current although the set of social circumstances to which it referred no longer necessarily obtains, in that it is now quite common for women literally to wear trousers and for women to hold positions of responsibility in their own right.

wear a hat is an idiom cliché indicating that one is currently assuming one of two or more positions or roles that one holds, as *He is a teacher at the school but he was wearing his parent's hat when he complained about the education cuts.* In origin the expression refers to the hats associated with different uniforms. It dates from the middle of the nineteenth century.

weather the storm is an idiom cliché meaning to survive some kind of difficulty or crisis, as *During the recession the firm had some financial difficulties but they succeeded in weathering the storm and are now very profitable.* The expression has been common since the middle of the nineteenth century, although it has been in use since the seventeenth century, and is still very widespread, being much used by journalists in particular. It derives from the idea of a ship surviving a heavy storm.

wedded bliss is a hackneyed phrase which refers to the happiness that marriage can bring, as *The old couple have been living in wedded bliss for fifty years.* The expression became popular in the late nineteenth century but nowadays when the phenomenon itself is becoming less common as a result of declining marriage rates and increasing divorce rates, the expression is used less commonly except in humorous or ironic situations, as *Mary and Jim had a real row in the pub last night. That's wedded bliss for you!*

weighed in the balance and found wanting is a quotation cliché meaning tested and found to be deficient in some way. It comes from the Bible and is a slight misquotation of part of the interpretation that Daniel gave to King Belshazzar of the handwriting on the wall 'Thou art weighed in the balances, and art found wanting.' (*Daniel* 5:27) The expression has been popular since the nineteenth century and is still in current use, especially in rather formal contexts, as *Several young men have asked for her hand in marriage but they have all been weighed in the balance and found wanting.*

welcome aboard is a hackneyed phrase used when someone new joins a firm, club, community, etc as *'Welcome aboard!' said the manager. 'I hope you will enjoy working here.'* As a cliché the expression dates from the first half of the twentieth century and is still used today, although mainly by older people and often in rather a pompous way. In origin the expression is probably naval although its use as a standard greeting welcoming passengers aboard aircraft has probably helped to popularize it.

welcome with open arms is a hackneyed phrase meaning to receive someone or something with great enthusiasm and warmth, as *The couple welcomed their new daughter-in-law with open arms*, and *The improvements to the shop have been welcomed by the customers with open arms*. It has been a cliché since the late eighteenth century and is still in widespread use. Indeed people hardly seem to welcome anyone or anything at all unless they do so with open arms.

well and truly is a doublet cliché used for emphasis, as *Our team was well and truly beaten in the first round*. It is extremely widespread, being particularly common in such situations as the opening of new shops, exhibitions, etc., as *I declare this new supermarket well and truly open*. As a cliché it dates from the late nineteenth century.

well-earned rest is a hackneyed phrase meaning a period of leisure or relaxation that is well-deserved following a period of activity, as *Just as she thought she was going to have a well-earned rest from child-rearing she was given her granddaughter to look after*. The expression has been common since the late nineteenth century and often refers to a period of rest at the end of one's career. In modern times it is often used as a euphemism relating to a situation in which someone has been forced to retire or leave a post, as *We are glad that several of our employees are taking advantage of our early retirement scheme and are going off to enjoy a well-earned rest*.

we'll let you know is a catchphrase cliché used to indicate that the speaker does not think very highly of whatever the person addressed is doing, particularly when that person is doing something that requires a degree of artistic talent such as singing, as *Whenever Mary plays the piano her brother annoys her by saying, 'We'll let you know.'* Like → **don't call us, we'll call you**, it has its origins in the entertainment industry, being a stock response to people auditioning for parts unsuccessfully. Although it seemed to offer a modicum of hope it was usually a euphemism for a direct rejection. It is often used in this way nowadays in a business context to reject applications for a job.

we'll see is a hackneyed phrase meaning much the same as → **wait and see** and is used in much the same way.

we must have lunch sometime is a modern hackneyed phrase used as a parting remark to a friend or acquaintance either in person or by telephone. It is often simply a stock response, sometimes even just a way to bring a lengthy or unwelcome conversation to as speedy an end as possible, rather than a serious promise of a future engagement, as *Well I'm running late and I'll really have to go. We must have lunch some time*.

wend one's way is a hackneyed phrase meaning to go or make one's way, the word 'wend' originally in this context meaning to turn. The expression was used originally in the fourteenth century but died out around the sixteenth century. It was later revived and became popular in the early nineteenth century and is now usually used either in a formal, literary or humorous context, as *If we are going to catch that train it is time we were wending our way to the station*.

we're just good friends is a hackneyed phrase used to indicate that there is no romantic or sexual element in a relationship. It usually takes the form of a public denial and is very frequently not the truth, as *'We're just good friends,' the politician told the reporter but he left his wife for his secretary the following week*. The expression dates from the twentieth century when mass communications led to an increased interest in the private lives of people in the public eye.

we shall keep your name on file is a hackneyed phrase which is more or less a euphemism, usually being simply a polite way of rejecting someone's application for a job, as *We are sorry that you have not been successful in your application for the present post but we shall keep your name on file in the event of future vacancies*. Given the number of applications that employers receive for every vacancy, it is extremely unlikely that they are going to store the name of applicants for future use. As a cliché it dates from the recession and consequent joblessness of the 1980s and 1990s.

we wiz/wuz robbed is a twentieth century catchphrase cliché, being an ungrammatical or dialectal form of 'we were robbed'. Originally a sports cliché, it is used to indicate that the users think that they have been treated unfairly in some way usually by the referee or umpire. It was used by boxers and then by football supporters. The expression has gradually begun to be used more widely in humorous contexts by people who would not normally use ungrammatical or dialectal speech, and who are consciously aping the sporting cliché, as *After the latest round of redundancies we all have to work so late that we asked management to pay us overtime but they refused. We wiz robbed!*

what are you going to do when you grow up? is a hackneyed phrase used by adults to children from an early age, usually in a patronizing way and often because the adult in question cannot think of anything else to say, as *What are you going to do when you grow up? I hope that you are going to study hard and get a good job*. It is often the first cliché to which people are exposed and is still used by some older people today despite the fact that the reduction in the number of jobs available in modern society has made the remark exceptionally inappropriate

what did your last slave die of? is a catchphrase cliché used ironically to someone who has asked one to do something that he or she could easily do without help, as *No, I'm not going upstairs to get your handbag. What did your last slave die of?* The expression has been popular since the early twentieth century and is still widespread.

whatever turns you on is a catchphrase cliché used in response to a statement by someone that he or she is going to do something of which one disapproves or feels disinclined to join in, as *No, I don't fancy camping in the rain but whatever turns you on*. The expression dates from the 1960s, 'turn on' being part of 1960s drug slang meaning to excite or stimulate.

what's your poison? is a hackneyed phrase used when asking someone what he or she would like to drink, as in *It's my turn to buy a round. What's your poison?* It dates from the 1920s and is now dated, being used mainly by older people. The reference to poison may be an allusion to the slogan of the Temperance Movement, 'Alcohol is poison'. An alternative form of the expression is **name your poison**.

what's the damage? is a hackneyed phrase used when asking the cost of something, as *That's all I need just now. What's the damage?* The expression has been common since the nineteenth century, having originated in America. It is found in informal contexts and is becoming rather dated.

what with one thing and another is a hackneyed phrase used to suggest a kind of semi-apology because someone is very busy or because there are several complications arising in a situation, as *What with one thing and another I just haven't had time to think about holidays.* The expression dates from the middle of the nineteenth century and is still widespread today

what you see is what you get is a modern catchphrase cliché indicating that someone or something is completely straightforward and above board, as *Some of the members of the committee may well try to deceive you but he is completely honest. With him what you see is what you get.* The cliché is often abbreviated to **wysiwyg** in the field of computers.

wheels within wheels is an idiom cliché indicating something extremely involved and complicated, and sometimes implying something dishonest, as *We tried to find out the cause of the firm's failure but there were wheels within wheels.* It has been a cliché since the nineteenth century and is still widespread. In origin the expression is probably Biblical 'Their appearance and their work was as it were a wheel in the middle of a wheel.' (*Ezekiel* 1:16)

when all is said and done is a filler cliché meaning in the end or often meaning virtually nothing, as *When all is said and done, we all have to die some time.* The expression dates from the sixteenth cen-

tury and has been a cliché since the late nineteenth century. It is still widespread.

when in Rome . . . is a hackneyed phrase advocating the advisability of conforming to the customs, conventions, etc of the environment in which one finds oneself, as *Women do not go out alone there. When in Rome* . . . The expression is a shortened form of **when in Rome do as the Romans do** which is also common. In origin it supposedly comes from the translation of the answer given by St Ambrose to St Augustine and his mother, St Monica, when they asked whether they should fast on Saturdays according to the custom practised in Rome, or whether they should adopt the Milanese custom and not fast. St Ambrose is said to have replied that when he was in Milan he did not fast on Saturday but when he was in Rome he did so.

when I was your age is a hackneyed phrase used by some older people when about to regale a member of a younger generation with tales of how much better, more moral, harder, etc things were in their youth than they are at the time of speaking, and how immeasurably better, more moral, thoughtful, hard-working, poorer, etc they were than the young person being addressed.

when one door closes another opens is a hackneyed phrase used to inspire optimism in someone who has just experienced some form of misfortune. It is often shortened to **when one door closes**, as *I know you've lost your job but you'll probably find a better one. When one door closes* . . . A more pessimistic and humorous form of the cliché is **when one door closes another one slams in your face**.

when one's ship comes in is an idiom cliché meaning when one has made one's fortune, when more affluent times arrive, as *They plan to buy a house of their own when their ship comes in.* The expression derives from the days when merchants used to await the arrival of their sailing ships from foreign parts hoping that they would arrive laden with goods that would make their fortune, there obviously being a degree of uncertainty involved. It has been common since the middle of the nineteenth century and is still widespread today.

when the cat's away the mice will play is an idiom cliché indicating that when a person in authority or control is not present those under his or her authority take advantage and break the rules, do no work, etc. As a cliché the expression is usually shortened to **when the cat's away . . .**, the rest of the saying being assumed to be understood, as *We cannot leave the children in the room without a teacher. When the cat's away . . .* The proverb has been in existence in English since the seventeenth century and the concept exists in other languages also.

when the going gets tough is a catchphrase cliché meaning when a situation becomes very difficult, as *There was no shortage of volunteers at the beginning of the protest campaign, but when the going got tough there was only a handful of us left.* The cliché is a shortened form of the catchphrase **when the going gets tough, the tough get going** which is also a cliché. The expression originated in America, probably in political circles. It has been attributed to Joseph Kennedy (1888–1969), father of President John F Kennedy. A joke form, **when the going gets tough, the tough go shopping**, became popular in the 1980s and since then various people have attached their own joke endings to the catchphrase.

when you gotta go, you gotta go is a twentieth century catchphrase cliché used in informal contexts when someone wants to go to the toilet, as *I was sorry to have to leave the hall and disturb the speaker but you know how it is. When you gotta go, you gotta go!* The expression at the time of the London Blitz in World War 2 indicated an acceptance that one might be killed and that there was nothing that one could do about it, the lavatorial association being a more recent development.

where have you been all my life? is a catchphrase cliché used to flatter and express an exaggerated interest in a member of the opposite sex, usually by a man to a woman, as *I have never met such a beautiful woman. Where have you been all my life?* It originated in America in the early 1920s and became established in Britain around the early 1940s. The expression is still used but it is most frequently used humorously or ironically.

whisper it not is rather a literary hackneyed phrase which is a shortened version of **whisper it not in Gath** and is no longer common. This in turn is a misquotation of a Biblical passage 'How are the mighty fallen! Tell it not in Gath, publish it not in the streets of Askelon.' (*2 Samuel*, I 19–20) As a cliché the expression became popular in the nineteenth century. Nowadays the shortened version is still used but usually only by people of a literary bent and often in humorous or ironic contexts, as *Whisper it not, but he is thinking of taking a bath.*

whiter than white is a twentieth century hackneyed phrase meaning extremely pure, often unbelievably so, as *She is always criticizing the morals of others but from what I hear she is not exactly whiter than white herself.* It refers to an advertising slogan describing the cleaning properties of soap powder.

who/which shall remain nameless is a hackneyed phrase indicating one's reluctance to mention by name the person or thing that one is talking about, as *Someone who shall remain nameless has been stealing money from the till*. The expression has been popular since the late nineteenth century. Nowadays it is found either in formal contexts or in humorous or ironic contexts, as *Someone who shall remain nameless has forgotten my birthday*.

whys and wherefores is a hackneyed phrase meaning all the reasons for something, the details of the background to a situation, as *I just know that they have divorced. I don't know the whys and wherefores*. The expression has been a cliché since around the middle of the nineteenth century and is still widespread today. **Whys and wherefores** could now be considered a doublet cliché, although originally why and wherefore were not synonymous, 'why' meaning the reason for something, and 'wherefore' meaning how something came to be.

wild horses would not drag me is a hackneyed phrase indicating that nothing whatsoever would persuade someone to do something, as *Wild horses would not drag me to a film with so much violence in it*. A related expression is **wild horses would not drag it from me** which means nothing would make me divulge it, which is a later form of **wild horses would not draw it from me** with its origin in medieval torture to make people confess. The expression has been popular since the middle of the nineteenth century.

win hands down is a hackneyed phrase meaning to win very easily or by a significant margin, as *We thought that it was going to be a close match, but our team won hands down*. The expression has been popular from around the beginning of the twentieth century and is still widespread. In origin it derives from racing, being a reference to the fact that jockeys tend to relax their hold on the reins, and so ride with their hands down, when they feel that they are going to win.

wish you were here is a twentieth century catchphrase cliché popular from having been a stock message on holiday postcards, communications which are extremely difficult to be inventive on. It is often now used humorously or ironically, as *The weather is very wet and the food terrible. Wish you were here!*

witching hour, the is a hackneyed phrase referring to midnight, supposedly the time when witches come out. It has been used as a cliché since the middle of the nineteenth century and is still used although its use now would be considered rather literary or pretentious, as *Come, it is time for us to go home. It will soon be the witching hour*. In origin it is probably an allusion to a passage from Shakespeare's *Hamlet* (3:2) 'The very witching time of night, when graveyards yawn.'

with bated breath is a hackneyed phrase meaning holding one's breath in anticipation, excitement, fear, etc, as *We waited with bated breath as they announced the results of the competition*. The verb 'bate' is an archaic verb meaning to restrain. This phrase has been a cliché since the late nineteenth century although it has been in the language much longer than that, having been used by Shakespeare in *The Merchant of Venice* (1:3) 'Shall I bend low, and in a bondsman key, with bated breath, and whispering humbleness.' Nowadays the cliché is often used humorously or ironically, as *I'm sure the villagers are all* waiting with bated breath for the result of the elections. Only about thirty percent of them bothered to vote.

without more ado is a hackneyed phrase meaning right away, as *I think that everything is ready, and so without more ado I shall declare the exhibition open*. It has been a cliché in this sense since the beginning of the twentieth century and is still current today, although usually in fairly formal contexts. 'Ado' means fuss.

wolf in sheep's clothing, a is an idiom cliché meaning a dangerous person who has in some way a deceptively kind or mild exterior, as *He was so charming to everyone outside his home that no one realized that he was a wolf in sheep's clothing and beat his wife and children*. The expression comes from Aesop's fable in which a wolf dresses up as a sheep, or in some versions as a shepherd, in order to get among the flock of sheep to seize one. There is also a Biblical reference in *Matthew* (7:15), where Jesus talks of 'false prophets which come to you in sheep's clothing but inwardly they are ravening wolves.' The figurative expression is an old one, going back to the fifteenth century and became popular enough to be considered a cliché in the middle of the eighteenth century. It is still widespread today.

wonders will never cease! is a hackneyed phrase indicating the speaker's great surprise at something. The expression dates from the late eighteenth century and is often now used in a humorous or ironically context, as *Wonders will never cease! Jim has arrived for work on time*.

word in your ear, a is a hackneyed phrase used to seek someone's attention, usually with a view to saying something relatively confidential, as *A word in your ear. The boss has been complaining about people spending*

too long on their coffee breaks. It dates from the late nineteenth century and is still popular.

words fail me! is a hackneyed phrase used as an exclamation when something is so surprising, dreadful, etc that it is difficult to find words to describe it. The expression has been common since the middle of the nineteenth century and is still current today. Although it sounds rather formal, it is common in everyday situations, as *When I think of the noise our neighbours make, words fail me!*

word to the wise, a is a hackneyed phrase indicating that the speaker is about to give the listener some good advice and that he or she is considered sensible enough to take note of it, as *A word to the wise, now would be a good time to buy property in that area of the city*. The concept of the expression is an old one, several of the classical Roman writers having used it. As an English expression it was used by the playwright Ben Jonson in his play *The Case is Altered* (circa 1600) 'Go to, a word to the wise.' It is still used nowadays especially by people of a literary bent and often in a humorous or ironic way.

working late at the office is a twentieth century hackneyed phrase used as a classic excuse to suggest that someone who is doing something that he or she should not be doing, especially having an illicit love affair, is in fact simply working overtime. It is often now used humorously or ironically, as *Jim never joins his colleagues for a drink after work. He is too busy working late at the office with his secretary*.

work one's fingers to the bone is an idiom cliché meaning to work extremely hard as though one were doing physical work for so long that the skin and flesh came off one's fingers, as *She was left a widow at an* *early age and had to work her fingers to the bone to look after her seven children.* The expression dates from the nineteenth century and is still commonly used today. In origin it possibly refers to seamstresses sewing until the flesh came off their hands.

world's your oyster, the is an idiom cliché used to try to inspire optimism in someone with the number of possible opportunities that offer themselves. It is usually used to console someone who has experienced some form of misfortune, such as a young person who has just been rejected for a job, and the optimism is often somewhat misplaced, especially in modern society where the number of opportunities is not large and seems to be ever-decreasing, as *If you stay on at school and take your exams the world will be your oyster.* It falls into that class of clichés which are used to console the unfortunate because they are the first thing that occurs to the speaker, rather than because it is likely that they are going to be in any way comforting or reassuring. As a cliché it has been popular since the nineteenth century and is still widely used. In origin the expression may derive from Shakespeare's *The Merry Wives of Windsor* (2:2) 'Why then, the world's mine oyster, which I with sword will open.' The implication is that the world is a place from which success and profit can easily be extracted just as a pearl can be extracted from an oyster.

world of good, do a see *do a world of good*

would you believe it? is a hackneyed phrase used as an exclamation expressing not so much surprise or disbelief, as exasperation, as *Would you believe it? The paper boy has delivered the wrong paper yet again.*

writing is on the wall, the is an allusion cliché used to indicate a prediction of impending disaster or misfortune, a suggestion that a certain event will lead to disaster, as *The writing was on the wall for the small shops when the hypermarket opened in the area.* It is an allusion to a Biblical passage, *Daniel* (5:5-31), in which in the course of a feast given by King Belshazzar a hand appears and writes some words on the wall. When Belshazzar asks Daniel to interpret the writing he tells him that it indicates his coming downfall and Belshazzar is killed later that night. The words concerned were *mene, mene, tekel, upharsin.* The expression has been widely used as a cliché since the nineteenth century and is still popular today. It is also found in the form **the handwriting is on the wall**.

wrong end of the stick, the is an idiom cliché meaning a mistaken impression, as in *Although we explained the situation in great detail he still managed to get the wrong end of the stick.* It has been popular since the nineteenth century and still much used today. In origin it refers to holding a walking stick by the wrong end.

X

X marks the spot is a catchphrase cliché indicating that a cross marks the place where something took place, is situated, etc, as *On the sketch of the area X marks the spot where the corpse was found.* The expression became popular in the 1920s and is still used today, although often in a humorous or light-hearted context, as *This is a postcard of our holiday hotel. X marks the spot where our room is*, or in connection with games or puzzles, such as 'spot the ball' competitions in newspapers in which competitors have to place a cross to indicate where they consider the ball to be in an action photograph of a football match, the actual ball having been blanked out. In origin the expression refers to treasure maps in stories about pirates, a cross being used to mark the supposed location of the treasure.

Y

year in, year out is a hackneyed phrase used to emphasize the relentless continuity, and usually monotony, of something, as *Year in, year out, she had to endure the pain which arose from the injuries she sustained in the accident.* The expression has been popular since the middle of the nineteenth century and is still widespread today.

you can lead/take a horse to water but you can't make it drink is an idiom cliché indicating that it is perfectly possible to establish a set of circumstances which will make it likely that someone will agree to do something, but you cannot force him or her actually to go ahead with it if he or she does not want to do so, as *You can certainly try to persuade all the villagers that moving to the new housing estate is a good idea, but just remember that you can lead a horse to water but you can't make it drink.* The figurative expression appeared in John Heywood's collection of proverbs in 1546 and was probably already in use long before then. It is still a popular expression today.

you can't make a silk purse out of a sow's ear is an idiom cliché meaning that it is not possible to turn something that is worthless into something of value, as *You cannot expect all your piano pupils to become professional musicians. After all, you cannot make a silk purse out of a sow's ear.* As a proverb the expression dates from the sixteenth century and as a cliché it is still widespread today.

you can't take it with you is a catchphrase cliché used to indicate that when you die you cannot take money or any material possessions with you, the implication being that you should enjoy the fruits of these while you are alive. The expression probably dates from around the middle of the nineteenth century and was popularized when it was used as the title of a hit comedy by George Kaufman and Moss Hart that opened on Broadway in 1936. The expression is still widely used today, as *Why don't you use some of your savings to visit your daughter in Australia? You can't take it with you, you know.* It may ultimately be a reference to a Biblical passage. 'For we brought nothing into this world and it is certain we can carry nothing out.' (*1 Timothy* 6:7)

you can't teach an old dog new tricks is a proverb cliché meaning that it is very difficult for older people or people with a great deal of experience in a certain area to be persuaded to adopt new ways, methods, attitudes, etc. The proverb dates from the sixteenth century, having appeared in John Heywood's collection (1546). As a cliché it is still widespread today, as *It is difficult for the older office workers to get used to the new technology. You can't teach an old dog new tricks.*

you can't win 'em all is a catchphrase cliché used to indicate a philosophic acceptance of failure or defeat, as *It's a pity that my application for the course was rejected but never mind – you can't win 'em all.*

The expression originated in America around 1940, becoming popular in Britain at the beginning of the 1960s. It is still widely used today.

you could have knocked me down with a feather is an idiom cliché used to express one's extreme suprise, as *You could have knocked me down with a feather when I walked into the room and saw all my friends. The children had arranged a surprise party for my birthday.* As a cliché it dates from the late nineteenth century.

you know what I mean is usually a filler cliché used virtually meaninglessly by people to whom it has become a habit, as *I am really in need of a holiday. You know what I mean.* Frequently they are not aware of the habit although people who regularly converse with them can find it very annoying. Of course, just occasionally, the phrase is used literally indicating that one assumes that someone understands what someone is getting at. As a cliché it has been established since the late nineteenth century and is still common.

you know what I think? is a filler cliché used in much the same way as **you know what I mean**. The listener is given no say in the matter, although the cliché is framed in the form of a question, since the speaker goes right on to say what he or she was going to say without waiting for a response. As a cliché it has been established since the late nineteenth century and is still common.

you'll look back on this and laugh is a hackneyed phrase of the second half of the twentieth century, used by well-meaning but thoughtless people in an effort to cheer up someone who has suffered some kind of misfortune. In common with other similar platitudes, it rarely has the desired effect,

since the person to whom the remark is addressed feels that he or she will never laugh again. Moreover the situations involved are often of the kind that no one would ever look back on with amusement, as *It does seem·hard that your husband has walked out on you and the children and cleaned out your joint bank account. Never mind, one day you'll look back on this and laugh.*

you'll thank me one day is a hackneyed phrase used to try to make some course of action seem more acceptable to the person who is at the receiving end of it. It is often used by older people in authority to young people, as *I know you don't like being made to stay in on a sunny evening to do your homework but you'll thank me one day.* Far from alleviating the situation, the remark usually simply makes the young person more annoyed and rebellious since it sounds so smug. As a cliché if dates from the twentieth century.

you mark my words is a hackneyed phrase which sometimes takes the form of a filler cliché. It is used to impress on a listener the importance and truth of what one is going to say or what one has just said, indicating that one will be proved right, as *You mark my words. He has no intention of marrying her.* As a cliché the expression dates from the middle of the nineteenth century.

you must be joking is a catchphrase cliché used to indicate that the user thinks that the speaker cannot possibly be serious about a remark just made. Frequently the speaker is being quite serious and is not trying in any way to be funny. It is used to express the user's disagreement with or displeasure at what has just been said. As a cliché it has been established since the middle of the twentieth century although it had been used in literary contexts from the nineteenth century. It is still very common today in all but the most formal contexts, as *You are advertising for an experienced chef at £3 an hour? You must be joking!* A slightly sharper form of the expression is **you're joking, of course**, while a more informal variant is **you must be kidding**.

young of all ages, the is a hackneyed phrase popular since the beginning of the twentieth century and used to emphasize the youthfulness in all but actual years of some members of a group. The expression is often used in semi-formal contexts, as in a speech opening a fair, exhibition, etc, as *The fête includes a funfair and we are sure that the young of all ages will enjoy it.* It has a tendency nowadays to sound rather pompous or patronizing.

your chariot awaits is a hackneyed phrase used to indicate that transport is standing by for someone, as *My son is going to drive you home and your chariot awaits.* It nowadays tends to be used by older people, being rather dated, and in a humorous way.

you're only young once is a twentieth century catchphrase cliché advocating that people should enjoy themselves and make the most of their lives while they are young, the implication being that this carefree period is all too transient, as *You should go out a bit more instead of spending all your spare time studying. After all, you're only young once.* It tends to be used by older people who know only too well the truth of the statement.

You're telling me see *tell me about it*.

your guess is as good as mine is a catchphrase cliché used to emphasize the lack of information or knowledge available about the situation in question, as *They may or may not attend the meeting. Your guess is as good as mine.* It dates from the early part of the twentieth century and originated in America. It is still widespread today, being used in all but the most formal contexts.

yours truly is a hackneyed phrase used in facetious informal contexts to mean I or me, as *Whenever the dog needs a walk it always seems to be yours truly who has to take it.* In this use the expression has has been current since the middle of the nineteenth century, although its use as a standard closing formula in letters is older.

❧ Z ❧

zero hour is a hackneyed phrase used to indicate the exact time at which something is due to begin, as *Are all the children ready for the prize-giving ceremony? Zero hour is 2 o'clock.* The expression is military in origin, being first used in World War 1. It gradually began to be used in situations that had no military connections and is still much used today in a wide range of contexts.